THE COLLECTED COURSES OF THE ACADEMY OF EUROPEAN LAW

Series Editors

PROFESSOR NEHA JAIN

PROFESSOR CLAIRE KILPATRICK

PROFESSOR SARAH NOUWEN

PROFESSOR JOANNE SCOTT

European University Institute, Florence

Assistant Editor

JOYCE DAVIES

European University Institute, Florence

Volume XXVIII/2

Reframing Human Rights in a Turbulent Era

THE COLLECTED COURSES OF THE ACADEMY OF EUROPEAN LAW

Edited by
PROFESSOR NEHA JAIN, PROFESSOR CLAIRE KILPATRICK
PROFESSOR SARAH NOUWEN, AND PROFESSOR JOANNE SCOTT

Assistant Editor
JOYCE DAVIES

Each year the Academy of European Law in Florence, Italy, invites a group of outstanding lecturers to teach at its summer courses on Human Rights Law and the Law of the European Union. A 'general course' is given in each of the two fields by a distinguished scholar or practitioner, who examines the field as a whole through a particular thematic, conceptual, or philosophical lens, or looks at a theme in the context of the overall body of law. In addition, a series of 'specialized courses' brings together a group of highly qualified scholars to explore and analyse a specific theme in relation to human rights law and EU law. The Academy's mission, to produce scholarly analyses which are at the cutting edge of the two fields, is achieved through publication of this series, the Collected Courses of the Academy of European Law.

Reframing Human Rights in a Turbulent Era

GRÁINNE DE BÚRCA

OXFORD
UNIVERSITY PRESS

OXFORD

UNIVERSITY PRESS

Great Clarendon Street, Oxford, OX2 6DP,
United Kingdom

Oxford University Press is a department of the University of Oxford.
It furthers the University's objective of excellence in research, scholarship,
and education by publishing worldwide. Oxford is a registered trade mark of
Oxford University Press in the UK and in certain other countries

Published in the United States of America by Oxford University Press
198 Madison Avenue, New York, NY 10016, United States of America

British Library Cataloguing in Publication Data

Data available

Library of Congress Control Number: 2021930829

ISBN 978-0-19-829957-8 (hbk.)
ISBN 978-0-19-924600-7 (pbk.)

DOI: 10.1093/oso/9780198299578.001.0001

Printed and bound by
CPI Group (UK) Ltd, Croydon, CR0 4YY

Links to third party websites are provided by Oxford in good faith and
for information only. Oxford disclaims any responsibility for the materials
contained in any third party website referenced in this work.

For Bernie

Acknowledgements

I am extremely grateful to the many people who helped me, in a variety of ways, to write this book.

The work of Charles Sabel on experimentalism has been a major influence on my thinking about transnational governance, and about human rights, for many years. My collaboration with him and with Robert Keohane over the past decade has been a source of immensely rewarding academic cross-fertilization. I am very grateful to both of them for their support, critique, encouragement and above all their friendship along the way, and for the extensive advice and input they gave me during the writing of this book. Chuck was also particularly helpful in prodding me along when various chapters were rather later to materialize than expected! The work of César Rodriguez Garavito has also been a significant influence on the book. His comments and advice have been invaluable, and his thoughtful scholarship—as well as the way in which he combines a commitment to critical thinking with a commitment to advancing human rights in practice—have been an inspiration for some of the ideas developed here. Sally Engle Merry's insightful and agenda-setting scholarship on human rights and vernacularization was also important in shaping my thinking, and her engagement and support were very much appreciated during the writing of the book. She passed away in September 2020, and her warm and generous friendship as well as her academic creativity and brilliance will be greatly missed.

I first presented the material which formed the seed of an idea for the book at a workshop at Brown University's Watson Institute in 2013, organized together with Chuck Sabel, Bob Keohane and Rick Locke. Since then, I have presented parts of the manuscript at multiple workshops and meetings and am indebted to all those who invited me, as well as to those who gave comments on the drafts presented. These include the participants at the Watson Institute workshops in 2013 and 2015, at the European University Institute's Max Weber lecture in 2015, the Tel-Aviv University international law workshop in 2018, the Aix-Marseilles University Aix Global Justice workshop in 2018, the European University Institute's Academy of European Law courses on human rights in 2017 and 2019, and finally at the book manuscript workshop organized at NYU law school in December 2019. The enormously helpful comments and probing criticisms I received at all of these events were vital to the writing and rewriting of the book.

Many colleagues and friends read and commented on parts of the manuscript or gave me feedback on presentations of parts of it at different stages. These include José Alvarez, Nehal Bhuta, Dennis Davis, Rosalind Dixon, Suzanne Egan, Veronika

Fikfak, Angelina Fisher, Ryan Goodman, Aeyal Gross, Ludovic Hennebel, Claire Kilpatrick, Benedict Kingsbury, Sarah Knuckey, Eliav Lieblich, Doreen Lustig, Tamar Megiddo, Sally Engle Merry, Ziba Mir-Hosseini, Gerard Quinn, Joanne Scott, Thomas Streinz, Julie Suk, Christiaan Van Veen, Neil Walker and Paula Wulff Fernandez.

I have also benefited greatly from the efforts of several excellent and dedicated research assistants who worked on the case studies, in particular Lauren Flanagan, Hilary Hogan, Nahuel Maisley, Sheherezade Malik and Sakeena Moeen. I am also grateful for their help and input at different stages to Victoria Adelmant, Judith Bauder and Molly Whelan.

Joyce Davies at the European University Institute in Florence was extremely helpful in steering the book through the copyediting process, assisting with the cover design, as well as liaising with Oxford University Press. Many thanks also to Kathryn Plunkett and Joe Matthews at OUP for their work during the production process.

Two people were central to the writing of this book in ways that combined moral support, practical assistance and incisive critique. Deirdre de Búrca continually nudged, encouraged and urged me to make progress particularly at times when energy was lacking. She supplied a stream of interesting and relevant material on civil society activism and made helpful suggestions and perceptive comments on multiple chapters. Philip Alston was deeply supportive both in terms of his unwavering commitment to doing an equal share of the household work and parenting, as well as in his academic advice, encouragement and substantive input at every stage. I should add that my teenage sons, Seán and Ross, while not intentionally engaging in naming and shaming, nonetheless helped to prod me into completing the manuscript by the genuine incredulity with which they asked: "are you really still writing that same book you were writing three years ago?".

The book is in large part about the way in which advocates and activists, including those whose lives are most affected by the denial of human rights, mobilize and engage with domestic and international institutions and laws to demand and vindicate their rights. In many parts of the world, activists who do so put themselves at risk, and are harassed, marginalized, threatened, and even killed. My profound admiration for their courage and commitment to justice and to progressive change has been an ongoing source of inspiration for this work.

Finally, I want to remember my mother, Bernadette de Búrca, who died in January 2020. Having been widowed early and left with four children to raise, she encouraged us constantly to take our education seriously, to work hard and to do something useful with our lives. I am not sure whether she would consider this book to be useful or not, but it is dedicated with love and gratitude to her memory.

Contents

1

Introduction

We live in a time of global turbulence. From the changing geopolitical order signalling the end of unipolar dominance and the global spread of political illiberalism, to the overwhelming planetary threat posed by climate change and the outbreak of a global pandemic which upended economies and politics worldwide, the current era is one of tumult and flux. Nationalism is on the rise, multilateralism is on the wane, and protest movements have erupted in countries across Asia, North Africa, Latin America, North America, and Europe. The COVID-19 pandemic has seen the widespread introduction of emergency powers, rule-by-decree, enhancement of surveillance, suspension of democratic safeguards, praise for authoritarian control, and state derogations from international human rights commitments.

This book addresses the role and relevance of international human rights in our turbulent era, at a time when human rights have been under political as well as intellectual attack. On the one hand, increasing political illiberalism, emboldened authoritarianism, and the crackdown on civil society would seem to suggest that even as they are targeted for repression, human rights movements are all the more important and urgent. Yet while it might have been assumed that intellectuals would leap to the defence of human rights under such geopolitical circumstances, the reality has been rather different, with some of the most vocal and most publicized academics and intellectuals expressing increasing scepticism about the effectiveness, significance, and normative desirability of international human rights. If the political tide appears, for now, to be turning definitively against human rights in so many countries, and if intellectual support for the idea of human rights is crumbling, what are we to make of the future, not to mention the past, of the international human rights movement?

In terms of the political trend, a growing array of populist and illiberal authoritarian leaders across the world, supported by the continued rise of the far-right and encouraged by the opportunities afforded by the pandemic, have overtly contested, distorted, and dismissed the idea of human rights. Domestically they enact and encourage increasingly repressive policies and practices against vulnerable parts of their population and against human rights defenders, as well as capturing and controlling independent institutions. Internationally they seek to undermine and weaken human rights institutions and processes. And while many human rights scholars have opted for a business-as-usual approach in the face of rising illiberalism, some of the loudest intellectual voices from both progressive and conservative quarters have expressed deep disenchantment with the human rights

Reframing Human Rights in a Turbulent Era. Gráinne de Búrca, Oxford University Press (2021). © G de Búrca.
DOI: 10.1093/oso/9780198299578.003.0001

enterprise. Prominent scholars and public intellectuals have variously dismissed the language, ideals, practices, and achievements of human rights law and advocacy as flawed, inadequate, hegemonic, confining, overreaching, apolitical, peripheral, or pointless. Human rights approaches have been accused of being tools of Western imperialism,[1] an elitist and bureaucratic legal paradigm,[2] a limiting expert discourse which crowds out emancipatory political alternatives,[3] which limits its ambitions and hides its own 'governmentality',[4] an intellectually 'autistic' culture,[5] an anti-politics,[6] and a companion to neoliberalism.[7]

Yet at the same time that scholars, particularly in the global north, have been outdoing one another with ever more scathing and dismissive critiques, human rights movements, protests, and practices have been abounding and spreading. There may be turbulence in the form of growing political repression and illiberalism, and the election of mendacious strongmen who have captured the institutions of state, repressed their opponents, and taken advantage of the pandemic, but there has also been turbulence in recent years in the form of widespread social justice protests and grassroots mobilizations. Many of the groups and movements which have mobilized for change across different parts of the world have invoked the discourse or activated the tools of human rights in their campaigns. Throughout 2019 and into 2020, before the COVID-19 shutdown, crowds rallied and protested in large numbers across several continents, including in Hong Kong, Lebanon, Chile, Indonesia, Ecuador, all across the United States and—as described in this book—Argentina, Pakistan, and Ireland, amongst others, to assert their demands, often in the language of rights. Black Lives Matter protests, large-scale women's marches, anti-rape demonstrations, and climate strikes and rallies around the globe in recent years have regularly invoked human rights, with Greta Thunberg and a group of children bringing a petition on the failure to take climate action before the UN Committee on the Rights of the Child.[8] The discourse of human rights continues to be used by many progressive social, environmental, indigenous, labour, and other movements and campaigns for justice, even as critical and sceptical scholars have

---

[1] M. Mutua, *Human Rights: A Political and Cultural Critique* (2002).

[2] M. Koskenniemi, *The Politics of International Law* (2011) Ch. 6.

[3] Kennedy, 'The International Human Rights Movement: Part of the Problem', 15 *Harvard Human Rights Journal* (2002) 101.

[4] Brown, '"The Most We Can Hope For ...": Human Rights and the Politics of Fatalism', 103 *South Atlantic Quarterly* (2004) 451.

[5] Koskenniemi, 'Rocking the Human Rights Boat: Reflections by a Fellow Passenger', in N. Bhuta *et al.* (eds) (forthcoming 2021).

[6] Marks, 'Four Human Rights Myths', in D. Kinley, W. Sadurski, and K. Walton, *Human Rights: Old Problems, New Possibilities* (2013) 217.

[7] Moyn, 'A Powerless Companion: Human Rights in an Age of Neoliberalism', 77 *Law and Contemporary Problems* (2015) 147.

[8] *Sacchi et al v. Argentina et al.*, Communication submitted under Article 5 of the Third Optional Protocol to the United Nations Convention on the Rights of the Child, 23 September 2019, available online at https://earthjustice.org/sites/default/files/files/CRC-communication-Sacchi-et-al-v.-Argentina-et-al.pdf.

continued to challenge and attempt to debunk it, and governments seek to undermine and distort it.

What is it that explains these two opposite sets of developments? Is the apparently continued vitality of the human rights movement and the conviction of the many actors worldwide who invoke human rights in their quest for social, economic, environmental, and other forms of justice, little more than the remains of a movement approaching its final stages—one which is fated to peter out in the face of the combined forces of widespread political repression and intellectual disillusionment, not to mention other major contemporary challenges such as the impact of new technologies, pandemics, rampant inequalities, and climate change? Or do the pessimistic and often scathing diagnoses of the human rights sceptics fail to give due credit to the drivers of human rights movements, to the conditions under which and the reasons why they continue to emerge, grow, and flourish?

This book argues that the human rights movement remains an inherently attractive and appealing one, due to the universally asserted values on which it is based, its continued vitality as one among various languages and tools for challenging injustice, and the adaptability and creative potential of human rights ideas, law, and advocacy to generate legitimacy and help to promote positive change and reform even under turbulent and rapidly changing national and global conditions. While acknowledging the many deficiencies and shortcomings of human rights law and practice—as is true of any human practice—I present an account of the international human rights movement that remains a powerful and appealing one with widespread traction in many parts of the world. This account draws from and builds on the practice of human rights by activists and advocates, and argues that far from being ineffective or marginal in its impact, human rights advocacy has played an important part in many movements for social, political, racial, economic, and environmental justice around the world. Further, in contrast to accounts that present the human rights movement as elitist, apolitical, top-down, or bureaucratic, the experimentalist account of international human rights law and advocacy which this book advances understands human rights instead as the product of ongoing interaction and contestation between an array of actors, institutions, and norms: between the claims and demands of people affected and concerned, the international norms and institutions which elaborate and monitor their implementation, and the domestic institutions and actors which reinforce and support those claims.

The potency and legitimacy of the human rights project rest on three main foundations. First, it is based on a deeply rooted and attractive moral discourse that integrates at least three core values: human dignity, human welfare, and human freedom. Second, these values and their more detailed elaboration in various international legal instruments have gained widespread (even if thin and uneven) agreement among states worldwide. Third, the human rights project is a dynamic one, which is activated, shaped, and given its meaning and impact through the ongoing mobilization of affected populations, groups, and individuals, and through their iterative engagement with an array of domestic and international institutions and processes over time.

Many of the critiques of human rights which have been articulated have been directed at specific aspects of human rights law or practice. Sceptical scholars on the left such as Martti Koskenniemi and David Kennedy focus on what they perceive as the managerialist and expertise-based elitism of institutionalized forms of human rights practice;[9] philosophers such as John Tasioulas address what they consider to be the overreach of human rights law;[10] Global South scholars such as Makau Mutua criticize its cultural imperialism;[11] law-and-economics scholars such as Eric Posner focus on the apparent lack of adequate enforceability or effectiveness of human rights law, as well as its allegedly top-down nature;[12] and historians such as Samuel Moyn on its perceived unsuitability for addressing economic inequality.[13] While certain parts of these and other critiques are well targeted and point to real problems affecting aspects of human rights law and practice, many others are caricatured, overblown, or overlook important dimensions of the human rights movement.

Furthermore, even to the extent that they are well-targeted, the blitz of intellectual criticisms do not signal the death or decay of the human rights movement, or the desirability of the death or decay of that movement, any more than well-targeted criticisms of democratic systems and their dysfunctions today in themselves signal the end of democracy or the desirability of the end of democracy. On the contrary, the most cogent of the criticisms may help to point the way towards reform and renewal—and indeed, as some of the best informed and most persuasive human rights scholar-practitioners have argued, towards creative disruption[14]—of human rights practices, institutions, and laws, so as to better fulfil the aspirations and promise of the movement's underlying ideals and to strengthen its future capacity for furthering justice.

---

[9] See e.g. Koskenniemi, 'The Effect of Rights on Political Culture', in *The Politics of International Law* (2010) ch. 5 and 'Human Rights Mainstreaming as a Strategy for Institutional Power', *Humanity* (2010) 47; and see Kennedy, 'The International Human Rights Movement: Part of the Problem?', 15 *Harvard Human Rights Journal* (2002) 101, and 'The International Human Rights Regime: Still Part of the Problem?', in R. Dickinson *et al.* (eds), *Examining Critical Perspectives on Human Rights* (2013) 19.

[10] Tasioulas, 'Saving Human Rights From Human Rights Law', 52 Vanderbilt Journal of Transnational Law (2019) 1167, and 'Are Human Rights Taking Over the Space Once Occupied by Politics?', *New Statesman*, 26 August 2019. For others making a similar argument, see Kaplan, 'When Everything Is A Human Right, Nothing Is', *Foreign Policy*, 6 September 2019 and H. Hannum, *Rescuing Human Rights: A Radically Moderate Approach* (2019).

[11] Mutua (n. 1).

[12] E. Posner, *The Twilight of Human Rights* (2014), at Chs 4 and 5.

[13] S. Moyn, *Not Enough: Human Rights in an Unequal World* (2018).

[14] Rodríguez-Garavito, 'The Future of Human Rights: From Gatekeeping to Symbiosis', *SUR: International Journal on Human Rights* (2014), available online at https://sur.conectas.org/en/the-future-of-human-rights-from-gatekeeping-to-symbiosis/ and 'Towards a Human Rights Ecosystem', in D. Lettinga and L. van Troost, *Debating the Endtimes of Human Rights: Activism and Institutions in a Neo-Westphalian World* (2014).

This book does not join the academic chorus of human rights sceptics and critics, not because there are no valid and important criticisms to make but because after years dominated by ever more expansive critiques, I join writers such César Rodríguez-Garavito,[15] Kathryn Sikkink,[16] and Philip Alston[17] in the view that constructive scholarly thinking about the human rights enterprise by those interested in social and other forms of justice is needed. Rather than engaging with sceptics who call on those concerned about injustice to abandon the human rights movement and to find other (generally unspecified) emancipatory paths, the more urgent task in my view for human rights activists and intellectuals concerned about socio-economic, political, environmental, and other forms of justice is to reflect on the most cogent and constructive of the critiques, with a view to providing ideas and impetus for strengthening and renewing a movement that has achieved much in the past, so as to better meet the challenges ahead.[18] In the final chapter I consider the contemporary challenges of illiberalism, climate change, and digitalization, in the context of a highly unequal world struggling with the aftermath of a global pandemic, and the capacity of the human rights movement, and of its tools, and strategies to address these challenges.

An argument regularly made by commentators who are sceptical—rather than merely critical—of the human rights project is that progressive energies would be better directed towards other means of challenging injustice, and that human rights approaches displace or crowd out such other means.[19] The displacement thesis remains thus far unproven,[20] but more importantly, the sceptics rarely if ever propose specific alternatives, generally confining themselves to gesturing towards politics and political action as the appropriate emancipatory path. Occasionally there is a hint as to what this politics might be—an undefined socialism, or perhaps revolution—but rarely is it elaborated or argued in any more detail than with the assertion, at the end of a lengthy critique, that 'politics' and not 'rights' provide the way forward.[21] But on the account of human rights advanced in this

---

[15] C. Rodríguez-Garavito and K. Gomez (eds), *Rising to the Populist Challenge: A New Playbook for Human Rights Actors* (2019).

[16] K. Sikkink, *Evidence for Hope* (2017), and *The Hidden Face of Rights: Towards a Politics of Responsibilities* (2020).

[17] Alston, 'The Populist Challenge to Human Rights', 9 *Journal of Human Rights Practice* (2017) 1. See also Dudai, 'Human Rights in the Populist Era: Mourn then (Re)Organize', 9 Journal of Human Rights Practice (2017) 16.

[18] For an author who argues against human rights as an emancipatory path and in favour of turning away from liberal freedom, see R. Kapur, *Gender, Alterity and Human Rights* (2020).

[19] For an articulation of the displacement thesis, see Moyn, 'Human Rights and the Crisis of Liberalism', in S. Hopgood, J. Snyder, and L. Vinjamuri, *Human Rights Futures* (2017) 261.

[20] For a challenge to the displacement thesis, see Song, 'Human Rights and Inequality', 47(4) *Philosophy and Public Affairs* (2019) 347. See also Simmons and Strezhnev, 'Human Rights and Human Welfare: Looking for a "Dark Side" to International Human Rights Law', in S. Hopgood, J. Snyder, and L. Vinjamuri (eds), *Human Rights Futures* (2017) 60.

[21] For a refreshing exception in the work of a scholar who seeks to combine critical theory with critical practice and to propose a role for human rights in emancipatory political movements, see O'Connell, 'On the Human Rights Question', 40 *Human Rights Quarterly* (2018) 962.

book—an activist-centred account that I believe provides a more descriptively ac-
curate and normatively persuasive account of the human rights movement than
that described by the sceptics—the practice of human rights is not a replacement
or a substitute for politics, or for redistribution. On the contrary, and even though
legal strategies have been and likely will remain important instruments for human
rights advocates, human rights law and advocacy is inevitably political.[22]

It is certainly—and unsurprisingly—true that the international bureaucracies that manage parts of the international human rights system often operate
in a formalistic or rigid way, and it is also true that various prominent North
American NGOs strove for years to present their human rights work as non-
political. But the reality of human rights practice for most of those involved
in human rights advocacy and practice—the legions of activists, grassroots
movements and organizations around the world—has always been political in
the sense that it is directed at bringing about political and social change, usually through contestation and struggle. And while it is true that human rights
law and practice are animated by essentially universally oriented values that are
neither partisan nor particular, namely by respect for human dignity, human
welfare, and human freedom, nevertheless human rights practice undoubtedly
aims to strengthen, redirect, and challenge other forms of political and economic action, to act as a catalyst or corrective to the dysfunctions of existing
political systems, and to help press for projects of social, economic, political,
and environmental reform.

While some critics have argued that human rights are 'not enough', the premise
of this book is that politics without human rights are not enough. I suggest that
a political system—whether capitalist, socialist, or any other—without the kind
of moral and institutional underpinning provided by a human rights framework,
with its explicit set of commitments to human dignity, freedom, and welfare, is
less likely to promote a just society. Every political system, democratic as well as
authoritarian, capitalist as well as socialist, at various times and to various degrees
neglects, marginalizes, and represses parts of its population. What the human
rights project at its best offers by way of keeping pressure on political systems and
societies to move in the direction of justice is a broad set of underlying values
with universal appeal, an array of internationally agreed laws as well as domestic
and international institutions to help develop and promote those values, and the
freedom and resources for social movements and their advocates to activate, demand and shape the realization of rights in practice through political, legal, and
other forms of advocacy and action.

---

[22] For an interesting account of how NGO human rights advocacy strategies in India, including liti-
gation, are neither depoliticized nor anti-political, see Bornstein and Sharma, 'The Righteous and the
Rightful: The Techno-Moral Politics of NGOs, Social Movements, and the State in India', 43 *American
Ethnologist* (2016) 76.

The book seeks to present a descriptive-theoretical account of human rights practice—which I present in more detail in the next chapter as an experimentalist account—drawing from examples of campaigns to advance disability rights, children's rights, gender justice, and reproductive rights in different parts of the world. Many other important examples and campaigns could have been chosen, such as indigenous rights, racial justice campaigns, or migrant rights movements, but the studies selected are intended mainly as exemplars of the ways in which human rights mobilization has worked in different contexts. The aim is to provide a closer look at the ways in which human rights advocacy has helped in the past to promote positive change, and in so doing to present an alternative and, I hope, more persuasive account of the international human rights movement than that which depicts it as ineffective, elitist, top-down, bureaucratic, or apolitical. I advance this experimentalist account of international human rights not in order to suggest that all actions taken in the name of human rights have been positive or benign, nor to deny that, as with all human systems, there are sclerotic, imperialist, and dysfunctional aspects of the broader international human rights regime complex. Rather, the aim is to present a fuller and more inclusive picture of the international human rights movement, and to reframe how it is perceived and what elements are included and prioritized in our understanding of how human rights law and advocacy operates. The experimentalist account brings to the fore, and places at the centre of the frame, what I view as the core elements that animate and shape the human rights movement, and that have made it an often important movement for those seeking justice around the world: namely the ongoing engagement and interaction between the claims and demands of domestic activists and advocates; the universal ideals which underpin the movement and the broad range of international human rights instruments agreed by states; and the array of international and domestic institutions which elaborate, monitor, and support these.

Nevertheless, even if an experimentalist account of the international human rights movement to date seems plausible, it may be asked whether a theory or approach built on past successes is adequate to meet the challenges of the current era. For even though human rights campaigns in the past have frequently emerged and flourished during turbulent times and in periods of political repression, the nature of the problems currently confronting the human rights movement are arguably different in kind and magnitude. Quite apart from the rapid spread of political illiberalism and the changing geopolitical order, the transformative nature of new technologies, the shock of the 2020 global pandemic, ever-increasing inequalities, and the rapid onset of climate change also present major new challenges which are likely to require human rights advocates to think urgently about reform and renewal of their traditional approaches, and to require any states and organizations which are concerned about these challenges to support and reinforce those efforts. But even so, and despite the mounting challenges, a source of hope and a cause for optimism in this era of global turbulence has been the renewed civic protest and creative adaptation of civic activism evident in many parts of the world, given that it is the energy and engagement of social movements which so often supplies the crucial motor for the most effective human rights advocacy and reform. The final chapter of this book considers whether and how an experimentalist approach to human rights could facilitate and further the kind of reform or change which the human rights movement may currently be contemplating.

To conclude, this book provides an account of the many and varied ways in which a rich and diverse human rights movement has helped to challenge injustice and to promote progressive change in the past. The aim is also to reframe the more typical mainstream academic presentation of a monolithic movement. The principal lesson to be derived from the analyses in the chapters which follow is that the daunting challenges of the current turbulent era provide powerful reasons to reform, innovate, and strengthen the tools and practices of the human rights movement for the future, rather than to abandon it, encourage others to abandon it, or to herald its demise.

2
The Effectiveness of Human Rights

1. Introduction

The project of international human rights seems to be at a critical and highly vulnerable juncture. On the one hand, during an era of rapidly spreading political and social illiberalism and emboldened authoritarianism across many parts of the world, international human rights norms are increasingly challenged and disparaged as illegitimate interventions into state sovereignty. Nationalism has been rising, exacerbated by the recent global pandemic. Political action has been taken to weaken and undermine international human rights institutions through withdrawal and de-funding, and a range of strategies has been pursued to limit, marginalize, and silence human rights advocates and civil society actors. On the other hand, from what is generally seen as the opposite side of the political spectrum, the human rights project has been sharply criticized, particularly by academic scholars who have denounced its alleged biases and normative imperialism, or who question its adequacy and effectiveness in promoting justice and positive social change. Buffeted in the middle, many human rights actors, advocates, and activists appear to be struggling, dealing with fears about repression, trauma caused by the nature of the work many are engaged in, and disillusionment in the face of the rising number of obstacles and setbacks.

The bleak pronouncements of the leading scholarly commentators who herald the failings and the coming demise of the international human rights project are particularly eye-catching. Their recent book titles speak volumes: *The Endtimes of Human Rights* by Stephen Hopgood,[1] *The Twilight of Human Rights Law* by Eric Posner,[2] and *Not Enough* by Samuel Moyn.[3] Hopgood tells us that an externally changing geopolitical context as well as internal contestation within the human rights movement mean that the end times are coming for human rights as effective global norms.[4] Posner tells us that human rights were never actually universal, that human rights law failed to accomplish its objectives, and that there is little evidence that human rights law has improved the wellbeing of people.[5] Moyn tells us that

---

[1] S. Hopgood, *The Endtimes of Human Rights* (2013).
[2] E. Posner, *The Twilight of Human Rights Law* (2014).
[3] S. Moyn, *Not Enough: Human Rights in an Unequal World* (2018).
[4] See for a summary account, Hopgood, 'The Endtimes of Human Rights', in D. Lettinga and L. Von Troost, *Debating the Endtimes of Human Rights* (2014) 11.
[5] See Posner, footnote 2 above.

Reframing Human Rights in a Turbulent Era. Gráinne de Búrca, Oxford University Press (2021). © G de Búrca.
DOI: 10.1093/oso/9780198299578.003.0002

human rights have become the language to indicate that our solidarity with our fellow human beings can remain weak and cheap, and that human rights have accommodated and humanized neoliberalism.[6]

What kind of future can there be for the international human rights project in view of these assessments, which are both deeply critical as to the past effectiveness of the project and deeply pessimistic as to its future? While the critical literature is broadly divided between those who view the human rights movement as having been powerful but pernicious,[7] and those such as the authors cited above who argue that it has been ineffective or marginal, and is destined for further marginality, this book addresses itself primarily to the critique of effectiveness. It argues that human rights advocacy has been an effective tool of social justice in many parts of the world, and offers a theory of its effectiveness that is premised on the power of social movements and civil society actors engaging with international and domestic human rights norms and institutions. While I do not directly address the arguments of those critics who see the international human rights movement as powerful and pernicious, the account of human rights advocacy advanced in this book nonetheless calls into question various aspects of the depiction of human rights as bureaucratic, elitist, top-down, and imperialist.

The book addresses both the critiques of past effectiveness and the pessimistic future prognosis. While acknowledging that human rights activism is not the only, or even the primary, means of pursuing social justice, and despite the major challenges confronting human rights advocates in the current era, I argue that the human rights movement has helped to advance important social and political change across many parts of the world in the face of both repression and neglect. Looking to the future, I argue that it should continue to be an important force for progressive change both in spite of and because of the rise of authoritarian illiberalism, the impact of the pandemic and the overwhelming threat of climate change, the transformative impact of technology, and the spread of extreme inequality.

In contrast to the deeply pessimistic accounts mentioned above, this chapter highlights a growing and empirically grounded body of scholarship which has focused with increasing sophistication and nuance on the ways in which human rights law and practice have promoted positive social change, and the chapters which follow use a number of case studies to illustrate in more detail the ways in which it has done so. Building on this literature and these examples, the book advances an experimentalist theory of the effectiveness of international human rights law and advocacy which is interactive (premised on the engagement of social movements, civil society actors, and international norms and institutions), iterative (dependent

---

[6] See Moyn, footnote 3 above, p.6 and p.218.

[7] See, as discussed in the Introduction, scholars such as M. Mutua, *Human Rights: A Political and Cultural Critique* (2002), M. Koskenniemi, *The Politics of International Law* (2011) ch. 6, and Kennedy, 'International Human Rights Movement: Part of the Problem', 15 *Harvard Human Rights Journal* (2002) 101.

on ongoing action) and long-term (pursuing the kinds of social and fundamental changes that are rarely rapidly achieved). This experimentalist account of human rights advocacy challenges one of the persistent dichotomies or oppositions in much of the scholarly literature which has presented contrasting sets of claims as to whether human rights reform has been (and should be) the result of 'top down' institutions and interventions secured through elite socialization and compliance, or whether it is (and should be) primarily a 'bottom-up' process best understood as internal mobilization from below. The experimentalist account, by comparison, builds on the suggestions in some of the more interesting recent scholarship as to how the *interaction* between local and global actors and institutions can work to promote human rights reform and progressive social change, and offers a more detailed account of this process.

While legally centred scholarly analyses of international human rights have traditionally tended to adopt a top-down perspective, emphasizing the importance of international laws and institutions and their impact on national governmental, judicial, and bureaucratic elites to secure human rights reform,[8] influential recent accounts of the impact of international human rights law have begun to turn towards bottom-up or grassroots theories of causality—perhaps in part as a reaction to emerging critiques of its allegedly elitist and top-down nature. Beth Simmons, in a major book on the impact of human rights treaties, compares the domestic mobilization 'bottom up' account with the 'elite-focused' theories of other scholars.[9] Stephen Hopgood has juxtaposed what he considers to be the elite and dysfunctional international Human Rights (uppercase) system composed of an array of global legal rules and institutions, with more promising (lower-case) grassroots human rights action.[10] Michael Ignatieff, in somewhat different vein, presents 'elite human rights discourse' as something distinct and separate from the ordinary virtues and moral operating systems of the majority of people, suggesting that it is the ordinary virtues rather than notions of human rights that are the real engines of solidarity.[11] These and other accounts present grassroots concerns and domestic mobilization as the real source of energy and social progress, with the international human rights system and its laws, institutions, and elites being viewed either as inadequate and dysfunctional or as peripheral in bringing about change.

---

[8] See e.g. Nowak, 'The Need for a World Court of Human Rights', 7 *Human Rights Law Review* (2007) 251.

[9] B. Simmons, *Mobilizing for Human Rights: International Law in Domestic Politics* (2009) 138, referring inter alia to the work of Harold Koh on how international human rights norms are domesticated. See e.g. Koh, 'How Is International Human Rights Law Enforced?', 74 *Indiana Law Journal* (1999) 1397.

[10] S. Hopgood, *The Endtimes of Human Rights* (2013). For a set of responses to this argument of Hopgood's, see D. Lettinga and L. van Troost (eds), *Debating the Endtimes of Human Rights* (2016).

[11] M. Ignatieff, *The Ordinary Virtues, Moral Order in a Divided World* (2017). For a somewhat contrary finding—also based on empirical research in various countries around the world—to the effect that ordinary people in the global south are broadly supportive of human rights discourse and do not necessarily view them sceptically, see J. Ron *et al.*, *Taking Root: Human Rights and Public Opinion in the Global South* (2017).

This juxtaposition between elite and grassroots, and the recent emphasis on bottom-up accounts of human rights progress in particular, are in many ways appealing and at first glance persuasive. International institutions and their networks seem remote, bureaucratic, and detached from the concerns of communities and populations as well as being focused on their own institutional self-interest and agendas, while governmental and judicial elites, although undoubtedly important for domestic public policy change, rarely have the incentives or experience the sense of urgency felt by those most directly affected. It is at the community level where grassroots mobilization takes place that passion and energy for change is generally to be found, and the level at which both the experience of deprivation or repression and the impetus, ideas, and action for reform tend to be situated.

This book however challenges the initial appeal of the dichotomous approach. I argue that moves to minimize or dismiss the role of international human rights law and institutions (the 'uppercase' Human Rights system) and to locate the real effectiveness of human rights reform instead in domestic action and activism, miss the importantly interactive and iterative dynamic of human rights-driven change.[12] The account of human rights law and advocacy reflected in the case studies locates the motor of change neither mainly in international law and institutions nor mainly in domestic activism, but instead in the ongoing engagement over time between an array of internal and external actors, institutions, and norms. The examples described in the book point to the productive effect of back-and-forth interaction between local, domestic, external, and global actors and institutions in advancing social and legal change, and suggest an iterative, multi-actor, and multi-directional theory of effective human rights reform. Drawing on these examples, the book advances an experimentalist theory of international human rights law and advocacy, arguing that human rights advocacy provides a powerful way of challenging injustice and catalysing social, political and legal reform. The focus is on progressive social change brought about by human rights advocacy, not just on doctrinal changes or the legal articulation of rights, but also on the enactment of laws, policies and practices that further the realization of rights in practice.

The argument advanced is not that the invocation of international human rights by domestic social movements or advocacy groups leads inevitably to human rights reform of this kind, nor that the reforms promoted by such groups are always uncontested or uncontroversial, or fully successful and positive in their impact. Some reforms, even when introduced, will not have their intended social impact, or will later be resisted or reversed. Many factors can impede progressive change,

---

[12] Another recent account which tends to juxtapose the dynamism of grassroots activism and 'law from below' with the 'top down, lawyer-driven, professional game' (as described by Lucie White and Jeremy Perelman) of human rights law as an elite discourse, in her discussion of the provisions for persons with disabilities in the Marrakesh Treaty on copyright exceptions to intellectual property, is Land, 'The Marrakesh Treaty as "Bottom Up" Lawmaking: Supporting Local or Neuronal Human Rights Action on IP Policies', 8 *UC Irvine Law Review* (2018) 513.

and human rights reform is far from being a story of unidirectional progress. The trajectory of change is almost always an uneven, contested, and multi-step one rather than a linear path of onward progress. Further, as illustrated by the various case studies, there is a complex relationship between legal, political, and social change, with legal change often remaining purely formal and unimplemented in the absence of underlying social support or demand. Legal change sometimes follows from and relies on antecedent social change, while at other times prior legal reforms help to galvanize subsequent social and political change.[13] Social mobilization for human rights is often messy and unpredictable, and there is invariably contestation both within and between social movements and parts of civil society as to what human rights require, and what kinds of reforms are needed or desirable.

The book does not purport to make any strong causal claim that international human rights advocacy has led directly to changes in substantive law and policy. A strong version of such a claim would, in most but not all cases, be impossible to sustain in a methodologically sound and analytically compelling way. The reality is messier and more complicated. While the campaigns for change described in the case studies were often successful and were generally framed in human rights language, they took place in the context of particular social, political, and economic developments unfolding in the relevant countries. Precisely because many different factors were at play, any attempt to isolate and define the precise contribution made by human rights advocacy to the outcomes is likely to fail. Nevertheless, the case studies provide ample grounds for suggesting that ongoing engagement over time between domestic social movements and activists, international human rights norms, institutions and networks, and national-level institutions and officials helped to advance outcomes which promote human rights in the case studies chosen from different countries and regions of the world.

The international human rights movement (like all other movements to date) may not have succeeded in overturning entrenched structures of economic injustice, but a world without international human rights commitments, institutions, and actors would be a bleaker one as far as human welfare and human freedom are concerned. Human rights advocacy has helped to promote reform, to empower subordinated groups, and to dis-entrench unjust or oppressive practices in many places. Further, in spite of the recent global spread of illiberal nationalism, human rights nonetheless appear to remain widely shared values rooted in respect for human dignity, human welfare, and human freedoms, which resonate with people around the world even if they are realized differently in different places.[14] Paradoxical as it may appear, the fact that authoritarian or illiberal governments

---

[13] On the sequencing of social, political, and legal change, see Koh (n. 9) 1413–1414.

[14] For some attempts to measure the extent of underlying public support for human rights and the factors which affect that in different parts of the world, see the Special Issue on Public Opinion Polling and Human Rights, 16(3) *Journal of Human Rights* (2017). See also Ron (n. 11).

have been voted into power and entrenched their power in various jurisdictions does not seem to mean that human rights have lost popular support there.[15]

Despite the political nature of much human rights practice and advocacy, however, human rights campaigns are not a substitute for politics. Rather, as part of a movement based on widely shared values and moral intuitions about dignity, welfare, freedom, and justice, the human rights framework provides a set of approaches, institutions, and tools to influence and challenge social, political, and economic action, and can function as an important corrective to the dysfunctions and distortions of existing political systems. As the case studies described in the following chapters suggest, human rights law and advocacy can play an important part in pressing for different kinds of change within different kinds of political systems—democratic and otherwise—even if the need for them may be most sharply felt in the face of illiberal repression of human freedoms or plutocratic neglect of human welfare.

Finally, even if the human rights movement has helped in the past to promote positive change, it is clear that in order to rise to the daunting array of contemporary challenges—climate change, digitalization, authoritarianism, pandemics, inequality and more—the movement and its supporters need to adapt and to devise new strategies and approaches that can adequately grapple with those challenges. Intensive reflection on how to respond to the many existing threats and criticisms has already begun within various communities of human rights practice, with an emphasis on what kind of reform—whether gradual, transformative, or disruptive—is needed as far as their assumptions, goals, practices, and future strategies are concerned.[16] The final chapter of the book reflects on the future of the human rights movement in the face of a number of these major contemporary challenges and on the need for change.

2. Theories of the effectiveness of human rights

A. The empirical debate

Lawyers and legal scholars in the past have generally tended to assume the relevance of international human rights law in bringing about change. In contrast to the work of social scientists, legal academic research has often focused on describing the establishment and functioning of international human rights institutions, the

---

[15] See e.g. Hartmann, 'Misdiagnosing the Human Rights Malaise: Possible Lessons from the Danish Chairmanship of the Council of Europe', in *Global Community: Yearbook of International Law and Jurisprudence* (2018) 153.

[16] C. Rodríguez-Garavito and K. Gomez, *Rising to the Populist Challenge: A New Playbook for Human Rights Actors* (2018). See also the biennial conference at the University of Dayton on the Social Practice of Human Rights, available at https://ecommons.udayton.edu/human_rights.

drafting and content of international human rights treaties and the debates surrounding them, and the interpretation of provisions of these treaties, whether by international tribunals and bodies or by domestic courts.[17] It has not, in the main, focused on the ways in which the interpretation of or pronouncements on the provisions of human rights treaties have moved beyond legal doctrine to advance human rights in practice. Traditional legal scholarship to this extent has largely assumed the importance and centrality of international human rights treaties, courts, and treaty bodies to the promotion of human rights, without necessarily extending the inquiry into the mechanisms and processes by which they take effect in practice.

Political and social science scholars, on the other hand, have extensively debated the extent to which international human rights law has or has not had an impact, although until recently most of the literature has focused less on the mechanisms and processes by which it might do so than on actually trying to demonstrate or deny impact. A persistent strand of critique in the scholarship has been that international human rights treaties, in particular, are not effective, and the past two decades have seen an array of empirical studies being marshalled with a view to either demonstrating or challenging this proposition. It has been argued by a variety of scholars that the adoption of human rights treaties has not improved government practices or human welfare, and even that the situation in certain countries worsened after human rights treaties were signed and ratified.[18] A growing group of scholars has challenged aspects of the methodologies underlying these more pessimistic studies, however,[19] and several have argued on the contrary that the ratification of particular human rights treaties under certain conditions clearly correlates with improved human rights outcomes.[20] While at least one scholar has

---

[17] Some examples of classic legal works of this kind in the field of international human rights law are S. Trechsel, *Human Rights Between Idealism and Realism* (2003); W. Kalin and J. Künzli, *The Law of International Human Rights Protection* (2009); K. Vasak and P. Alston (eds), *The International Dimensions of Human Rights* (1982) Vols 1 and 2.

[18] See e.g. Hathaway, 'Do Human Rights Treaties Make a Difference', 111 *Yale Law Journal* (2002) 1935; Hafner-Burton and Tsutsui, 'Human Rights in a Globalizing World: The Paradox of Empty Promises', 110 *American Journal of Sociology* (2005) 1373; Keith, 'The United Nations International Covenant on Civil and Political Rights: Does It Make a Difference in Human Rights Behavior?', 36 *Journal of Peace Research* (1999) 85; Hill, 'Estimating the Effects of Human Rights Treaties on State Behavior', 72 *Journal of Politics* (2010) 1161; Hollyer and Rosendorff, 'Why Do Authoritarian Regimes Sign the Convention Against Torture? Signaling, Domestic Politics and Non-Compliance', 6 *Quarterly Journal of Political Science* (2011) 275, and E. Posner, *The Twilight of Human Rights Law* (2014).

[19] See e.g. Simmons, 'From Ratification to Compliance', in T. Risse, S. Ropp, and K. Sikkink, *The Persistent Power of Human Rights* (2012) and Dai, 'The Conditional Effects of International Human Rights Institutions', 36 *Human Rights Quarterly* (2014) 569.

[20] See e.g. Lupu, 'Best Evidence: The Role of Information in Domestic Judicial Enforcement of International Human Rights Treaties', 67 *International Organization* (2013) 469 and 'Legislative Veto Players and the Effects of International Human Rights Agreements', 59 *American Journal of Political Science* (2015) 578. Beth Simmons' book, *Mobilizing for Human Rights* (n. 9), provides one of the most sustained arguments to the effect that human rights treaties do make a difference particularly in countries in a transitional democratic state where there is civil society mobilization. For a challenge to the Hafner-Burton/Tsutsui thesis (n.18), about the impact of human rights treaty commitment on

expressed the view that none of the reforms advanced in connection with the implementation of human rights treaties amount to much more than 'tweaking' so long as economic inequality exists,[21] the more widely held view is that all kinds of human rights and human rights advances are important, including but not restricted to those related to economic inequality. The debate in recent years has grown in both size and sophistication as studies have multiplied and become more nuanced.[22]

What lessons, then, about the past successes of international human rights advocacy can be drawn, given the continued debate over the extent of effectiveness of international human rights law? This book does not add to or contest the empirical studies, but instead builds on the consensus within that literature around a particular proposition. That proposition is that in circumstances where there is a certain degree of political liberalization and hence at least some space for domestic civil society and for social mobilization, the presence of international human rights treaties ratified by a state correlates with a measurable improvement in human rights outcomes.[23] Indeed, an increasing number of scholars have argued that even in the most illiberal and repressive political systems, there is always some degree of civic space for action, and that human rights mobilization of different kinds can take place within these contexts.[24] Lynette Chua's work in particular challenges

---

government repression, see Conrad and Ritter, 'Do Human Rights Treaties Protect Rights', in C. R. Conrad and E. H. Ritter, *Contentious Compliance* (2019).

[21] Samuel Moyn uses scathing terms to dismiss the significance of the empirical debates by characterizing them as 'diverting', their focus as 'picayune', and at best showing that human rights 'tweak the world a tiny bit'. See Moyn, 'Beyond the Human Rights Measurement Controversy', 81 *Law and Contemporary Problems* (2018) 121, responding in particular to the exchange between Beth Simmons and Eric Posner on some aspects of the methodology and arguments underlying Simmons' book, *Mobilizing for Human Rights* (n. 9) in Simmons, 'Reflections on Mobilizing for Human Rights', 44 *NYU Journal of International Law and Policy* (2012) 729.

[22] See e.g. the response by Cope and Creamer, 'Disaggregating the Human Rights Treaty Regime', 56 *Virginia Journal of International Law* (2016) 459 to the argument of Adam Chilton and Eric Posner in 'The Influence of History on States Compliance with Human Rights Obligations', 56 *Virginia Journal of International Law* (2016) 211 that it may be other long-running trends and not human rights treaties that have a positive impact on human rights conditions throughout the world. For the argument that the empirical scholarship shows correlation rather than causation, see Chilton, 'Experimentally Testing the Effects of Human Rights Treaties', 18 *Chicago Journal of International Law* (2017) 164.

[23] Simmons (n. 9); Neumayer, 'Do International Human Rights Treaties Improve Respect for Human Rights', 49 *Journal of Conflict Resolution* (2005) 925; Dai, 'The "Compliance Gap" and the Efficacy of International Human Rights Institutions', in T. Risse, S. Ropp, and K. Sikkink, *The Persistent Power of Human Rights* (2013). For further discussion of this literature, see de Búrca, 'Human Rights Experimentalism', 111 *American Journal of International Law* (2017) 277.

[24] According to Kaldor and Kostovicova, 'Global Civil Society and Illiberal Regimes', in M. Albrow, H. Anheier, M. Glasius, and M. Price (eds), *Global Civil Society Yearbook 2007/8*, 'In all illiberal regimes, it is possible to identify some kind of space—underground or open, private or public, virtual or real, at home or abroad—for autonomous activity'. On gay rights activism in authoritarian states, see L. Chua, *Mobilizing Gay Singapore: Rights and Resistance in an Authoritarian State* (2015). See also Stobb, 'A Shield in Battle: The Contingent Value of Human Rights Treaties to NGOs in Autocracies', 23(4) *International Journal of Human Rights* (2018) 555. For a challenge to a simple liberal/illiberal binary as a way of categorizing political systems and state types, see Teo, 'Conduct and Counter-Conduct in the "Nonliberal" State: Singapore's Headscarf Affairs', 33 *Global Society* (2019) 201.

the purely political definition of 'authoritarianism', arguing that societal authoritarianism is ubiquitous, and that societal as well as public power can impede legal and other forms of mobilization.[25] Certainly, given the fragility and volatility of even supposedly stable democratic political systems in recent years, and the shift towards authoritarian regimes as well as so-called 'illiberal democracies',[26] particularly in a time of pandemic, the potential for human rights mobilization within illiberal systems of different kinds needs to be studied more closely.[27]

As will be outlined in further detail below, this book introduces and uses three detailed qualitative case studies from within different kinds of democratic political system in different parts of the world to look more closely at some of the ways in which interaction between domestic advocacy movements and international human rights law and institutions has helped to promote progressive human rights reform in the past, and to consider what might be learned from these in terms of the current and future challenges facing the human rights project.

B. Explanatory accounts of the effectiveness of human rights law and advocacy

While much of the social science scholarship on the impact of international human rights law has, as indicated above, been empirical and quantitative in nature, focusing on the question whether a causal relation or correlation can be shown rather than seeking to explain the mechanisms of change, a number of influential explanatory theories of change have also been advanced. Amongst the two most developed and influential of these explanatory theories are the *boomerang* thesis of Sikkink and Keck (focusing not so much on law but on human rights norms more broadly), and the *domestic mobilization* thesis of Simmons (focusing primarily on human rights treaties). In proposing their original boomerang thesis, Kathryn Sikkink and Margaret Keck argued that domestic constituencies—particularly within states that are not responsive to human rights norms and claims—seek to encourage and leverage international connections and transnational networks to impose pressure from above and from outside on the state.[28] Keck and Sikkink

[25] Chua, 'Legal Mobilization and Authoritarianism', 15 *Annual Review of Law and Social Science* (2019) 355.

[26] Several scholars have argued that 'illiberal democracy' is an oxymoron or at least a misnomer in the circumstances in which it is being used: J. Werner Müller, 'The Problem with "Illiberal Democracy"' *Project Syndicate*, 27 January 2016. And see in relation to Poland in particular, W. Sadurski, *Poland's Constitutional Breakdown* (2019), at Ch. 9.

[27] For some examples, see the case studies on human rights activism in Venezuela, Turkey, Egypt, and India, contained in C. Rodriguez Garavito and K. Gomez, *Rising to the Populist Challenge: A New Playbook for Human Rights Actors* (2018). See also for a study of two campaigns in Iran, Barlow, and Akbarzadeh, 'Human Rights and Agents of Change in Iran: Towards a Theory of Change', 10 *Journal of Human Rights Practice* (2018) 229.

[28] M. Keck and K. Sikkink, *Activists Beyond Borders: Advocacy Networks in International Politics* (1998). There is now a significant literature on the impact of international NGOs (INGOs) and naming

describe these international and transnational networks as operating to provide alternative sources of information and to draw attention to issues by targeting other states, international organizations, financial institutions, and companies in order to mobilize and shame or pressure states into honouring the human rights commitments they have entered into. According to the boomerang theory, the external actors and transnational networks have particular importance and prominence in view of the resistance or inaction of the state in the face of domestic advocacy and pressure. This international and external dimension is presented in the boomerang theory as being crucial to generating and securing the kind of pressure needed to make recalcitrant states comply with their human rights commitments.[29]

A second influential theory of the effectiveness of international human rights, which remains the most developed of existing theories to date and which focuses particularly on the efficacy of human rights treaties, is the domestic mobilization thesis advanced by Beth Simmons. In a major book in 2009 and in her subsequent work, Simmons proposed this theory to explain how it is that the international human rights treaty commitments entered by states eventually translate into improved human rights outcomes.[30] Pointing out that the act of a government in signing international treaties does not in itself achieve much other than signalling commitment, Simmons drew attention to the array of domestic responses that often follow after human rights treaty ratification, including national legislative changes, the initiation of civil litigation, and the empowerment of other kinds of political mobilization. The focus of the domestic mobilization theory is on what happens within the country in question after signature and ratification of a treaty, and Simmons argued that the response of domestic constituencies provides the crucial ingredient that enables international human rights law to operate to produce positive change. Without domestic actors who are motivated, empowered, and equipped to persuade and challenge the behaviour of state actors and others to change existing laws and practices that impede or prevent the realization of

and shaming techniques on states that sign human rights treaties. See e.g. A. Murdie, *Help or Harm: The Human Security Effects of International NGOs* (2014); S. Tarrow, *The New Transnational Activism* (2005); Meernik et al., 'The Impact of Human Rights Organizations on Naming and Shaming Campaigns', 56 *Journal of Conflict Resolution* (2012) 233; Hendrix and Wong, 'When is the Pen Truly Mighty? Regime Type and the Efficacy of Naming and Shaming in Curbing Human Rights Abuses', 43 *British Journal of Political Science* (2013) 651. For more recent scholarship on how authoritarian states can use critical pressure from external sources—especially from rival states—to bolster their domestic support, see Gruyffyd-Jones, 'Citizen Condemnation: Strategic Uses of International Human Rights Pressure in Authoritarian States', *Comparative Political Studies* (2018).

[29] While a group of authors have tested and challenged aspects of the boomerang thesis, arguing that the negative effects of external third party pressure actually diminish the positive effects, their study focuses on coercive external action and in particular on economic sanctions and military intervention, rather than persuasive or accountability-enhancing interventions: see Allendoerfer, Murdie, and Welch, 'The Path of the Boomerang: Human Rights Campaigns, Third-Party Pressure, and Human Rights', 64 *International Studies Quarterly* (2020) 111.

[30] Simmons (n. 9).

rights, treaty ratification would achieve little. Simmons presents her theory as an explicitly 'bottom up' account of the effects of human rights treaties, contrasting with what she describes as elite-focused theories which emphasize the role of international organizations and transnational elites in influencing domestic elites to comply with human rights.[31]

Both the domestic mobilization and boomerang theories attach importance to the role of domestic actors in realizing the potential of international human rights, although Simmons' theory focuses closely on treaties and places considerably more weight on the actions of domestic actors themselves, while Sikkink and Keck emphasize the importance of external and international actors, other states and transnational networks in supplying pressure from outside to bring about the requisite compliance with human rights norms. And while Sikkink and Keck's account may appear to rely strongly on mechanisms of pressure or coercion from above (inducement), and Simmons' account on ideational change (persuasion) from below, in fact elements of both of these mechanisms seem present in each of their accounts, as arguably they are present—alongside other causal mechanisms such as socialization and acculturation[32]—in many campaigns for human rights reform.

Broader accounts of the series of steps by which initially repressive governments have gradually been brought to respect human rights law and norms, and which incorporate elements of both the boomerang and domestic mobilization thesis, include the 'spiral model' of human rights progress developed by Risse and others.[33] The spiral model, in both its original and its updated version,[34] proposes a five-stage account of how initially resistant governments gradually respond positively to the pressures created by human rights advocates and others to sign, to ratify, and eventually to implement human rights agreements, though it does not go beyond this stage to examine what happens after implementation. Goodman and Jinks have also added to the existing 'persuasion' and 'inducement' accounts of state compliance with human rights their own distinctive socialization/acculturation model, which focuses on the adaptation of elite (state) behaviour to the prevailing norms in the environments they inhabit.[35] Goodman and Jinks' account of human rights compliance does not focus on external pressure or persuasive influence from below, but considers the additional possible mechanism of mimetic or normative isomorphism on the part of elites, while other studies have examined

[31] Ibid. 138.
[32] See R. Goodman and D. Jinks, *Socializing States: Promoting Human Rights Through International Law* (2013). Their work contains an interesting discussion of the possible interactions between these three different mechanisms of human rights influence (persuasion, acculturation, and inducement), including questions as to whether crowding-out or countermanding of one mode of influence by the other may occur: see in particular Ch. 9.
[33] T. Risse, S. Ropp, and K. Sikkink, *The Power of Human Rights* (1999).
[34] T. Risse, S. Ropp, and K. Sikkink, *The Persistent Power of Human Rights* (2013).
[35] Goodman and Jinks (n. 32).

the sequencing and the relationship between domestic-mobilization explanations and state-socialization explanations for particular human rights reforms.[36]

C. The new human rights scholarship: examining the interaction of the global and the local

Recent years, however, have seen an emerging multidisciplinary body of scholarship on human rights law and practice that is notable for two reasons. In the first place, in their detailed analyses of how human rights law and practice work and how they help to promote change, these accounts contrast with the verdicts of failure and predictions of the demise of human rights described at the outset of this chapter. In the second place, some of the more recent accounts eschew a primarily binary or dichotomous analysis, and rather than comparing or juxtaposing bottom-up with top-down or elite influence, they explore aspects of the idea that human rights reform is often advanced through interaction between the international and the local levels.[37]

At least three clusters of research can be discerned within this emerging body of scholarship. Some of it is the more recent work of political scientists who—like Sikkink and Simmons—are seeking to explain the ways in which international human rights, and particularly international human rights law, make a difference. A second cluster includes a range of anthropological and sociological studies of the ways in which the language of human rights is filtered through local experience, or is changed through domestic interaction with international institutions and norms. A third cluster includes contributions by practitioners and advocates who have been reflecting critically on how best to conduct human rights advocacy so as to advance human rights in practice.

The first of these clusters of social science scholarship pointing to a more interactive account of the impact of international human rights includes the more recent work of Sikkink herself. In some of her later writing she has suggested that the boomerang thesis is probably most applicable to repressive or authoritarian contexts, while in more open political systems 'insider-outsider coalitions' involving the interaction of international and domestic opportunity structures have been created and have given rise 'to new forms of dynamic multi-level governance'.[38]

---

[36] See in particular on the adoption of domestic violence legislation in states of North and South America, and the interesting relationship between domestic mobilization on the one hand and state socialization through international engagement on the other: Hawkins and Humes, 'Human Rights and Domestic Violence', 117 *Political Science Quarterly* (2002) 231.

[37] For an early attempt at articulating the importance of interaction between the local and the global in human rights advocacy, although with the emphasis on bringing back in the local, and emphasizing bottom-up involvement with international human rights norms, see K. De Feyter, 'Localizing Human Rights', University of Antwerp Discussion Paper 2006/02.

[38] Sikkink, 'Patterns of Dynamic Multilevel Governance and the Insider Outsider Coalition', in D. Della Porta and S. Tarrow (eds), *Transnational Protest and Global Activism* (2005) 151–173. Similarly

Beth Simmons too in her recent work has begun to look at the interaction between domestic civil society and international institutions through the treaty reporting process, a process which did not figure in her major book, discussed earlier.[39] Shareen Hertel has applied Amitav Acharya's conception of localization to the issue of labour rights, describing processes of 'blocking' and 'backdooring' when local activists reject or change international interpretations of norms and press for different or additional rights,[40] while Kiyoteru Tsutsui and Jackie Smith have referred to a 'sandwich effect' to describe their understanding of the interaction of global and local levels in the promotion of human rights.[41] In his book-length study of the interaction of domestic social movements with international human rights law, Tsutsui describes in detail the ways in which minority groups in Japan were galvanized by and used international human rights law and institutions to successfully advance their claims.[42] Focusing on human rights advocacy in Latin America, historian Patrick William Kelly has traced some of the ways in which 'transnational forces interacted with local realities—and how local particularities, in turn, inflected the approach of transnational actors.'[43] And in their collaborative study of economic and social rights advocacy, LaDawn Haglund and Robin Stryker have advanced a series of hypotheses about the ways in which interaction and engagement between global and local human rights norms and actors lead to improvements in the lives of those who are marginalized or living in poverty.[44] While many of these works are quite different in their focus and aim, they have in

Thomas Risse, one of the scholars who coined the 'spiral model', in recent work has acknowledged the importance of studying the processes of 'localization and translation': Risse, 'Human Rights in Areas of Limited Statehood: From the Spiral Model to Localization and Translation', in S. Hopgood, J. Snyder, and L. Vinjamuri (eds), *Human Rights Futures* (2018) 135. Risse cites the work of Tobias Berger, who studies how transnational notions of the 'rule of law' were received and translated in Bangladesh in T. Berger, *Global Norms and Local Courts: Translating the Rule of Law in Bangladesh* (2018).

[39] See Simmons (n. 9). In Simmons and Creamer, 'Do Self-Reporting Regimes Matter? Evidence from the Convention Against Torture', 63 *International Studies Quarterly* (2019) 1051, Beth Simmons and Cosette Creamer cite to the literature on experimentalist governance (discussed further below) and expressly acknowledge the importance of the iterative and interactive dimensions of engagement between the international and domestic levels in treaty reporting. See also Creamer and Simmons, 'The Dynamic Impact of Periodic Review on Women's Rights', 81 *Law and Contemporary Problems* (2018) 31.

[40] Hertel, 'Re-Framing Human Rights Advocacy: The Rise of Economic Rights', in S. Hopgood, J. Snyder, and L. Vinjamuri (eds), *Human Rights Futures* (2018) 237 drawing on Acharya, 'How Ideas Spread: Whose Norms Matter? Norm Localization and Institutional Change in Asian Regionalism', 58 *International Organizations* (2004) 239.

[41] Tsutsui and Smith, 'Human Rights and Social Movements: From the Boomerang Pattern to a Sandwich Effect', in *The Wiley Blackwell Companion to Social Movements* (2nd ed., 2018) 586. See also Boesenecker and Vinjamuri, 'Lost in Translation? Civil Society, Faith-Based Organizations and the Negotiation of International Norms', 5 *International Journal of Transitional Justice* (2011) 345.

[42] K. Tsutsui, *Rights Make Might: Global Human Rights and Minority Social Movements in Japan* (2018). See also Tobias Berger's account of the translation of the rule of law in Bangladesh (albeit not focused specifically on human rights): T. Berger, *Global Norms and Local Courts* (2017).

[43] P. W. Kelly, *Sovereign Emergencies: Latin America and the Making of Global Human Rights Politics* (2018).

[44] L. Haglund and R. Stryker, *Closing the Rights Gap: From Human Rights to Social Transformation* (2015).

common an account of international human rights advocacy and reform which looks closely at examples in practice and brings out the complexity and range of interactions between local, international, internal, and external actors and sites in different parts of the world.

The second cluster within this growing body of 'multidirectional' human rights-related scholarship is a broadly anthropological literature on the relationship between local experience and international human rights norms. One of the most influential and original bodies of work in this vein has been Sally Engle Merry's research on the vernacularization of human rights, which has drawn attention to the ways in which local actors and intermediaries translate, use, and make sense of international norms in specific contexts.[45] Drawing inspiration from Engle Merry's research, Tina Destrooper assembled a group of anthropologists and critical human rights scholars to consider the multiple directions of 'travel' of human rights norms, including not only 'upstream' and 'downstream' directions from the global to the local and vice versa, but also across and between organizations and sites.[46] While they are not necessarily seeking either to explain human rights outcomes or to develop a theory of how international human rights law becomes effective, these anthropological accounts contribute to a better understanding of the complex relationships between local actors and experiences on the one hand, and international human rights norms and institutions on the other.[47]

The third cluster within this emerging body of scholarship includes scholar-practitioners who are critically exploring the relationship between local and grassroots action and international human rights norms, usually in order to provide a better account of how and under what circumstances human rights advocacy is likely to work, and with a view to improving the effectiveness of practice. Koen de Feyter led a collective research project on localizing human rights focused on how the global human rights regime is used at local level by people facing unjust or repressive conditions, with the aim of understanding not just how international human rights law was used locally but also how local experience may inform and help develop the global framework.[48] César Rodríguez-Garavito, a leading

[45] See Merry and Levitt, 'Vernacularization on the Ground: Local Uses of Global Women's Rights in Peru, China, India and the United States', 9 *Global Networks* (2009) 441 and Merry and Stern, 'The Female Inheritance Movement in Hong Kong: Theorising the Local/Global Interface', 46 *Current Anthropology* (2005) 387. See also M. Goodale and S. E. Merry, *The Practice of Human Rights: Tracking Law between the Global and the Local* (2007).

[46] Destrooper, 'On Travel, Translation and Transformation', in T. Destrooper and S. E. Merry, *Human Rights Transformation in Practice* (2018). For an interesting anthropological study of the interaction between the global and the local in the context of women's rights movements in Morocco, see A. Evrard, *The Moroccan Women's Rights Movement* (2014).

[47] For a study of the impact of the interaction between local mobilization and international and transnational networks of support in the context of mining in Peru by a sociologist of development, see Paredes, 'The Glocalization of Mining Conflict: Cases from Peru', 3 *The Extractive Industries and Society* (2016) 1046.

[48] For a proposed practical methodology for human rights advocates that would help to localize human rights so as to serve the needs of those most affected on the ground, see G. Oré Aguilar, 'The Local Relevance of Human Rights: A Methodological Approach', in K. De Feyter et al. (eds), *The Local*

scholar-practitioner, has suggested that the notion of 'multiple boomerangs' better captures the currently changing field of human rights advocacy than Sikkink's original boomerang idea, since it points to less hierarchical existing models of collaboration, and encompasses internal as well as external coalitions and groupings.[49] He has also proposed the metaphor of an 'ecosystem' to describe the kind of human rights system which is evolving, so as to better reflect as well as promote its complex, horizontal, and multi-actor nature.[50]

Rather than arguing or assuming that the levers of human rights reform operate either mainly through the interventions of international actors, or mainly bottom up through local activism, the emphasis in these diverse disciplinary clusters of research is on examining different dimensions of the interaction between various actors and sites, including how globally articulated norms are localized, vernacularized, resisted, or transformed through domestic action and vice versa. They aim to enhance understanding of the varying relationships between the global and the local in the field of human rights, and offer valuable insights in a range of contexts and detailed examples.

This emerging body of scholarship is for the most part both critical and constructive in nature, neither idealizing human rights law and practice nor suggesting that it is the main or only answer to injustice, and addressing the complexities and limitations of human rights advocacy. Nevertheless, and by comparison with the more pessimistically critical or sceptical academic commentaries mentioned earlier, neither do they take the view that human rights law is inadequate or peripheral because it has not overturned neoliberal capitalism,[51] nor do they trivialize its impact in helping to galvanize meaningful social and political reform in many parts of the world.[52] Even while they grapple with the challenges and limitations of the international human rights movement as a set of mechanisms and strategies for contesting injustice, many of the studies contain detailed and insightful accounts of the ways in which human rights movements have or have not helped to advance reforms, and they do so in the main by focusing on the interaction between domestic movements and international human rights law and institutions.

Relevance of Human Rights (2011). Many of the other contributions to this volume address aspects of local-global interactions in the practice of human rights.

[49] See C. Rodríguez-Garavito, *Multiple Boomerangs: New Models of Global Human Rights Advocacy*, Open Global Rights, 21 January 2015, available at https://www.openglobalrights.org/multiple-boomerangs-new-models-of-global-human-rights-advoc. Also Evans and Rodríguez-Garavito, 'Introduction: Building and Sustaining the Ecosystem of Transnational Advocacy', in P. Evans and C. Rodríguez-Garavito (eds), *Transnational Advocacy Networks: Twenty Years of Evolving Theory and Practice* (2018).

[50] C. Rodríguez-Garavito, 'The Human Rights Movement: From Gatekeeping to Symbiosis', 11 *Sur—International Journal on Human Rights* (2014) 499.

[51] See Moyn (n. 3).

[52] See Posner (n. 2).

This book advances a broader explanatory theory of the effectiveness of inter-national human rights. It does so in part by building on three detailed studies of human rights advocacy and reform in different parts of the world. While they are quite different in their detail, context and focus, each of the studies suggests to varying degrees that the dynamic created by iterative interaction over time be-tween at least three broad sets of internal and external actors and institutions—domestic movements and activists, international and transnational institutions and networks, and independent national institutions and actors—has been key to the process of realizing human rights-promoting reform in practice. This iterative, interactive, and multi-actor dynamic of international human rights advocacy will be described in further detail below as an example of transnational experimen-talism in action.[53]

To conclude, I am not arguing that there have been no interesting examples of human rights activism which are primarily or entirely local (other than in the uni-versalism inherent in the use of the language of human rights), and which make no use of formal international institutions or processes.[54] And there are undoubtedly instances in which the lack of capacity or interest of state actors means that en-gagement between civil society activists and international institutions is the main driver of human rights reform.[55] Neither am I seeking to argue that there are no examples of human rights reform which are brought about primarily by means of elite behavioural change, or by 'acculturation', in the way that Goodman and Jinks suggest.[56] Rather, the argument advanced in this book is that a particularly ef-fective model of human rights promotion which can be observed from campaigns in many parts of the world is one that combines robust domestic mobilization with external accountability and independent internal support in an ongoing process of change over time. My emphasis on the 'iterative' nature of human rights reform is not at all intended to imply that change is likely to be a calmly adaptive, rou-tine, or mechanical process, since most campaigns for human rights entail contest-ation, opposition, disruption, and challenge, but rather is intended to underscore the fact that one-shot campaigns or short-term mobilization rarely bring about

---

[53] On global experimentalist governance, see de Búrca, Keohane, and Sabel, 'New Modes of Pluralist Global Governance', 45 NYU Journal of International Law and Politics (2013) 723, and 'Global Experimentalist Governance', 44(3) British Journal of Politics (2014) 477. For an introduction to the idea of transnational experimentalist governance and its application to the field of human rights, see de Búrca (n. 23).

[54] An interesting example of human rights action in a jurisdiction which cannot officially participate in international legal processes due to China's opposition to its recognition as a state, but which none-theless opts to shadow international norms and processes, is Taiwan. Taiwan has chosen to bind itself to international human rights treaties and procedures, including inviting international human rights experts to monitor its compliance. See Chen, 'Human Rights Treaty Monitoring 2.0: Taiwan's Local Innovation and Implications for Global Practice', in Taiwan and International Human Rights (forth-coming), available online at https://papers.ssrn.com/sol3/papers.cfm?abstract_id=3536921.

[55] I am grateful to Sarah Knuckey, who gave a recent example from the Central African Republic, for this point.

[56] Goodman and Jinks (n. 32).

fundamental or transformative change of the kind that is so often sought through human rights advocacy.

3. Three case studies

The three case studies which are used to illustrate the theory advanced in this book are drawn from a variety of jurisdictions and regions, and involve different issues and claims. In spite of their differences, each shows a range of ways in which social mobilization and activation by domestic advocates of human rights law through ongoing engagement over time with international and national institutions, networks, and actors has helped to advance social and political reform across a range of important issue areas. The studies have not been chosen in order to make any kind of empirical claim about the success of human rights advocacy. While they were deliberately chosen from different jurisdictions and continents, and each intentionally deals with a different set of rights, the main aim of the studies is to examine and illustrate in greater detail *the ways in which* human rights campaigns can further rights-promoting change in different contexts and on different issues, rather than to prove or demonstrate with any methodological rigour the circumstances under which they are likely do so.

Drawing out common themes from the various accounts, this book argues that the case studies illustrate a model of domestic–transnational mobilization and engagement which has been effective in helping to advance human rights in practice. The human rights norms themselves have generally been agreed by states in the treaties or other instruments they sign, whether for strategic or sincere reasons. Increasingly, international human rights instruments are being drawn up in consultation with or at the instigation of other stakeholders including civil society organizations[57]—and even, in recent times, occasionally drawing in corporate actors whose buy-in will be crucial if rights are to be implemented in practice.[58] Sometimes themselves the product of social mobilization and advocacy, these human rights measures, once enacted, are generally activated and used in a variety of ways by advocates within states to promote rights, to build on and mobilize broader support for issues, and to engage domestic actors and officials as well as

---

[57] The involvement of 'non state actors' of various kinds can be seen prominently in a range of recent human rights treaty-making forums such as the Ottawa Mine Ban Convention, the Rome Statute on the establishment of the International Criminal Court, the UN Convention on the Rights of Persons with Disabilities, and the currently proposed draft Treaty on Business and Human Rights. For earlier discussions see e.g. Charnovitz, 'Two Centuries of Participation: NGOs and International Governance', 18 *Michigan Journal of International Law* (1997) 183; Raustiala, 'The Role of NGOs in International Treaty Making', in *The Oxford Guide to Treaties* (2012) and Spiro, 'NGOs and Human Rights: Channels of Power', in S. Joseph and A. McBeth (eds), *Research Handbook on International Human Rights Law* (2010).

[58] A key example of this are the UN Guiding Principles on Human Rights (the so-called Ruggie Principles): see https://www.ohchr.org/documents/publications/guidingprinciplesbusinesshr_en.pdf.

international institutions in an effort to challenge the status quo and to further change. The studies describe the uses that an array of civil society actors and activists, often driven or accompanied by broader social movements in these different jurisdictions, have made of various international human rights laws and institutions as part of their campaigns for reform, and more specifically the ways in which domestic constituencies used those provisions and the institutions established to monitor their implementation as part of their campaign to press successfully for rights-promoting social and political change.

The first case study looks mainly at the use made in Pakistan of the Convention on the Elimination of All Forms of Discrimination against Women (CEDAW), a key instrument intended to combat gender inequality globally, and more particularly at the processes and outcomes of social mobilization and domestic advocacy in the country around CEDAW and other international human rights norms on gender equality. The second study examines the part played by international human rights law and advocacy in two recent movements for social and political reform in Ireland. One concerns domestic advocacy and action around the Convention on the Rights of the Child (CRC) and the treaty body charged with implementation, and the range of legal and policy reforms which were adopted in part through this engagement over the years since the treaty's ratification. The other concerns recent changes to Irish law and policy governing reproductive autonomy, and the role that the use by domestic social movements and advocacy groups of international human rights norms and institutions played in the reform of Irish abortion law which took place. The third case study examines some reforms of disability policy in Argentina, particularly but not only in the area of inclusive education, which were brought about in part through the engagement of domestic advocacy groups with international human rights institutions including the UN Convention on the Rights of Persons with Disabilities and its Committee, and with state institutions and actors.

The three clusters of rights which are the focus of each of the studies exemplify the close relationship between the supposedly distinct categories of civil and political rights on the one hand and socioeconomic rights on the other. For women, children, and persons with disabilities, as indeed for many others, the distinction has little traction since their access to civil and political liberties are interwoven with their access to social and economic welfare and vice versa.

And even while they are obviously quite different in many respects, the case studies have a number of key features in common. In particular, three interacting dimensions were important to the progress achieved in each of the cases, in which continued engagement over a sustained period of time between domestic and international actors, institutions, and norms contributed to a process of domestic legal and policy change. The first is domestic social mobilization and advocacy around an issue framed in human rights terms; the second is engagement on the part of some of these domestic actors with an external system of accountability and reinforcement such as that provided by international human rights institutions, and with transnational and regional networks of support; and the third is their engagement with a range of independent domestic actors and institutions such as courts, ombudspersons, media, and legislators including legislative veto-players who were able to provide national traction. Finally, the interaction of these dimensions over time appears to have been important to generating political responsiveness and to the eventual achievement of what will hopefully be meaningful and durable reform.

Three of the studies focus primarily on domestic advocacy for change centred around one particular human rights treaty, while one of them examines domestic advocacy focused on a specific issue—reproductive rights—which is addressed by a range of different treaties and normative sources. Each of the three main international human rights treaties in question focuses on a section of the population: women under CEDAW, children under the CRC, and persons with disabilities under the CRPD. The three treaties cover not just civil and political rights such as torture or freedom of expression, which have been the focus of many of the existing empirical studies and attempts at measurement of impact, but also economic and social rights such as the right to education (e.g. inclusive education for persons with disabilities), health (e.g. reproductive rights for women) and welfare (in particular child welfare). The Convention on the Rights of Persons with Disabilities is a particularly comprehensive example of a human rights treaty which covers a wide range of types of rights, including civil, political, economic, social, and cultural rights.[59] Each of these treaties provides group-specific protection, which may partly explain the extensive and focused mobilization which has taken place around them.

The countries in which the case studies are based are located in Europe, Asia, and South America respectively, and their political systems are somewhat different. Currently, Ireland is considered to be a relatively stable democracy, while Pakistan is characterized, according to the Democracy Index developed by the Economist's Intelligence Unit, as a hybrid democracy.[60] Argentina is at present a fairly vibrant democracy albeit with a relatively recent history of military dictatorship, and it is currently characterized by the Democracy Index as 'flawed'. The characterization as 'hybrid' or 'flawed' reflects the score attributed to those countries based on five categories including electoral process and pluralism, civil liberties, the functioning of government, political participation, and political culture. Indeed, the simple

---

[59] Mégret, 'The Disabilities Convention: Towards a Holistic Concept of Rights', 12 *International Journal of Human Rights* (2008) 261. For an evaluation and analysis of the UN CRPD that contrasts a 'new governance' approach with a traditional litigation approach, see Lorion, 'A Model for National Human Rights Systems? New Governance and the Convention on the Rights of Persons with Disabilities', 37 *Nordic Journal of Human Rights* (2019) 234.

[60] The Economist Intelligence Unit Democracy Index rates countries on a scale of 1 to 10 and classifies them either as full democracies, flawed democracies, hybrid democracies or autocracies.

binary distinction between 'liberal' and 'illiberal' states has been questioned, with scholars pointing to "the similarities across liberal and non-liberal societies where freedom and authoritarianism coexist",[61] and offering a definition of societal authoritarianism which blurs the sharpness of the proposed distinction between authoritarian and non-authoritarian states.[62] Further and pertinently, it has become clear in recent years that countries and their political systems are liable to move back-and-forth between authoritarianism, transitional systems, hybrid democracy, and more robust democratic systems. The proliferation of formal states-of-emergency and repressive measures across all types of political system during the COVID-19 pandemic has added further salience to this existing trend. There is certainly no clear trajectory whereby authoritarian regimes and flawed or hybrid democracies move gradually towards fuller and more stable democracy, but rather there is movement back and forth between these various systems: many formerly robust or apparently stable democracies having begun to backslide significantly, putting the health of liberal democracy overall in question.[63] Nevertheless, given the importance of civil society activism to an experimentalist theory of human rights effectiveness, an interesting future research agenda would be to examine the relative success or otherwise of comparable human rights advocacy campaigns across a spectrum of different kinds of political system, ranging from highly repressive authoritarian on one end to robust constitutional democracy on the other, with an array of intermediate systems in between.

The case studies chosen for the book examine democracies of different kinds in which there is some civil society presence, and the focus of the studies is on the processes by which human rights reform occurs. The developments they depict call into question the assumption that human rights treaties and human rights activism are irrelevant or make little difference in vibrant or stable democracies. Instead, they suggest that the extent to which international human rights norms are liable to help advance domestic reform within a reasonably robust democracy is likely to depend on the issue in question.[64] Even within stable democracies, for instance, there are many neglected minorities and vulnerable population groups, as is clear from several of the examples. Persons with disabilities, for example, have often been overlooked or marginalized in many societies, while children have often not been viewed as rights-holders whose voices should be heard or heeded separately from those of their families. Democracies that are otherwise pluralistic

---

[61] Teo, 'Conduct and Counter-conduct in the "Nonliberal" State: Singapore's Headscarf Affairs', 33 *Global Society* (2019) 201.

[62] See Chua (n. 25).

[63] See e.g. Varieties of Democracy Institute (V-Dem), *Democracy for All? V-Dem Annual Democracy Report 2018* and S. Levitsky and D. Ziblatt, *How Democracies Die* (2018).

[64] For a similar recent argument in the context of CEDAW, see Hill and Watson, 'Democracy and Compliance with Human Rights Treaties: The Conditional Effectiveness of the Convention on the Elimination of All Forms of Discrimination Against Women', 63 *International Studies Quarterly* (2019) 127.

and inclusive may privilege the views of a particular religion within public policy, as was the case for many decades in relation to reproductive rights in Ireland. Women are significantly socially, politically, and economically disadvantaged in many parts of the world despite their numerical strength. And the poor are marginalized in virtually all societies. While some previous large-n empirical studies, such as in Beth Simmons' major book, have suggested that human rights treaties and international human rights advocacy appear to make little difference in stable democracies, a close look at particular campaigns such as reproductive rights and children's rights in Ireland and disability rights in Argentina indicate that international human rights law and advocacy have had a meaningful role to play in advancing reform in some robust democratic systems just as they have in partial, flawed, or hybrid democracies.

While none of the rights at issue in the various studies were uncontroversial, it is certainly true that human rights advocacy and reform is likely to be significantly more difficult to pursue in the absence of some degree of underlying social support for the rights in question, or in the face of strong state resistance. Human rights are far from being a monolithic category, and different kinds of rights are likely to require very different kinds of campaign and to generate different kinds of responses from governments as well as societies.[65] Advocating for the rights of migrants, for example, particularly during an era of illiberal nationalism, is likely to be far more challenging than advocating for the rights of children or persons with disabilities. And advocating for the rights of prisoners or detainees during a political context which is presented as a national security emergency is unlikely to be easy or popular. More pertinently, as the world has recently seen, a whole array of human rights are quickly seen as unwelcome impediments and brushed to the side during a time of pandemic. At the same time, it is worth noting that promoting gender equality in a highly patriarchal social and political system, or advocating for reproductive rights in a predominantly Catholic society has also presented profound challenges for activists, and yet human rights advocacy helped to advance social change in those contexts too. More generally, human rights movements have often begun and gained traction precisely during times of significant repression, and they have experienced some success even when advocating on behalf of supposedly socially despised or unpopular minorities. It is already clear at the time of writing that human rights advocates and civil society groups have not remained silent during the states of emergency and repressive measures brought in during

---

[65] According to research carried out on behalf of USAID, the relative success of domestic human rights campaigns is likely to depend on factors including: (i) the regime type of the state in question; (ii) the degree of poverty prevalent in the country in which mobilization takes place; and (iii) the lack of domestic contestation of and degree of recognition afforded to the right in question: 'Struggles from Below: Literature Review on Human Rights Struggles by Domestic Actors', Research and Innovation Grants Working Papers Series, 21 February 2017, available online at https://www.iie.org/Research-and-Insights/Publications/DFG-DU-Lit-Review-Publication.

the coronavirus pandemic, nor in relation to the profound impact of the virus on economic and social rights, but have been finding alternative ways to mobilize virtually and to press for remedial action.

4. Social movements and civil society as key actors in 'human rights experimentalism'

Unlike some other examples of 'transnational experimentalist governance'[66] described in the literature, in more technocratic or specialized fields such as ozone governance or dolphin mortality, domestic activists and social movements are particularly important actors in the human rights field.[67] As will be seen in the case studies which follow, the longer-term success of human rights campaigns often depends on the level of underlying social support and wider mobilization, even when committed and 'expert' advocates are leading the campaign.

Throughout the book, the terms 'activists', 'advocates' and 'civil society' are used interchangeably to refer to groups of actors who are concerned about particular issues, committed to shared values, and who act together in an effort to advance social, economic or political reform on those issues. And since the book is concerned with human rights law and advocacy, its focus is on civil society groups, activists, and advocates who mobilize to promote human rights rather than other shared values (whether religious, commercial, or other political values). However, as will be explained in more detail below, the category of civil society is a very broad and heterogeneous one. Further, a relevant distinction is often drawn between activists and advocates who are part of what might be called 'organized civil society' on the one hand, and wider, often more organic, social movements on the other.[68] The relationship between these two groups, broadly understood, is important to understanding the field of human rights mobilization and advocacy.

There is an extensive existing literature on the concept of civil society with varying definitions on offer, but there is a reasonably broad consensus around the idea that civil society constitutes a kind of mediating institution between the state and the individual, or between the state and social movements.[69] Civil society, as the concept has developed, refers to a category distinct both from the state and from the profit-seeking private sector. And a wide range of critiques has been advanced of the role of both domestic and transnational civil society in seeking to

---

[66] On experimentalist governance in general, and human rights experimentalism in particular, see the literature cited at n. 53 above.

[67] De Búrca, Keohane, and Sabel (n. 53).

[68] For a helpful analysis, see Nash, 'Human Rights, Movements, and Law: On Not Researching Legitimacy', 46 *Sociology* (2012) 797.

[69] For a principles-based theory of civil society along these lines, see A. Arato and J. Cohen, *Civil Society and Political Theory* (1994). See also Foley and Edwards, 'The Paradox of Civil Society', 7 *Journal of Democracy* (1996) 38.

promote social change,[70] including the risks of 'governmentality',[71] of the professionalization, 'NGO-ization' and bureaucratization of movements through the activities of civil society,[72] and of the domestication and cooptation of civil society to neoliberal or other particular international or domestic agendas.[73]

Furthermore civil society, as with all socio-political institutions, is very far from monolithic or homogenous.[74] While this book is concerned with civil society actors and social movements which focus on the promotion of human rights, there are many domestic and transnational interest groups which focus on the promotion of conservative rather than liberal values.[75] While some of these have chosen to use the language of rights, particularly religious organizations or movements,[76] many conservative civil society movements instead frame their claims in opposition or contrast to those of progressive human rights activists. The US government in 2019, for example, announced its intention to establish a 'commission on unalienable rights' intended to promote 'reform of human rights discourse where it has departed from our nation's founding principles of natural law and natural

[70] See J. Howell and J. Pearce, *Civil Society and Development: A Critical Exploration* (2001).

[71] Lipschutz, 'Power, Politics and Global Civil Society', 33 Millennium (2005) 747. On the risks for feminist movements and gay movements respectively of engaging with international power structures of governance, see Otto, 'Power and Danger: Feminist Engagement with International Law through the UN Human Rights Council', *Australian Feminist Law Journal* (2010) 97 and Gross, 'Homoglobalism: The Emergence of Gay Global Governance', in D. Otto (ed.), *Queering International Law* (2017).

[72] See e.g. S. Lang, *NGOs, Civil Society and the Public Sphere* (2013); J. W. Van Deth and W. Moloney, *New Participatory Dimensions in Civil Society* (2011); B. K. Koch and V. Buth, 'Civil Society in EU Governance: Lobby Groups like Any Other?', TranState Working Papers, No. 108 (2009). For one of the critiques focused on civil society activism in Palestine, see Hammami, 'NGOs: The Professionalization of Politics', 37 *Race and Class* (1995) 51. For an argument to the effect that this kind of professionalization or 'institutionalization' of social movements has not occurred in the context of indigenous peoples' advocacy around the UN, see Morgan, 'On Political institutions and Social Movement Dynamics: The Case of the UN and the Global Indigenous Movement', 28 *International Political Science Review* (2007) 273.

[73] Seethi, 'Postmodernism, Neoliberalism and Civil Society', 62 *The Indian Journal of Political Science* (2001) 307; Mohantry, 'Civil Society and NGOs', 63 *Indian Journal of Political Science* (2002) 213; Chakravartty, 'Governance without Politics: Civil Society, Development and the Post-colonial State', 1 *International Journal of Communication* (2007) 297. See however Bornstein and Sharma, 'The Righteous and the Rightful: The Techno-Moral Politics of NGOs, Social Movements, and the State in India', 43 *American Ethnologist* (2016) 76.

[74] Amoore and Langley, 'Ambiguities of Global Civil Society', 30 *Review of International Studies* (2004) 89.

[75] R. Youngs (ed.), *The Mobilization of Conservative Civil Society* (2018). See also Arato and Cohen, 'Civil Society, Populism and Religion', 24 *Constellations* (2017) 283.

[76] Religious claims advanced under human rights law can—like other competing contentions—present significant challenges for human rights institutions and courts, as they often require weighing up the claims of groups and individuals against those of other individuals or groups, and sometimes appear to subordinate individual rights to group interests. On the ways in which faith-based and religious groups, just like secular liberal groups, are using international human rights law and institutions to pursue their claims see McCrudden, 'Transnational Culture Wars', 13 *International Journal of Constitutional Law* (2015) 434. For a related argument about the use of the discourse of transnational NGO mobilization (though not international human rights) by Islamist groups, see Atalay, 'Vernacularization of Liberal Civil Society by Transnational Islamist NGO Networks', 16 *Global Networks* (2016) 391.

rights'[77] This reflects the then conservative government's opposition to many of the precepts and provisions of international (and domestic) human rights law, in particular those opposed by Christian conservative movements, such as reproductive rights, sexual orientation recognition, and transgender rights. By way of an attempt to reverse the social, political, and legal recognition gained for those rights in previous decades, the US government aimed to use the language of rights to promote an agenda focused on limiting the freedom and welfare of women and LGBTQ persons in order to meet the preferences of various religious constituencies. One reason for their avoidance, for the most part, of the language of international human rights law is that international human rights law does not purport to establish recognition or protection for religious views to the extent that they negate or undermine the welfare and freedom of others.[78] Hence the US State Department evidently chose the language of 'natural rights' and 'natural law' precisely in order to challenge some of the corpus of international human rights law and to seek to reverse reforms to which that body of law and practice has so far given rise in the field of gender, sexual orientation, and transgender rights for people whose identities and behaviour had previously been criminalized or repressed, or who had been subject to social control or subordination. Similarly, examples have been given of the vernacularization of global norms by grassroots groups which do not share the liberal agenda of international human rights law, such as the use by Islamist NGO networks of the discourse of transnational civil society.[79] However, to the extent that such networks in question see their normative commitments as being discordant with international human rights, they do not use or invoke human rights law or discourse but generally focus on their faith and its precepts.[80]

More generally and even beyond issues of gender and religion, with the renewed rise of far-right and hyper-nationalist movements in many parts of the world, there is a growing number of social movements and groupings focused on promoting strongly illiberal, exclusionary, repressive, and sometimes even violent aims.[81] The

---

[77] US Department of State notice of 30 May 2019, available online at https://www.federalregister.gov/documents/2019/05/30/2019-11300/department-of-state-commission-on-unalienable-rights.

[78] While the Universal Declaration on Human Rights was mentioned in the charter establishing the so-called Pompeo Commission, no reference was made to the many binding international human rights treaties which contain specific commitments to which the US has bound itself, including limits on rights such as religious freedom. See Huckerby and Knuckey, 'Pompeo's Rights Commission is Worse than Feared: 7 Concerns to Watch', *Just Security*, 16 April 2020, available online at https://www.justsecurity.org/69708/pompeos-rights-commission-is-worse-than-feared-7-concerns-to-watch. For the Charter establishing the Commission on Unalienable Rights, see https://www.state.gov/charter-for-the-commission-on-unalienable-rights.

[79] Atalay (n. 76).

[80] Ibid. For religious groups which do use human rights law to advance their claims, see McCrudden, 'Transnational Culture Wars', 13 *International Journal of Constitutional Law* (2015) 434.

[81] For an earlier historic parallel, see the account by D. Riley, *The Civic Foundations of Fascism in Europe* (2010) of the relationship between civil society mobilization and the rise of fascism in Europe in the last part of the 19th and first half of the 20th century. More recently see A. Hug (ed.), *The Rise of Illiberal Civil Society in the Former Soviet Union* (2018), available online at https://fpc.org.uk/wp-content/uploads/2018/07/The-rise-of-illiberal-civil-society-in-the-former-Soviet-Union.pdf.

label 'bad' or 'uncivil' society has been used at times to connote illiberal and re-pressive movements, or to distinguish them from civil society organizations which promote liberal values, and more generally to convey the fact that civil society worldwide is neither monolithic nor largely left-leaning.[82] Scholars have warned of the risks of the generation and articulation of counter-norms[83] and of the role of 'norm-spoilers' in seeking to corrode and undermine existing human rights norms.[84]

Nevertheless, while grassroots mobilization in itself is not associated with the promotion of any particular set of issues, groups that mobilize using human rights norms and treaties cannot easily succeed to the extent that they aim to use these norms and institutions to advance repressive or illiberal aims, at least not unless and until the relevant human rights institutions or courts become more thor-oughly captured. While repressive and illiberal groups have often drawn on the language and discourse of rights to advance reactionary agendas or to control mi-norities, it is generally quite difficult to do so using international human rights law. International human rights treaties and other international human rights instru-ments that have been developed to date contain strong commitments to a wide range of liberal values which begin from an articulation of the fundamental prem-ises of human dignity, human welfare, and human freedom, which makes it less likely—though not impossible[85]—that they will successfully be invoked as part of a campaign for repressing or subordinating particular groups or individuals or for significantly reversing rights or freedoms that have previously been advanced.[86] Illiberal movements instead generally use the language of 'natural rights' or other kinds of 'traditional' rights to challenge those contained in contemporary inter-national human rights instruments and to introduce 'counter-norms' such as sov-ereignty and stability when seeking to advance their goals, or to suppress moves towards gender equality, transgender recognition, and protection of the rights of various minorities.[87] 'Norm spoilers' and the producers of 'counter-norms' usually

---

[82] See Chambers and Kopstein, 'Bad Civil Society', 29 *Political Theory* (2001) 837. Clifford Bob points to a very wide array of active conservative transnational networks: C. Bob, *Global Right Wing and the Clash of World Politics* (2011). See also C. Bob, 'Civil and Uncivil Society', in M. D. Edwards (ed.), *Oxford Handbook of Civil Society* (2011) 209; Ruzza, 'Populism and Euroscepticism: Towards Uncivil Society', 28 *Policy and Society* (2009) 87 and C. Monga, 'Uncivil Societies: A Theory of Socio-Political Change', World Bank Development Economics Policy Research Working Paper 4942.

[83] See Vinjamuri, 'Human Rights Backlash', in S. Hopgood, J. Snyder, and L. Vinjamuri (eds), *Human Rights Futures* (2017).

[84] Sanders, 'Norm Spoiling: Undermining the International Women's Rights Agenda', 94 *International Affairs* (2018) 271.

[85] See C. Bob, *Rights As Weapons: Instruments of Conflict, Tools of Power* (2019).

[86] See however the argument put forward by Linos and Guzman, 'Human Rights Backsliding', 102 *California Law Review* (2014) 603, and Schneiker, 'The New Defenders of Human Rights? How Radical Right-Wing TNGOs are Using the Human Rights Discourse to Promote their Ideas', 33 *Global Society* (2019) 149.

[87] See n. 77 above. See also the discussion in Vinjamuri, 'Human Rights Backlash' and Cooley and Schaaf, 'Grounding the Backlash: Regional Security Treaties, Counternorms, and Human Rights in Eurasia', both in S. Hopgood, J. Snyder, and L. Vinjamuri (eds), *Human Rights Futures* (2017).

seek to introduce alternative ideas that challenge the language and corpus of inter-national human rights, such as cultural identity, the sanctity of life, or the natural unit of the family, rather than invoking international human rights law and institutions to advance illiberal agendas.[88]

Sometimes too, social movements which are not illiberal and which seek to ad-vance progressive social justice aims choose unruly, disruptive or 'uncivil' tactics to pursue their goals.[89] And while some of the overall goals of unruly protest move-ments may be very similar to those pursued by other social-justice focused civil society organizations and social movements, there may nonetheless be a mismatch between the discourses, methods, and targets of the two sets of groups. Lettinga and Kaulingfreks have suggested of social protest movements that 'it may be that the advancement of human rights is indeed not seen as the most useful for the ultimate attainment of social and economic justice goals [a]nd that international human rights organizations with their legal instruments are seen as too institution-alized, too hierarchal, too modest in their aim, and too polite in their civil society discourse to achieve the radical system change the protestors deem is needed'.[90] The authors argue that many radical activists—take Extinction Rebellion, for example—see human rights advocates as insufficiently political and inadequately challenging to the status quo, and that more radical activists reject the mediation and framing of their message by institutionalized actors. On the other hand, civil society groups and NGOs for their part sometimes view protest movements as too antagonistic or unruly to help further the goal of inclusive, rights-respecting, durable, and effective governance.[91] Nevertheless, some of those who are engaged in the field suggest that organized civil society and radical protest movements do not need to reach consensus amongst themselves in order for there to be pro-ductive synergies between the two different sets of actors and strategies in their pursuit of progressive social change.[92] This intuition is to some extent borne out by the empirical work carried by other scholars who have found that institution-alized human rights NGOs, even if they prefer to support non-violent over violent groups, continue to engage in activities that support a wide range of different do-mestic actors and strategies, including unruly protest.[93] The possible relationship

---

[88]   Sanders (n. 84).

[89]   See Lettinga and Kaulingfreks, 'Clashing Activisms: International Human Rights Organizations and Unruly Politics', 7 *Journal of Human Rights Practice* (2015) 343. On the different waves and types of social activism, including over the past decade, see Biekhart and Fowler, 'Transforming Activisms 2010+: Exploring Ways and Waves', 44 *Development and Change* (2013) 527.

[90]   Lettinga and Kaulingfreks (n. 89).

[91]   Ibid.

[92]   Amongst other things, Lettinga and Kaulingfreks (n. 89) recommend that NGOs should defend the basic civil and political rights of protesters even if they resort to unconventional or violent means. See also Lettinga, 'International Human Rights Advocacy and "New" Civic Activisms: Divergences, Contestations and Complementarity', in P. Evans and C. Rodríguez-Garavito (eds), *Transnational Activists Networks: Twenty Years of Evolving Theory and Practice* (2018) 151, at 166.

[93]   Murdie and Bhasin, 'Aiding and Abetting: Human Rights INGOs and Domestic Protest', 55 *Journal of Conflict Resolution* (2011) 163.

between protest movements and other kinds of grassroots mobilization on the one hand, and organized civil society on the other, in the pursuit of human rights, will be discussed further in the final chapter of this book.

A further important distinction to be drawn between the various kinds of civil society actors mobilizing for human rights is the distinction between advocates or actors who aim to *represent* the constituencies whose rights are affected, and advocates or actors who claim themselves to be affected. In general, nongovernmental organizations (NGOs), both at the domestic and international level, position themselves as representatives of affected communities, aiming to work on their behalf and to advocate for them. In recent years, however, there has been a move on the part of affected communities and constituencies to represent and advocate for themselves in domestic and international settings, rather than relying on NGOs or professional advocates to represent them.[94] Some of the best known include the movement for peasants' rights and food security, La Via Campesina, which has grown significantly in scale and action since its establishment in 1992.[95] Other groups which have increasingly insisted on the importance of the direct involvement of affected persons, rather than being represented by NGOs, include indigenous peoples and people affected by specific diseases such as HIV/Aids.[96]

In the case studies detailed in this book, the array of civil society groups and activists mobilizing around various human rights campaigns was in some cases broad and quite diverse, pluralistic and loosely organized, while in others the actors were more cohesive and integrated. Some of the campaigns were driven mainly by professional nongovernmental organizations (NGOs) which were established specifically to advocate for particular issues, while others involved wider coalitions and movements including those directly affected, in which NGOs sometimes played a part but did not supply the primary motor or energy behind the demands for reform. The various studies, as will be seen in the specific chapters as well as in the final chapter, suggest that the outcomes of the different advocacy campaigns and the extent and significance of their engagement with international human rights are likely to vary according to the nature and scale of the groups mobilizing for reform. Wider mobilization of a social movement or set of movements, whether

---

[94] See the special issue of Third World Thematics on the subject, with an introduction by Sändig, Von Bernstorff, and Hasenclever, 'Affectedness in International Institutions: The Promises and Pitfalls of Involving the Most Affected', 3 *Third World Thematics: A TWQ Journal* (2019) 587.

[95] https://viacampesina.org/en. See e.g. P. Claeys, *Human Rights and the Food Sovereignty Movement: Reclaiming Control* (2016), and Vandenbogaerde, 'Localizing the Human Rights Council: A Case Study of the Declaration on the Rights of Peasants', 16 *Journal of Human Rights* (2017) 220. For reflection on the advantages and disadvantages for the peasant movement of recourse to the language and institutions of international human rights, see Larking, 'Mobilising for Food Sovereignty: The Pitfalls of International Human Rights Strategies and an Exploration of Alternatives', 23 *International Journal of Human Rights* (2019) 758.

[96] For discussion see Schramm and Sändig, 'Affectedness Alliances: Affected People at the Center of Transnational Advocacy', 3 *Third World Thematics: A TWQ Journal* (2019) 664.

unruly or not, brings with it a legitimacy, embeddedness and urgency that NGOs or organized networks of civil society generally do not enjoy.[97]

An example of a campaign that was conducted mostly by specialized civil society advocates and not based on or linked to a broader social movement is that of children's rights in Ireland, detailed in Chapter 5, in which the numerous advocacy groups mobilizing domestically around these issues became fairly united, working mainly through the Children's Rights Alliance although alongside a number of issue-specific or group-specific organizations such as Travellers' Rights Groups, reproductive rights groups, and prison reform organizations. In Pakistan, as outlined in Chapter 3, the number and variety of groups mobilizing around a range of gender reform issues was extensive and varied, although a relatively small number of professionalized NGOs took the lead in engaging with the international human rights monitoring system and review processes. At times the campaigns were boosted by widespread social action, as for example with the women's day marches in Pakistan, which both drew attention to the scale and ubiquity of gender injustice and also, predictably, generated a conservative and male backlash.[98] Nevertheless, it points to the beginnings of a cultural shift which is likely to be crucial in supporting the ongoing work of civil society advocacy groups in Pakistan.[99] In Argentina, as described in Chapter 4, the modern disability rights movement emerged from the activities of a number of different kinds of movements and entities, including service-oriented groups as well as more rights-oriented and also radical groups. Although the various groups were very different in their origins and approaches, many of them came together at particular junctures around a focus on changing the paradigm of disability and the way in which people with disabilities are perceived, treated, and participate in social, economic, and political life. And they gained particular impetus at times when a broader social movement—such as the strong opposition to pension cuts which would particularly affect persons with disabilities—attracted popular support and increased public pressure for reform.

The case studies indicate that even when the focus is on those parts of civil society advocating specifically for progressive human rights (as opposed to illiberal causes), and even within 'organized' civil society, the picture is still quite diverse, complex, and far from unified or cohesive. The campaigns examined involved a range of groups with very different starting points, underlying values, priorities, and agendas, with some gaining more prominence and influence than others. There was often significant contestation both within and between advocacy

---

[97] For an analysis of the differences and the relationships between social movements and advocacy networks, and their engagement with the language and institutions of human rights, see Nash (n. 68).

[98] Azeem, 'Women Marched for Their Rights. Then the Backlash Came', *The Diplomat*, 20 March 2019.

[99] Shahid, 'Women Will March on Despite Public Backlash', *Asia Times*, 13 March 2019, and Bina Shah, 'The Real Enemy of Pakistan's Women is not Men: it is Society's Acceptance of Patriarchy', *New York Times*, 14 April 2019.

groups, as is evident in the differences between grassroots local groups and urban professionalized NGOs addressing gender reform in Pakistan, or between advocates of inclusive education and other groups such as deafness advocates arguing for the importance of special education in the context of disability in Argentina, or between more radical anti-capitalist critics and other human rights advocates in the Latin American disability movements, or between the many different groups advocating for aspects of reproductive reform in Ireland. The tensions and differences which can arise between grassroots groups and professional civil society, such as, between feminist advocacy groups and human rights organizations, or between victims and NGOs, have already been well-documented and described in the case of campaigns concerning violence against women.[100]

It is also not always easy to clearly distinguish external or international influence from local influence and action in the field of human rights activism, given that many domestic, not only international advocacy groups and NGOs, receive support—when not prohibited from doing so by domestic law—from international funders and networks.[101] Nevertheless, even if they receive some of their funding from international donors, the term 'domestic civil society' as used in this book refers broadly to those groups and organizations which are based within a particular state and focused on problems and issues occurring within the state, rather than being internationally based or being a domestic branch of an international organization, or focused on issues taking place outside the state.

The case studies focus not just on core civil and political rights such as freedom of expression and association, life, and liberty, but also on various socio-economic rights, and they concern advocacy for change on behalf of groups in a position of subordination or neglect, including women in religious or patriarchal societies, persons with disabilities in many if not most societies, and children in societies with a traditional or paternalistic approach to family authority. A significant dimension of each of the case studies concerns the role of human rights treaty reporting and other kinds of periodic review and engagement with international human rights institutions, although litigation and individual complaints have also been an important part of a wider reform process in several instances. Nevertheless, although they are often an important component of other ongoing campaigns, individual petitions and particular instances of litigation—such as the inclusive education cases detailed in the chapter on Argentina—risk remaining as one-shot events if

---

[100] See e.g. MacDowell Santos, 'Mobilizing Women's Human Rights: What/Whose Knowledge Counts for Transnational Legal Mobilization?', 10 *Journal of Human Rights Practice* (2018) 191.

[101] External sources of funding for domestic NGOs of course have become a focus of scrutiny in many of those states which are seeking to restrict civil society activity. This is a development that began some time ago but has accelerated with the rise of illiberal and authoritarian governments worldwide: see Vernon, 'Closing the Door on Aid', 11(4) *International Journal of Not-for-Profit Law* (2009); Watson and Burles, 'Regulating NGO Funding: Securitizing the Political', 32 *International Relations* (2018) 430, Chaudhary and Heiss, 'Who's afraid of the Activists? Causes and Consequences of the Global Crackdown on NGOs' (2018).

they are not accompanied by the kind of follow-up procedures and public pressure which often characterize the international reporting processes and longer-term campaigns. The kind of change sought through the pressure generated by treaty reporting and wider mobilization processes is also often more systemic, entailing legislative, institutional, and policy reform. Enduring or system change does not often follow from individual complaints and cases unless they are part of a broader campaign. Similarly, collective mobilization in the form of grassroots protest often arises in response to a particular outrage or specific event—such as the response to the 'honour killing' murder of Qandeel Baloch in Pakistan, for example,[102] or following the introduction of a new extradition bill in Hong Kong in 2019, or the brutal police killing of George Floyd in the US in 2020. While it may not be sustainable in the longer term, protest in response to a specific outrage can nonetheless be energizing and powerful in providing a strong social signal of the desire for change, and can also strengthen and underpin more sustained, focused, and ongoing processes of advocacy and pressure. And it will also be clear from the various case studies, for example in the context of some of the 'alphabet' litigation brought by women seeking abortion in Ireland, that although the focus of the studies and of the book overall is on wider processes of mobilization and change, nonetheless individual cases, litigation, and complaints have often formed an important dimension in such overall campaigns and provided a crucial impetus and support for those ongoing processes and strategies.

5. A transnational experimentalist theory of human rights law and advocacy

Reflecting on the examples in the case studies, and building on the insights of the new human rights scholarship which focuses on the interaction between the domestic and international levels, this book draws on the ideas of transnational experimentalism to offer an account of the effectiveness of human rights law. Experimentalist thinking proposes that social and political action and change can—and should—come about not by means of hierarchical direction or systems of control from above, but through an iterative system of contestation and learning from on-the-ground experience, in conjunction with ongoing collective reflection, reaction, and institutional response, and in the interaction over time between multiple actors and institutions at various levels.[103]

---

[102]   See Chapter 3.

[103]   Charles Sabel, who draws on philosopher John Dewey's work, is the leading contemporary scholar of experimentalist governance theory and has written extensively on both the theory and its application to different policy contexts. For an overview see Sabel and Simon, 'Democratic Experimentalism', in J. Desautels-Stein and C. Tomlins (eds), *Searching for Contemporary Legal Thought* (2017) 477. For an earlier scholarly development of Dewey's ideas of pragmatic experimentalism in the context of democratic renewal, see R. Unger, *Democracy Realized: The Progressive Alternative* (1998).

Experimentalist governance theory, in particular, has been expounded as a theory of multi-level governing that proposes how a set of broad political commitments or goals can be agreed, elaborated, and implemented in a multilevel setting, including in a transnational context. On one description, 'experimentalist governance represents a form of adaptive, open-ended, participatory, and information-rich cooperation in world politics, in which the local and the transnational interact through the localized elaboration and adaption of transnationally agreed general norms, subject to periodic revision in light of knowledge locally generated'.[104] Sabel and Zeitlin argue that an experimentalist approach responds to the weaknesses and failures of 'command-and-control' or top-down regulation, and is particularly suited to the transnational domain in which there is no sovereign with authority to set common goals, and where the diversity of local conditions and practices makes adoption and enforcement of uniform norms even less feasible than in domestic settings.[105] Importantly, rather than being considered second-best to a supposedly more effective hierarchical or integrated regime of norm-elaboration and enforcement, the attraction of an experimentalist system lies precisely in its decentralized, participatory, and iterative character.

It has been suggested that the international system as designed and developed in the twentieth century post-war era envisaged a landscape of integrated international regimes, closely answerable—on a principal-agent conception of accountability—to states, with comprehensive and centralized institutions intended to manage social and political coordination in various fields, such as trade through the WTO, or security through the UN Security Council, amongst others.[106] In the human rights field, the UN Commission on Human Rights (now the Human Rights Council) was at the apex of a regime which included a system of UN 'special procedures', as well as multiple international human rights treaties, all of which were to be implemented and enforced domestically but also monitored through international procedures, including political reporting to the Human Rights Council.

But with major geopolitical changes taking place, there was decreasing support from the mid-1990s for the creation of new integrated international regimes, and existing regimes began to weaken and fragment. More decentralized and fragmented 'regime complexes' have been emerging and changing,[107] while various

---

[104] On global experimentalist governance, see de Búrca, O. Keohane, and F. Sabel, 'New Modes of Pluralist Global Governance' (n. 53) and 'Global Experimentalist Governance' (n. 53). See also Sabel and Zeitlin, 'Experimentalism in Transnational Governance: Emergent Pathways and Diffusion Mechanisms', GREEN (Global Reordering: Evolution through European Networks) Working Paper No. 3 (2011).

[105] Sabel and Zeitlin, 'Experimentalist Governance', in D. Levi-Faur (ed.), *The Oxford Handbook of Governance* (2012) 169.

[106] De Búrca, Keohane, and Sabel, 'New Modes of Pluralist Global Governance' (n. 53).

[107] See e.g. Alter and Meunier, 'The Politics of International Regime Complexity: Symposium', 7 *Perspectives on Politics* (2009) 13; Keohane and Victor, 'The Regime Complex for Climate Change', 9 *Perspectives on Politics* (2011).

international organizations have shifted their focus and modus to operate more as 'orchestrators' and to engage with networks of non-state actors in pursuing their mandates.[108] At the present time, in the third decade of the twenty-first century, the international system has moved far from anything that could be described as a model of integrated, coherent, or comprehensive order, and the current multi-polar environment in which international institutions and treaty systems are being destabilized and challenged, not least by re-invigorated nationalism, seems likely to be the environment in which human rights advocates will find themselves for some time to come.

For many concerned observers, a looser, more fragmented, de-centred, and pluralist system will not serve the promotion of human rights well, and there have been renewed calls in recent years for a World Court of Human Rights that would bring stronger centralized enforcement to the human rights field.[109] But apart from the reality that the international order at present is indeed very fragmented, and likely to remain so for some time, one of the arguments advanced by this book is that human rights advocacy can in fact survive and even thrive under such condi-tions, despite the challenges and changes taking place. Indeed, I suggest that the effectiveness of much human rights law and advocacy to date can be explained in experimentalist terms. In particular, where the conditions are such that domestic civil society has some freedom to mobilize and to advocate, and where an array of international and regional institutions, networks, and fora can supply a degree of external accountability and support, and there are domestic institutions and actors with sufficient independence and status to bolster and reinforce the rights claimed and promoted by activists, human rights advocacy has proven effective in many in-stances and contexts in helping to advance social and political change.

Experimentalist theory posits that common values and goals—such as the re-spect for human dignity, human welfare and human freedom which underpins international human rights law—can be advanced when they are articulated and developed through the iterative interaction of a multiplicity of actors and institu-tions situated at different levels and locations within a multilevel political system. And while the language of 'shared values' or 'common norms' may seem to depol-iticize contentious issues, the reality is that although agreement can quite often be reached at a fairly high level of generality on goals such as reversing climate change, reducing poverty, promoting public health etc., there is inevitably contestation over the meaning of those values and over how the goals should be pursued in practice. This is also true of the provisions contained in international human rights instru-ments on which agreement can often be reached in the abstract (human dignity,

---

[108] See K. Abbott *et al.*, *International Organizations as Orchestrators* (2015).

[109] See e.g. M. Scheinin, *Towards a World Court for Human Rights*, available online at http://www.eui.eu/Documents/DepartmentsCentres/Law/Professors/Scheinin/WorldCourtReport30April2009.pdf and Nowak, 'A World Court for Human Rights', in G. Oberleitner (ed.), *International Human Rights Institutions, Tribunals, and Courts* (2018).

the right to life, freedom of expression etc.), even though further contestation and struggle inevitably takes place over the activation, elaboration, and implementation of the rights in practice and in specific contexts.

Experimentalism emphasizes the importance of the active participation of those most affected, and of learning from different local or contextualized experiences in the implementation of a common framework. The conceptual model of transnational experimentalist governance developed in the literature to date suggests that an effective and deliberative multilevel system can emerge where a number of key features are present.[110] These features include the establishment—ideally through an experimentalist system—of agreement on a common problem or challenge across diverse settings and the articulation of a shared set of norms or goals; activation and implementation of these norms by contextually situated or local actors and ongoing active participation of key stakeholders with knowledge and experience of local conditions who invoke, use, and adapt the norms to different contexts; feedback from local contexts allowing for external accountability and monitoring across a range of contexts with outcomes subject to some form of review; and periodic re-evaluation with possible revision of the basic norms and the practices in light of what is learned from the ongoing review.

While the real world of human rights law and practice of course does not conform precisely or even very closely to this model, nevertheless there are many aspects of the way in which human rights advocacy works to promote rights-based social change that resonate with the premises and assumptions of experimentalism. In terms of how agreement is reached on human rights laws and norms in the first place, while in the earlier days of the international human rights regime the establishment of human rights protections in international treaties took place in a highly state-centric and elite-dominated way, with little room for input by civil society or other interest groups, this has begun to change in recent years. New human rights instruments have been created and have resulted from the mobilization and engagement of affected groups and advocates. Examples are the Landmines Treaty (the Ottawa Convention), the Convention on the rights of Persons with Disabilities, the UN Declaration on the Rights of Indigenous Persons, the UN Guiding Principles on Business and Human Rights, and the Marrakech Treaty to Facilitate Access to Published Works by Visually Impaired Persons. These international instruments resulted from sustained advocacy and mobilization on the part of affected persons as well as representative NGOs, and they were adopted through less conventional and more participatory processes than the traditionally state-centred treaty negotiation procedures.

And while experimentalist theory was developed and applied in relation to more technocratic policy contexts such as the implementation of the Montreal Protocol

---

[110] For a short account, see de Búrca, Keohane, and Sabel, 'Global Experimentalist Governance' (n. 53).

on the protection of the ozone layer,[111] or the development of child welfare policy in federal systems,[112] several of its key elements are present in the more overtly political context of transnational human rights mobilization.[113] In the human rights context, the interaction of domestic activism, external or international accountability and legitimation, and pressure from independent domestic actors, can be observed at work in human rights campaigns. Social movements, activists and advocates identify and raise claims and assert rights to challenge laws and practices, often with support from national, regional, or international networks of advocates and activists; the external accountability institutions—which often also serve a legitimation function for the claims of domestic activists which might otherwise be suppressed or dismissed—include the array of treaty bodies, international courts, commissions, special procedures, and other external bodies that evaluate the implementation of these instruments; and the independent domestic actors comprise domestic courts, the media (including new media forms), ombudspersons, legislators, and others who sharpen pressure and generate additional leverage for change. Of course it is possible that media may be state-owned or state-controlled, or that certain courts may be packed or politically subservient, but to the extent that there are some domestic institutions which remain fairly independent, they play an important role in an experimentalist human rights system. Finally, the targets of change and the actors towards which human rights advocacy and pressure is directed are governmental or corporate actors, and increasingly today, both.

Social movements and domestic activists identify and highlight injustices, they articulate the rights implicated, build social movements, and generate awareness and support for reform. They do this by gathering and publicizing information often with support from transnational networks; by challenging official accounts and advocating for change through protest, public campaigns, media and social media, litigation, and parliamentary lobbying. Domestic advocacy and activism alone may occasionally be enough to generate change, but more often the targets of activism, namely the governmental, corporate or other powerful actors whose conduct affects the extent to which rights are realized, are resistant—even within robust democratic systems—to acknowledging or acting upon such claims. This may be the case for reasons of ideological or political opposition, economic cost, inertia, a focus on other priorities, or sometimes lack of recognition of the implications of the laws and norms in question. Despite the widespread ratification and acceptance of numerous international human rights treaties and instruments, domestic pressure is often insufficient to bring about change to promote or realize those commitments, regardless of the political system or the nature of the democracy in

---

[111] De Búrca, Keohane, and Sabel, 'New Modes of Pluralist Global Governance' (n. 53).

[112] Noonan, Sabel, and Simon, 'Legal Accountability in the Service-Based Welfare State: Lessons from Child Welfare Reform', *Journal of Law and Social Inquiry* (2009) 523.

[113] For an experimentalist interpretation of international human rights treaty implementation see de Búrca (n. 23).

question, and particularly when the interests and rights affected are ones which are neglected or controversial within the domestic system.

This is why the impetus provided by engagement with external, accountability-forcing actors such as international human rights treaty bodies or other institutions is important to much human rights advocacy. International institutions such as courts, commissions, and treaty bodies provide a forum for accountability, highlighting the issues raised by domestic activists and requiring state actors to justify and explain their actions or omissions, and they can also help to provide a kind of external legitimacy rooted in universalist norms for local activists.[114] The pressure created by international institutions and attention can activate a wider set of dynamics that help bring about change.[115] Equally, however, the intervention or pronouncements of such international institutions, even in conjunction with domestic advocates, can often be insufficient to bring about significant social or political change without further pressure from national institutional actors, and without broader underlying social support. While both the original impetus for human rights reform and the eventual leverage that brings about change are usually in significant part domestic, their engagement with international actors and institutions supplies a crucial degree of external accountability and often the kind of irritant or catalyst that furthers disruption of the internal status quo and helps to promote change.

The engagement of domestic activists with *international actors and institutions*, such as treaty bodies, commissions, and courts, as well as with transnational networks of support thus helps to generate external accountability, to highlight normative standards, and to create a stimulus for further mobilization and change. International actors, institutions, and networks provide a high-profile external forum in which rights claims and grievances can be aired; they incentivize the generation and circulation of information about compliance or non-compliance; they develop and pool experience and knowledge of practices from different contexts; they share expertise in the ongoing interpretation and elaboration of human rights standards, they generate and supply external accountability by requiring state

---

[114] On the legitimating function of international norms for domestic activists, see Levitt and Merry, 'The Vernacularization of Women's Human Rights', in L. Vinjamuri, J. Snyder, and S. Hopgood (eds), *Human Rights Futures* (2016). For an argument that international treaty body procedures need to be more accessible to local activists, see Bowe and Cooper, 'Putting People at the Heart of the Human Rights Treaty Body System', *Open Global Rights*, 17 June 2020, available online at https://www.openglobalrights.org/putting-people-at-the-heart-of-the-human-rights-treaty-body-system/?lang=English.

[115] For some recent analyses of the distinctive role of human rights treaty bodies and their output, see Barkholdt and Reiners, 'Pronouncements of Expert Treaty Bodies: From Black Boxes to Key Catalysts in International Law', KFG Working Paper Series, No. 40, Berlin Potsdam Research Group, 'The International Rule of Law—Rise or Decline?' *and* Borlino and Crema, 'The Legal Status of Decisions by Human Rights Treaty Bodies: International Supervision, Authoritative Interpretations or Mission Éducatrice?', European Society of International Law Annual Research Forum 2019 Conference paper No. 3/2019.

actors to publicly engage and respond to the information, claims, and complaints brought, and they follow up and help to bring pressure to bear on the responsible organs of the state. Transnational, regional and domestic networks also provide support of various kinds to domestic activists, whether in amplifying advocacy or supplying capacity and information, sharing resources and experiences, coalition-building and devising new strategies, and connecting them to actors and activists elsewhere engaged in similar advocacy. International institutions and bodies routinely comment and provide influential views on the meaning and application of human rights norms to specific situations and on the development of human rights standards, and they generate further information and input from state and civil society actors.

Continuing this experimentalist analysis of human rights advocacy, the third group which forms part of the dynamic circuit of international human rights mobilization and change is comprised of *independent domestic actors and institutions*, including ombudspersons, courts, the media—traditional as well as new and social media—agencies, parliamentary committees, national human rights bodies, and others. Independent national institutions of this kind supply domestic levers and opportunity structures enabling activists to follow up on and publicize the output and outcomes of international engagement, to generate and amplify domestic advocacy and international standards, and to create additional social, legal as well as political pressure on governmental and corporate actors to respond.[116] The diagram reproduced below attempts to represent the iterative dynamic of human rights law and advocacy in graphic form (see Figure 2.1).

Apart from the dynamic interaction between these three sets of actors and the pressure they bring to bear on the powerful targets of reform (generally states and corporate actors), the other key element of an experimentalist theory of international human rights effectiveness—which also emerges from the case studies in the chapters which follow—is the iterative and continuous nature of many of the processes which lead to change. Few if any of the issues or campaigns described in the following chapters were short-term or one-shot campaigns. On the contrary, each entailed a longer-term process of mobilization, advocacy, and pressure punctuated by numerous and repeated sets of interactions between domestic and international actors over a period of time. In none of the cases did significant or lasting change come about in the short term, but rather in stages and over time. This does not imply that important reforms can never be achieved in a shorter period, or that significant individual steps are not constantly being taken, but rather that the kinds

---

[116] On the importance of domestic institutions for furthering human rights, see Jensen, Lagoutte, and Lorion, 'The Domestic Institutionalisation of Human Rights: An Introduction', 37 *Nordic Journal of Human Rights* (2019) 165.

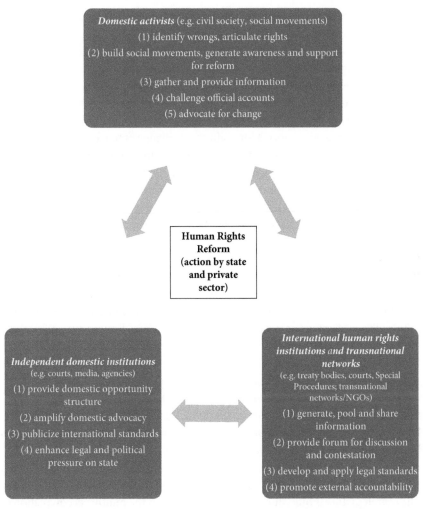

Figure 2.1 The Iterative Dynamic of International Human Rights Advocacy

of reforms which human rights-related activism seeks to bring about often entail major social, political, and economic change that is unlikely to be brought about without sustained and ongoing processes of mobilization, advocacy, and pressure. The deep social, economic, and political structures and patterns that underlie many if not most human rights injustices are rarely susceptible to rapid or easy change. Further, the iterative nature of human rights advocacy also regularly brings about change not only to domestic laws and policies but also to the international norms themselves. This can be seen in some of the case studies—for example, the emergence of new international human rights norms against the criminalization of abortion promoted through the Irish reproductive rights campaigns—but in other fields of human rights advocacy such as violence against women,[117] and the free, prior, and informed consent of indigenous peoples.[118]

Hence an experimentalist account of international human rights law suggests that human rights law becomes effective as a consequence of the long-term, ongoing, dynamic, and often contentious engagement between these main groups of domestic and international actors, movements, networks and institutions. Human rights experimentalism in particular describes a cycle of active engagement between locally situated actors who mobilize to challenge practices, highlight injustices, and claim rights; transnational or international institutions and forums which provide an external accountability forum by hearing claims from various domestic settings, facilitating contestation and debate of claims and issues, and articulating normative standards; and domestic and other independent actors and institutions which amplify and increase pressure on the state and translate or localize normative inputs.

Compare this experimentalist account of human rights with other theories of the effectiveness of human rights. For those who view international human rights law as a largely top-down practice, the picture they envisage is one of implementation of a set of existing ('out there') international human rights provisions. For others who understand international human rights as a bottom-up practice, the picture they present is one of ongoing contestation and demand by local actors (who sometimes use an international framework to help them) to challenge the injustices they have identified and named. The experimentalist account of the case studies in this book suggests, however, that these two perspectives each provides only a partial picture of much effective human rights advocacy and reform. Drawing on those studies I argue that a particularly effective form of human rights practice is an interactive one involving input from various levels and sets of actors, each of which depend in ways on the other to advance the claims articulated from below or within, and the norms monitored and supported from above or outside. The overall picture is one which could be described as the multilevel co-creation of human rights law and practice, with reform coming about through domestic mobilization involving the articulation of rights claims and demands, through the generation and provision of information to external accountability institutions which promote debate and contestation, and reflect on existing practices and goals; which in turn create normative pressure, generate leverage, and increase political impetus for domestic reform. In terms of the causal mechanisms of change on which the experimentalist account rests, it seems likely that a combination of mechanisms are at work. The ideational change by persuasion identified by Beth Simmons is

---

[117] For this and related examples in the field of children's rights and the rights of persons with disabilities, see de Búrca (n. 23) at 293–297.

[118] C. Rodríguez-Garavito, forthcoming in P. Alston (ed.), *Essays in Honor of Sally Engle Merry* (2021).

clearly at work in the mobilization of domestic advocates and activists; and the inducement of change through external pressure identified by Keck and Sikkink is also at least partly at work in the intervention of international institutions such as treaty bodies, regional or international courts, and special procedures; while the repeated engagement of state actors with these international institutions also provides a context in which socialization or acculturation, as identified by Goodman and Jinks, takes place.

International human rights law in practice, on an experimentalist account, is not to be understood as a set of norms and legal standards created and shaped from above and imposed or applied to a set of actors and institutions below. Equally, claims for justice from below which might otherwise go unheeded can gain additional normative authority, social support and political traction through their engagement with international institutions and external networks. International human rights law, according to the experimentalist theory advanced here, is a set of norms and standards which are mutually constituted through the continual iterative interaction of domestic and international actors and institutions, underpinned and activated by the support of domestic and transnational social movements. Human rights law is co-created through this process, and the real motor of change in much human rights advocacy is neither international institutions on the one hand nor domestic activism on the other, but rather the ongoing engagement over time between these and other internal and external actors, institutions, and norms.

3

Mobilization for gender equality in Pakistan and the role of international human rights

1. Introduction

Chapter 2 has introduced the experimentalist account of international human rights law and practice, arguing that some of the most effective and durable human rights progress is advanced not through hierarchical intervention from 'above' by international bodies and actors, or through purely local or domestic advocacy, but instead through ongoing interaction over time between domestic activists and transnational actors and institutions invoking and activating human rights norms to bring pressure to bear on governmental and other actors to promote domestic change.

This chapter examines the struggle for women's rights and gender equality in Pakistan in recent decades through the lens of that experimentalist framework. It describes the work of women's groups and other activists in Pakistan to advance the rights of women, and their engagement over time with international human rights law and institutions as part of those efforts, in particular the UN Convention on the Elimination of All Forms of Discrimination against Women (CEDAW). Many different kinds of groups and organizations have advocated at various times for change to the entrenched patterns of social, economic, political, and legal subordination of women in Pakistan. Some of the most prominent groups have sought the support of transnational networks and used international human rights institutions, including CEDAW as well as the Universal Periodic Review of the UN Human Rights Council, to bring pressure to bear on governmental and other domestic actors to introduce change. And despite the size and extent of the social and political obstacles facing their efforts at reform, many significant changes have been introduced as a consequence of domestic mobilization and engagement. The discussion that follows outlines some of these contested legal and political processes over time and the reforms that have gradually been brought about, as well as the limitations they have confronted.

Reframing Human Rights in a Turbulent Era. Gráinne de Búrca, Oxford University Press (2021). © G de Búrca.
DOI: 10.1093/oso/9780198299578.003.0003

2. Pakistan and international human rights law

Pakistan presents considerable challenges to the agenda of advancing gender equality and implementing CEDAW. The overwhelming majority of the population is Muslim, and Islam is the state religion. It is given prominent status in the national constitution and plays a dominant role in social and political life. At the same time, Pakistan is a constitutional democracy and has been an active participant in the international political community since its foundation in 1947, enjoying periods of democratic rule interrupted by army coups and cycles of military rule. Pakistan has been elected four times to a seat on the UN Human Rights Council, and following a slow start, the state has signed and ratified many of the major UN human rights treaties including the two Covenants (i.e. the International Covenant on Economic Social and Cultural Rights (ICESCR) and the International Covenant on Civil and Political Rights (ICCPR)), as well as the Convention on the Rights of the Child, the Convention on the Elimination of Racial Discrimination, the Convention on the Rights of Persons with Disabilities, and CEDAW.

Yet in spite of this international engagement and the decision to ratify a range of human rights treaties, Pakistan still confronts major challenges as far as the goals of gender equality and women's empowerment are concerned. It is ranked almost at the bottom of several major global rankings of countries from the perspective of gender and the situation of women. The World Economic Forum Global Gender Gap Index in 2020 ranked Pakistan third from the bottom, at 151 out of 153,[1] and the Georgetown Institute for Women Peace and Security in 2017 ranked Pakistan 150 out of 152.[2] Women in Pakistan experience systematic gender subordination across all aspects of social, economic, and political life, with the situation being particularly oppressive in rural areas and for the non-elite social classes and castes. Gender violence, including 'honour' killings, acid attacks, domestic abuse, and workplace harassment, is endemic. Widespread patriarchal cultural practices include forced marriage and child marriage, and women experience profound inequality in law and in fact, including discrimination in access to education, economic opportunity, and political participation. Customary norms and misogynist practices such as *ghag* (forced marriage) and *watta-satta* (bride exchange) are amongst the edicts which emerge from *jirgas*—an informal justice system where men from a village or tribe assemble to impose judgment for a wrong committed—and which continue to coexist alongside and outside the formal legal system.[3] Jirga decisions have notably included various forms of revenge judgment against the innocent family members of alleged wrongdoers, for example that a female family member of the wrongdoer should be raped, or that a child of the

---

[1] Available online at http://www3.weforum.org/docs/WEF_GGGR_2020.pdf.
[2] Available online at https://giwps.georgetown.edu/index-rankings/.
[3] See N. Brohi, *Women, Violence and Jirgas: Consensus and Impunity in Pakistan* (2016).

wrongdoer's family should be handed over to the wronged family as a future bride. At the same time, while the religious nationalism that characterized Pakistan's founding has been a powerful force hindering the development of democracy and gender equality, the rise of the Taliban and of the Islamic State (Daesh) in recent decades has added an exceptionally repressive and violent dimension to the resistance to women's rights.[4]

While CEDAW was adopted by the UN in 1979, its eventual ratification by Pakistan took place 17 years later at a time when Benazir Bhutto was prime minister, following a long and sustained campaign waged by domestic women's groups and NGOs.[5] At the time of ratification, CEDAW was only the third of the UN human rights treaties to be ratified by Pakistan, following its ratification of the Convention on the Elimination of Racial Discrimination in 1966 and the Convention on the Rights of the Child in 1990.[6]

Much of the resistance to ratifying CEDAW concerned its alleged incompatibility with Islamic law, and the Ministry of Religious Affairs was particularly staunchly opposed to ratification. There was concern amongst religious forces, the most prominent of which has been the Council of Islamic Ideology, that CEDAW would lead to the revocation of a set of laws known as the Hudood Ordinances, which were introduced during the period of 'Islamization' of Pakistan under the rule of General Zia-ul-Haq in the late 1970s.[7] The Hudood Ordinances, which included the infamous Zina and Qazf Ordinances, effectively equated rape with adultery, imposed discriminatory and other onerous evidentiary rules (such as the four-witness requirement) on rape victims, conferring effective impunity on rapists and frequently resulted in victims instead of perpetrators being punished.[8] But with organized public pressure from below, international pressure from above, and a more supportive government, which included a significant number of female members during a period of non-military rule, the Convention was ultimately signed and ratified in 1996,[9] joining the two other human rights treaties which

---

[4] R. Saigol, *Feminism and the Women's Movement in Pakistan: Actors, Debates and Strategies* (2016).

[5] For a helpful account of the long campaign, see Ali, 'From Ratification to Implementation: "Domesticating" the CEDAW In State, Government and Society. A Case Study of Pakistan', in A. Hellum (ed.), *Women's Human Rights: CEDAW International, Regional and National Law* (2013) 430.

[6] Pakistan ratified the two UN Covenants, the Covenant on Economic Social and Cultural Rights and the Covenant on Civil and Political Rights, in 2008 and 2010 respectively.

[7] Kennedy, 'Islamization in Pakistan: Implementation of the Hudood Ordinances', 28 *Asian Survey* (1988) 307. For an description of some of the consequences of this period of Islamization for women in Pakistan and its 'damaging legacy' see Shaheed, 'Contested Identities: Gendered Politics, Gendered Religion in Pakistan', 31 *Third World Quarterly* (2010) 851.

[8] Although some aspects of the Hudood ordinances were reformed in 2006, many of the core provisions remain in force: Lau, 'Twenty Five Years of Hudood Ordinances: A Review', 64 *Washington and Lee Law Review* (2007) 1291 and M. A. Rathore, *Women's Rights in Pakistan: The Zina Ordinance and the Need for Reform* (2015), available online at scholarworks.umass.edu/cppa_capstones/38/.

[9] For an account of the campaign to have CEDAW ratified and its impact since then, see S. Ali, *Modern Challenges to Islamic Law* (2016), at ch. 5, and A. Weiss, *Interpreting Islam, Modernity and Women's Rights in Pakistan* (2014), at ch. 2.

Pakistan had already signed and ratified. However, as part of its ratification of the Convention, the government entered a declaration which specified that ratification was to be subject to the provisions of the Pakistani Constitution. The significance of this declaration from the point of view of CEDAW is that the Constitution declares Islam to be the state religion, and declares that no law is to be enacted which is repugnant to Islamic injunctions. Pakistan also entered a reservation declaring that it did not consider itself bound by Article 29(1) of CEDAW, which requires signatory states to submit to arbitration or to the jurisdiction of the ICJ to resolve a dispute over the interpretation or application of the Convention.

The prospect that ratification of CEDAW could help to promote change in Pakistan was a daunting one, given the dominance of religious and patriarchal forces in the country, and particularly after the rule of Zia-ul-Haq from 1978 to 1988. According to one Pakistani scholar and activist's account of the aftermath of the period of Islamization: 'post-Zia, while pockets of liberalism have surfaced and the pressure on professional working women and upper and middle class women has eased considerably, no ruler has taken on the challenge of reversing state sponsorship of religious orthopraxy'.[10] And indeed, the story of CEDAW's implementation in Pakistan is a mixed and partial one. However, it is also a story of very gradual and incremental legal and political change. It is unquestionably the case that considerably deeper and more widespread social and cultural change will be necessary before most women in Pakistan—and particularly those in rural and tribal areas—can benefit from the legal changes that have taken place since the ratification of CEDAW. In this chapter, the gradual steps which have been taken to reform some of the most egregious legal and political barriers to women's emancipation will be outlined, and the ways in which civil society organizations, women's groups, and NGOs have mobilized to give effect to the provisions of CEDAW will be described.

Three factors seem key to explaining both the ratification of CEDAW and more particularly how it has operated to help bring about a number of significant legal reforms in Pakistan to date. These are: first, the existence of a substantial and active civil society focused on women's rights; second, the presence of governments which at various stages have been open to gender reforms, focused at least in part on the country's international reputation and acceptance (in particular under Musharraf's rule from 2001 to 2007, but also more recently), and willing to establish and permit the existence of independent domestic institutions and media; and, third, regular review and engagement with international and external networks and institutions focused on gender issues. The influence and interaction of these factors will be discussed below.

---

[10] Shaheed (n. 7) 861.

3. Women's activism and civil society in Pakistan

The existence of an active civil society in Pakistan in the area of women's rights and gender equality long pre-dated the ratification of CEDAW. In 1949 the All Pakistan Women's Association (APWA) was formed, the first organization of its kind in the newly established state. Describing itself as 'an organization committed to the furtherance of the general economic welfare of the women and children of Pakistan', it has been perceived mainly as a service organization, focusing its work over the decades primarily on 'education, health and women's empowerment'.[11] Nevertheless, in addition to the social focus on domestic improvements in the conditions of women, this association from the outset also lobbied for Pakistan's accession to international human rights instruments including an earlier UN Convention on the Political Rights of Women, and for enhancing the legal and constitutional status of women's rights within Pakistan.[12] Nevertheless, APWA was a less overtly political organization which chose to work alongside the state in bringing about reform rather than in challenging it directly. In addition to APWA, there were many specific organizations working on issues relevant to women, including the Democratic Women's Association which was founded in 1950, but it was not until the early 1980s that the women's movement in Pakistan erupted powerfully and changed quite dramatically.

Prompted by resistance to the Islamization program of Zia-ul-Haq and to the passage of the Hudood Ordinances, the Women's Action Forum (WAF) was established in 1981.[13] Describing itself as 'a non-partisan, non-hierarchical and non-funded organization ... supportive of all aspects of women's rights and related issues', the Women's Action Forum focused on advocacy and awareness-raising, as well as on challenging discriminatory legislation against women, the invisibility of women in public life, violence against women, the exclusion of women from social and cultural activities, the exclusion of women from media, sports and cultural activities, dress codes for women, violence against women, and the seclusion of women.[14] By comparison with the somewhat more cautious, establishment-oriented, and service-focused APWA, the Women's Action Forum was self-consciously activist, political, and rights-oriented, and helped to catalyse many other women's rights groups and resource centres, launching a campaign of information and mobilization in an attempt to draw in women at every level across the country.[15] As will be discussed further below, the

---

[11] See https://apwapakistan.com.
[12] See Weiss (n. 9) Ch 2, at 22–24. For the 1953 Convention, see http://www.un.org.ua/images/Convention_on_the_Political_Rights_of_Women_engl.pdf.
[13] For a history of the Women's Action Forum, see A. Khan, *The Women's Movement in Pakistan: Activism, Islam and Democracy* (2018).
[14] See http://www.wluml.org/contact/wrrc/content/womens-action-forum-waf.
[15] S. Rouse, *Women's Movement in Pakistan: State, Class, Gender* (1998), available online at http://www.wluml.org/sites/wluml.org/files/import/english/pubs/pdf/dossier3/D3-06-Pakistan.pdf.

Women's Action Forum at the time of its establishment also chose to adopt a secular approach founded on human rights, rather than to argue through the interpretation of Islamic law. This was partly because of how radically restrictive prevailing interpretations of Muslim law had become under the Zia regime, although members of the Forum later acknowledged the need to address gender injustice and discrimination through the lens of Islam in order to reach many of Pakistan's women. The Women's Action Forum participated actively in the Beijing 4th World Conference on Women in 1985, supported the establishment of the Pakistan Human Rights Commission in 1986, and was subsequently active in mobilizing and advocating for the ratification of CEDAW, for example by organizing seminars and arguing for the compatibility of the Convention with the spirit of Islamic law.[16] There were a number of other non-urban based and provincial women's movements, such as the Sindhiani Tehrik, based in the province of Sindh.[17]

Following the successful campaign to have CEDAW ratified, this array of domestic groups, networks, and NGOs focused on gender issues in Pakistan has continued to grow and remains active in the field.[18] In addition to general human rights organizations and NGOs, there is at present a large number of domestic groups working on gender equality and women's rights, including several influential professionalized organizations such as Aurat[19] and Shirkat Gah,[20] the Pakistani Women's Human Rights organization, as well as a substantial number of smaller, specialized organizations, including activist theatre, writing and film-making groups,[21] and a wide array of provincial and grassroots groups and networks. Some of these organizations were actively involved in the campaign to have CEDAW signed and ratified, and have continued to work for its implementation and enforcement since then. Further, a number of prominent international bodies like UN Women and USAID as well as numerous large international NGOs also work in Pakistan on these issues.

As will be discussed further below, critical accounts of the work of professional NGOs have been articulated, including the charge that many (though certainly not all) are run by urban, educated, and westernized elites, that they are distant from or inadequately representative of the communities and women on whose behalf they

---

[16] See 'Pakistan-Women: Activists Pressurise Government to Ratify Cedaw', *IPS News*, 21 June 1995, available online at http://www.ipsnews.net/1995/06/pakistan-women-activists-pressurise-government-to-ratify-cedaw/.

[17] For a critical comparison of the Women's Action Forum and Sindhiani Tehrik, see Ali, 'Elitist View of Women's Struggle in Pakistan', 23(20) *Economic and Political Weekly* (1988) 1034.

[18] For some general accounts, see A. Jafar, *Women's NGOs in Pakistan* (2011); Saigol (n. 4); Imran and Munir, 'Defying Marginalization: Emergence of Women's Organizations and the Resistance Movement in Pakistan: A Historical Overview', 19 *Journal of International Women's Studies* (2018) 132; and F. Shaheed and K. Mumtaz, *Women of Pakistan: Two Steps Forward, One Step Back?* (1987).

[19] https://www.af.org.pk/about.php.

[20] http://shirkatgah.org/.

[21] See Imran and Munir (n. 18) 146–152.

work, and that when such work becomes just a 'paid job' it ceases to be committed, autonomous activism.[22] Despite the undoubted force of these criticisms and their implications for the ways in which gender issues have been tackled and addressed within the country, there is unquestionably a large number of active domestically focused organizations, some of which are internationally networked while others are more local and grassroots in nature, all working in different ways—some within Islam, some outside it—to advocate for women's empowerment and various aspects of gender justice in Pakistan.

Nonetheless, even with this active and diverse civil society mobilizing for gender equality, campaigns for women's empowerment have faced enormous challenges in Pakistan's predominantly religious and patriarchal society, particularly during periods when the government in power was repressive or disinterested. However, there have been periods during which Pakistan's political leadership has been, for various reasons, relatively open to the agenda of promoting women's rights. During the period of General Musharraf's presidency in particular, the country was concerned with its international reputation and with its programme of 'modernization', which resulted in sustained attention to issues of gender for some years, and more recently the government—at least in international fora—has declared gender equality to be again a priority.[23]

Farida Shaheed recently summarized the trajectory of the women's movement in Pakistan by identifying three distinct phases.[24] She suggests that the first phase in the 1980s was defined by opposition to a military dictatorship intent on restricting women's rights; while the second phase in the 1990s was marked by a coincidence of democratization within Pakistan with the transnationalization of women's movements, when international developments were used to leverage change at home. She identifies a third—current—phase as a stage of domestic advocacy for the adoption of legislative and policy changes, arguing that the various diverse strands of the women's and feminist movement have not yet developed a common vision or unity of purpose, nor an adequate roadmap and strategy for transforming social and political realities for women in Pakistan, and identifies this as a crucial step for future progress. A range of different approaches and areas of contestation amongst women's organizations and reform advocates in Pakistan, particularly as regards the role and relevance of international human rights norms such as CEDAW, are discussed in the following section.

---

[22] Saigol (n. 4) 38.

[23] SAMAA, *At UN, Pakistan Says Gender Equality Among Top Priorities*, 15 February 2017, available online at https://www.samaa.tv/pakistan/2017/02/at-un-pakistan-says-gender-equality-among-top-priorities/.

[24] Shaheed, 'Pakistan's Women's Movement: Protests, Programmes, and Revitalization', in A. Basu (ed.), *Women's Movements in the Global Era: The Power of Local Feminisms* (2017) 89.

4. The contested localization of human rights in Pakistan

Anthropologist Sally Engle Merry has described how the domestic application of international norms, including CEDAW provisions, takes place through a process of what she terms vernacularization, where locally situated actors use and make sense of the content of international norms by appropriating and translating them into locally relevant ideas and terms.[25] She and others have depicted a 'fractured process' whereby norms which are created through diverse social movements in various parts of the world crystallize into a form of symbolically universal law, which is then reappropriated by local groups in different settings and translated into terms that resonate domestically.[26] They studied campaigns around a series of specific issues in cities in India, Peru, China, and the USA, to observe local groups 'remaking human rights in the vernacular'.

A lively debate over the process of vernacularization has certainly character-ized the campaign for gender reform in Pakistan, where there have been sharp differences of view amongst those committed to advancing gender equality as to the feasibility and desirability of invoking international human rights norms and processes for this purpose, as well as about how those norms should be trans-lated into the domestic context. Similar debates—although varying in kind from country to country—have taken place not just in Pakistan but even more actively in other Muslim-majority countries in which women have sought to advance gender equality in the face of conservative religious laws and norms. There have been passionate discussions and struggles over the question of how to address the conflicts and tensions between human rights commitments to gender equality and non-discrimination on the one hand and Islamic laws and precepts on the other.[27]

NGOs such as Women Living Under Muslim Laws,[28] as well as Sisters in Islam[29] and its related organization Musawah[30] have dedicated themselves to finding ways, as Muslim women acting within the context of their faith and culture, to challenge gender discrimination and to promote women's rights. According to Sisters in Islam, which was founded in Malaysia in 1987, their movement began with a recog-nition that legal reform was insufficient to promote real change for women, given that Islam itself was being 'referred to and used as a source of injustice and oppres-sion', and they felt 'the urgent need to re-read the Qur'an to discover if the Text truly

---

[25] For a recent account, see Merry and Levitt, 'The Vernacularization of Women's Rights', in S. Hopgood, J. Snyder, and L. Vinjamuri (eds), *Human Rights Futures* (2017) 213.

[26] Ibid.

[27] See e.g. Hashim, 'Reconciling Islam and Feminism', 7 *Gender and Development* (1999) 7; Grami, 'Islamic Feminism: A New Feminist Movement or a Strategy by Women for Acquiring Rights?', 6 *Contemporary Arab Affairs* (2013) 102. For a review of some of the foundational work on the notion of Islamic feminism, see R. Rhouni, *Secular and Islamic Feminist Critiques in the Work of Fatima Merniss* (2009).

[28] http://www.wluml.org/node/5408.

[29] http://www.sistersinislam.org.my/BM/.

[30] http://www.musawah.org/.

supported the oppression and ill-treatment of women.[31] The organization states that it seeks to 'promote an understanding of Islam that recognizes the principles of justice, equality, freedom and dignity within a democratic nation state'. According to the Musawah organization, which focuses attention in particular on the family, its movement is 'led by Muslim women who seek to publicly reclaim Islam's spirit of justice for all', and seeks 'to build and share knowledge that supports equality and justice in the Muslim family using a holistic approach that combines Islamic principles and jurisprudence, international human rights standards, national laws and constitutional guarantees of equality and non-discrimination, and the lived realities of women and men'.[32] Each of these organizations, along with others, seeks to articulate a different relationship between human rights principles and the precepts of Islam other than the sharp and fundamental conflict assumed by many, and in particular they seek to challenge the assumption that Islamic texts must necessarily be read in a way that subjugates and subordinates women. Hence, while they engage with international human rights processes such as CEDAW to promote the rights of women, they do not generally do so by challenging Islamic law and practice as being incompatible with international law and with human rights law in particular, but rather they argue that the Qu'ran does not have to be read in ways that result in serious injustice for women.[33] Musawah, for example, published a research project on CEDAW that examined the justifications advanced by 44 states (all countries with Muslim majority or substantial Muslim minority populations) for their failure to implement provisions of CEDAW in relation to family laws and practices that discriminate against women.[34] In this report, Musawah has provided a range of responses to many of these justifications and argued for 'more meaningful dialogue on the connections between Muslim family laws and practices and international human rights law'.

Although this project of creative re-interpretation of Islamic law in harmony with human rights has spread and taken different forms across a range of countries, it did not initially have prominence among the women's organizations in Pakistan which were most engaged with CEDAW. While a leading activist and scholar has pointed out that 'differing conclusions over women's inequality produced by diverse lines of argument based on Islam and Islamic law are evident from the debate on whether Pakistan should become party to CEDAW', and cited examples

---

[31] https://sistersinislam.org/article/in-search-of-common-ground-reconciling-islam-and-human-rights/.

[32] See e.g. Musawah Knowledge Building Brief No. 4, *CEDAW and Muslim Family Laws*, available online at https://www.musawah.org/resources/knowledge-building-brief-4-cedaw-and-muslim-family-laws-en/.

[33] See Mir-Hosseini, 'Women in Search of Common Ground: Between Islamic and International Human Rights Law', in A. M. Emon, M. S. Ellis, and B. Glahn (eds), *Islamic Law and International Human Rights Law: Searching for Common Ground* (2012) 291.

[34] *CEDAW and Family Laws: In Search of Common Ground* (2011), available online at http://www.peacewomen.org/assets/file/Resources/NGO/wps_cedawandmuslimfamilylaws_march2011.pdf.

of Islamic law being interpreted in far more restrictive ways than the text would suggest due to their being filtered through the lens of cultural and social expectations,[35] others have argued that by comparison with reform efforts by feminist groups such as Sisters in Islam in other Muslim countries like Iran and Malaysia, women's NGOs in Pakistan did not generally engage in debates about the interpretation of the text of the Qu'ran or try to present alternative interpretations of parts of the text which are relevant to women.[36] Rather, they chose to present their arguments primarily in terms of international human rights and to challenge the very idea that women's rights should be limited by Islamic injunctions.[37] Organizations such as the Women's Action Forum engaged initially in long and contentious debates over the question of whether to pursue a secular strategy or one which also made room for a religious framework, but settled eventually on one which championed a secular and democratic state.[38]

Over time, however, it seems that several of the women's rights groups, including the influential organization, Shirgat Gah, shifted to a position of accepting the strategic importance of recognizing religious arguments.[39] According to activist Leena Khan, 'there is no other way of getting through to so much of the public unless we use religious language, especially ... when working with women in rural areas'.[40] She points to the argument made by the organization Women living under Muslim Laws, that while women should work within an Islamic framework, they should 'explore feminist ways of interpreting, thinking and relating'.[41] Others have noted, along similar lines, that it is virtually impossible for women's NGOs in Pakistan not to engage with religion given the reality and ubiquity of religious fundamentalism across the country, and that they must 'compromise in order to survive'.[42] A leading Pakistani activist and sociology scholar, Farida Shaheed, has argued that reliance on a global human rights framework and discourse and keeping the primary focus on the state is bound to greatly limit any impact activists may have. She has suggested that 'activists, who have developed fairly well-established political state-oriented initiatives, must also devise strategies for the social terrain'.[43] She points

---

[35] Ali (n. 9) 187. She provides the following example: 'Islamic law accords women inheritance rights, yet cultural articulations negate this by denying daughters the right to inherit land; male child preference continues as a cultural norm but has no support in Islam, as the Prophet Muhammad himself had no male offspring to survive him and his preference for his daughter Fatima was exceptional in its explicitness; adult women have the right to marry of their own choice, but societal norms expect women to defer to the spouse chosen by the family'.

[36] Weiss (n. 9) ch. 4, 77–78, and Saigol (n. 4).

[37] Ibid.

[38] Saigol (n. 4) 15–16.

[39] L. Z. Khan, 'Women's Activism and Politics in Pakistan', *IWCA Letters – South Asia* (2001), available online at http://www.icwa.org/wp-content/uploads/2015/09/LZK-2.pdf.

[40] Ibid.

[41] Ibid.

[42] Jafar, 'Engaging Fundamentalism: The Case of Women's NGOs in Pakistan', *Social Problems* (2007) 256, at 271.

[43] Shaheed (n. 7) 865.

to the risk that women's rights activists will be labelled as 'Westerners' and aliens, and argues in terms similar to Engle Merry's vernacularization thesis that 'the discourse of women's rights in particular and human rights in general would have greater resonance if, without abandoning references to international human rights, it were also embedded within society's more liberal popular traditions and idiom'.[44]

Yet the view that the movement for gender reform should seek to work with and within a religious framework has been sharply challenged by others, who argue that the originally strong secular feminist movement of the 1980s in the country 'paved the way for its own marginalization' by giving feminist legitimacy to religious and Islamic feminism, and empowering 'neo-Islamic political feminism'.[45] Shehrbano Zia has argued that the Women's Action Forum—which had initially been clearly committed to secularism and the liberal cause—became marginalized because it became too much of an inclusive forum without criteria for membership and did not sufficiently organize itself 'as a practicing secular, feminist, street activist, like-minded, oppositional organization', which challenged religious movements and religious organizations headed by women.[46] Zia perceives what she describes as a new iteration of a revisionist school of gender reform that seeks to find feminist and even secular tendencies amongst conservative, organized religious forces. She contests Farida Shaheed's claim that middle class feminist activists should be wary about challenging religious feminists' interpretations of Islam and should avoid 'subjugating' culturally challenging practices including religion, and argues instead that 'the historical lesson should have taught us that, repeatedly, spaces made to accommodate cultural expressions of religion have merely eclipsed, negated and delegitimized the progressive feminist movement in Pakistan'.[47] She draws on the work of Saba Mahmood emphasizing the political dimension of grassroots Islamic women's 'piety' movements[48] and argues that the soft inclusivity of much of the women's reform movement in Pakistan ends up rendering secular political feminism a 'marginal, westernized and outside' voice on women's issues, instead of a legal, political, economic, and personal challenge to all forms of patriarchal expression including religion.[49]

The heated debate amongst women's groups about what place international norms and institutions have in promoting domestic gender reform in Pakistan (and elsewhere) has extended beyond the question whether activists should embrace a religious framework or not in their integration of human rights principles, and has also addressed what kinds of groups are best placed to advance women's

---

[44] Ibid.
[45] Zia, 'The Reinvention of Feminism in Pakistan', *Feminist Review* (2009) 29. For similar scepticism of the phenomenon of Islamic feminism, see Grami (n. 27).
[46] Zia (n. 45). 43.
[47] Ibid.
[48] S. Mahmood, *Politics of Piety: The Islamic Revival and the Feminist Subject* (2004).
[49] Zia (n. 45) 44.

rights. For some, grassroots activism is more authentic and meaningful—and potentially more effective—than the work of professional NGOs which are dependent on donor funding and media support to promote social and political change.[50] There have been sharp critiques of the 'NGO-ization' and bureaucratization of the women's movement, and indeed of other social movements for reform in developing countries.[51] Similarly, the cleavage in the women's rights movement between urban, educated, middle-class activists with strong connections to transnational and international networks and institutions on the one hand, and women from lower socio-economic and rural backgrounds on the other has been criticized.[52] Other observers, however, have reacted against this critique to argue that 'consistent efforts to mobilize women across class and location have produced some positive results, and the actual movement composition is more nuanced'.[53] Shaheed acknowledges that some in Pakistan have questioned 'whether the robust activism of women in the 1980s, acknowledged locally and internationally as a women's movement' really qualifies as a movement given that it never became a mass movement and remained state-oriented, but her response to this scepticism is that movements can take many forms, being on the streets at certain points while working within institutions at others.[54] Further, developments in recent years, such as the growing countrywide support for the annual women's march organized by a coalition of activist groups since 2018, suggest that a new and broader social movement to promote the rights of women may be underway in Pakistan.

This kind of contestation amongst women's groups and feminist activists as to how best to promote gender reform, and in particular how best to mobilize and generate support on the ground across the country, reflects the complexity of domestic engagement with international human rights as well as the range and diversity of the social groups and working for (and against[55]) change. The account below describes the ways in which international human rights and institutions have played a significant part in the process bringing about change in Pakistan, both through the normative commitments they express and the external accountability,

---

[50]   See the discussion with Lala Rukh and Afiya Zia in Saigol (n. 4) 38.

[51]   Jad, 'The NGOisation of Arab Women's Movements', 35 *IDS Bulletin* (2004) 34.

[52]   For an example in another jurisdiction of this tension between advocacy on behalf of middle class and educated women, on the one hand, and marginalized minority groups—in this case Dalit women in India—see Atrey, 'Women's Human Rights from Progress to Transformation: An Intersectional Response to Martha Nussbaum', 40 *Human Rights Quarterly* (2018) 859.

[53]   Critelli and Willett, 'Struggle and Hope: Challenging Gender Violence in Pakistan', 39 *Critical Sociology* (2012) 201.

[54]   Shaheed, 'Pakistan's Women's Movement: Protests, Programmes and Revitalization', in A. Basu (ed.), *Women's Movements in the Global Era: The Power of Local Feminisms* (2017) 89, ch. 3.

[55]   On the growth and popularity of conservative, piety based movements which challenge liberal notions of gender equality, and which encourage women to be submissive to male authority, see Su, 'The Rising Voices of Women in Pakistan', *National Geographic*, 2 February 2019. And on the spread of the Al-Huda movement, a conservative middle-class religious movement led by a woman, see Mushtaq, 'A Controversial Role Model for Pakistani Women', 4 *South Asia Multidisciplinary Academic Journal* (2010), available online at https://journals.openedition.org/samaj/3030.

information-generation mechanism and discussion forum that they have provided, as well as the ways in which they have been used domestically to advocate and press for reform. Nevertheless, the processes of domestic advocacy for reform have been neither monolithic nor harmonious, but have involved lively contestation and sometimes sharp divisions over the relationship of these international norms and institutions to religious faith and local culture, and over the best strategies and the most effective interlocutors for their vernacularization. In the following section, the active engagement of Pakistani NGOs and others with the CEDAW processes, and their advocacy around CEDAW and the Universal Periodic Review (UPR) to promote domestic gender reforms, are described in further detail.

5. Pakistan's engagement with CEDAW

Despite the successful campaign to have CEDAW ratified in 1996, Pakistan did not submit any reports to the treaty body which monitors the Convention (the Committee on the Elimination of Discrimination Against Women) until 2005, in part due to political instability in the country and in part due to the attitude of the government towards the Convention at the time.[56] It thus effectively missed two earlier cycles of reporting as, under the terms of the Convention, each country is required to submit a report on its implementation of the treaty within a year of its entry into force and thereafter every four years, which meant that Pakistan should have reported in 1997 and 2001. By way of explanation for the long delay, it has been argued that the Pakistan government's view of CEDAW and its implementation was that this was merely a 'project' to be taken up when sufficient funding was made available by donor agencies, rather than a governmental commitment to be budgeted for and pursued like any other.[57]

A. 2007 treaty body review

By the time the government eventually made its first report to the CEDAW committee, the report was supposed to cover three cycles of reporting from the time of accession until the end of December 2004. It was submitted late in 2005 and came before the CEDAW committee for consideration in 2007. The government declared that the report had been created with the assistance of contributions from civil society, that the draft report had been posted on the internet with an invitation

---

[56] See Noreen and Musarrat, 'Protection of Women's Rights through Legal Reform in Pakistan', 3 *Journal of Public Administration and Governance* (2013) 119, who refer to the decade of political instability in Pakistan from the late 1980s to the late 1990s.
[57] Ali (n. 9) 194.

to comment, and that it had been sent to all leading human rights and women's activists and NGOs for their views.[58] This account was however challenged by one of the two civil society shadow reports which stated that NGOs 'were ignored in the preparation of the government's report'.[59]

The government's report mainly presented a positive account of the actions it had adopted to comply with the Convention, emphasizing a range of domestic laws, policies, and new bodies which had been created after ratification in order to give effect to provisions of the Convention. Examples were the amendment of the Pakistan Citizenship Act 1951 to give children born to Pakistani women married to foreigners the right to Pakistani nationality, and the adoption of the Prevention and Control of Human Trafficking Ordinance 2002. The government claimed that it had facilitated the prosecution of 'honour' killings, and pointed to its establishment of the National Commission on the Status of Women (NCSW) in 2000. It listed the creation of crisis centres for women in several cities and the establishment of an Access to Justice Programme aimed at judicial and law enforcement gender sensitization,[60] as well as a national plan and national policy for the advancement of women.[61] The report also highlighted the challenges faced by the government in protecting and promoting women's rights, including lack of awareness, funding, and training, and also low literacy levels especially among the female population. While pointing to the role of courts in awarding decisions or damages for discrimination against women;[62] it acknowledged the difficulties of access to justice within the country.[63]

This broadly optimistic account of the state of affairs for women in Pakistan and of the implementation of CEDAW was challenged by two shadow reports which were submitted around the same time as the state's official report to the committee. The first was submitted by a collective of 60 NGOs in Pakistan with the support of external NGOs,[64] and the second was submitted by Shirkat Gah, a leading domestic women's rights organization which had been founded in 1975 as a voluntary collective.[65]

---

[58] *Consideration of reports submitted by States parties under article 18 of the Convention on the Elimination of All Forms of Discrimination against Women: Combined initial, second and third periodic reports of States parties—Pakistan* CEDAW/C/PAK/1-3 (3 August 2005), point 23 at 11.

[59] Democratic Commission for Human Development & National Commission for Justice and Peace (Pakistan), *Discrimination Lingers On: A Report on the Compliance of CEDAW in Pakistan* 6 (2007).

[60] CEDAW/C/PAK/1-3 (n. 58), at 18–19, 23.

[61] Ibid. 19.

[62] The report included an example of using the court system to successfully eliminate the 'fixed quota system' for female admission to medical college, instead creating a merit-based admission process. CEDAW/C/PAK/1-3 (n. 58), at 22.

[63] CEDAW/C/PAK/1-3 (n. 58), at 21–22.

[64] See *Discrimination Lingers On* (n. 59). Also Dominicans for Justice and Peace, *Shadow Report Presented to the UN Committee on the Elimination of All Forms of Discrimination against Women (CEDAW) at the United Nations in New York* (15 June 2007), available online at http://un.op.org/en/node/2790.

[65] See n. 20. Shirkat Gah's shadow report to CEDAW was entitled *Talibanisation & Poor Governance: Undermining CEDAW in Pakistan* (2007).

The first shadow report, *Discrimination Lingers On*, highlighted the enormous challenges confronting the goal of tackling discrimination against women in Pakistan and the need for the government to undertake more concrete, committed, and faster steps to do so.[66] The basic fact that the government had failed to create a legal framework for translating the provisions of CEDAW into domestic law was highlighted. Amongst the issues which the report claimed the government had not adequately addressed in its report were: the existence of discriminatory laws; the effectiveness of policy changes; the pervasive violence against women which was sanctioned by widespread social and religious practices; and the absence of any legislation criminalizing domestic violence.[67] Amongst the recommendations made by the first shadow report were: formulate a constitutional definition of 'discrimination' against women; revise discriminatory laws including the Hudood Ordinances; register all marriages and births; reduce the female illiteracy rate; remove gender stereotypes in educational materials; adopt a comprehensive approach to ending forced and child marriages; and ratify all human rights treaties.[68] Attention was drawn to the failure of the political quotas which had been introduced to reserve one third of local government seats for women, due to the many practices which barred women from exercising these political rights and prevented them from participating in the political process. The report also called on the government to ratify the Optional Protocol to CEDAW which grants a right of individual complaint to the treaty body, and to withdraw the limiting declaration it made upon accession to the Convention.[69] Finally, the report emphasized the need to improve the state of law, to inculcate democratic values, and to create an environment which would enable women to participate in the political process.

The second report, submitted by Shirkat Gah and to which 22 other organizations contributed, argued strongly that unless the government of Pakistan acted to curb growing 'Talibanisation' in the country—(which was described as the commission of violence by 'men who sport beards' referencing Islam, exempting themselves from the law and holding the country hostage) and establish adequate basic governance structures, discrimination against women would only strengthen.[70] With its primary emphasis on the need to combat religious extremism, the shadow report argued that the government had become nonchalant in the face of armed groups denouncing polio vaccinations and contraceptives, threatening and attacking girls' schools and development and women's NGOs, and coercing women to wear Taliban-prescribed clothing.[71] The report echoed many of the concerns of the first shadow report, arguing for the government to strengthen its underlying

---

[66] *Discrimination Lingers On* (n. 59), at 2.
[67] Ibid.
[68] Dominicans for Justice and Peace (n. 64).
[69] Ibid.
[70] Shirkat Gah (n. 65) 8, 11–12.
[71] Ibid. 7–8.

commitment to CEDAW,[72] to combat Talibanisation, to develop and enhance the role of the NCSW,[73] and to foster education,[74] governance,[75] and the prevention of violence against women. The report strongly emphasized the need for the government to directly address discrimination against women based on 'customs, practices and misinterpretation of religion'.[76] The lack of adequate record-keeping mechanisms and effective data collection were identified as significant problems, given that the failure to record births enables child marriages, and the lack of marriage and divorce records open women to criminal prosecution and harassment by ex-husbands.[77] Barriers to women's participation in the political process were highlighted, including the prevention of women from registering to vote, the failure to hold elections for women's reserved seats,[78] and the lack of national identity cards which are required to vote and to access government schemes.[79]

The CEDAW Committee in its concluding observations on Pakistan following the 2007 review focused on many of the issues that were raised in the two shadow reports, and especially on the systemic issues. The Committee welcomed some of the recent initiatives adopted by the government such as the establishment of the NCSW and the Gender Reform Action Plan. Reference to the Taliban and other extremist groups was made in urging prompt action to counteract the influence of 'non-State actors, which, through the misinterpretation of Islam and the use of

---

[72] The report called upon the Committee to press the government on issues such as the withdrawal of Pakistan's general declaration, the ratification of the Optional Protocol, incorporation of the CEDAW definition of discrimination into domestic law or policy, the promotion of 'cross-sectoral, inter-ministerial ownership' and creation of an enabling environment to implement CEDAW provisions, and the institutionalization of partnership between the government and civil society organizations to monitor the impact of programs and policies to give effect to CEDAW: Shirkat Gah (n. 65) 2.

[73] The report encouraged the government to make the National Commission on the Status of Women (NCSW) a permanent statutory commission, increasing its autonomy and granting it greater monitoring power over compliance of laws and policies, enabling the NCSW's direct access to the highest levels of decision-making, and obligating the government to respond to NCSW recommendation within an allotted timeframe: Shirkat Gah (n. 65) 3. Further, the report argued (at 10) that the government had misled the committee as to the clout and role of the NCSW in its report.

[74] On education, questions posed by the Shirkat Gah report included whether any measures had been adopted to ensure the security of female staff and students, replacement of education materials promoting female stereotypes, religious misconceptions, and collaboration with civil society organizations to create female-positive textbooks, mechanisms to track students through the primary cycle ('identifying reasons for non-enrolment and drop-outs') and promote student retention, to enhance educational quality and ensure, at a district level, educational opportunities for females in every village: Shirkat Gah (n. 65) 3.

[75] On governance, questions posed by the report included what measures the government had taken to ensure adequate record-keeping of births, marriages, divorces, and deaths, to collect gender disaggregated data across all socio-economic strata, to change operational definitions of 'work' and 'economic productivity' to accurately reflect the economic contributions of females in both the informal and formal sectors, to register women to vote and to record gender disaggregated data on political participation, to educate the population on women's rights, to train NGOS, law enforcement, and the judiciary on women-sensitive issues, and to train those administering Muslim family laws. Shirkat Gah (n. 65) 3.

[76] Ibid. 11.

[77] Ibid. 10.

[78] Ibid. 12.

[79] Ibid. 18.

intimidation and violence, are undermining the enjoyment by women and girls of their human rights'.[80] In terms of necessary reforms, the Committee urged the government to do the following: pass legislation to implement CEDAW domestically as well as systematically review all existing discriminatory laws; provide capacity-building and training; cooperate closely and consult with civil society; ensure proper implementation of national gender reform plans and policies; collect adequate data on the participation of women in public and political life; ensure the registration of births and marriages and that all women are issued a national identity card; promote awareness-raising of women's rights; and address fundamental issues such as violence against women, child and forced marriages, trafficking, education, and health.[81]

Hence the CEDAW committee in this first review of Pakistan was highly responsive to the issues raised by the two shadow reports submitted on behalf of the array of domestic NGOs and organizations which had prepared them. While acknowledging some of the positive steps taken by Pakistan's government, especially the broader systemic reforms, the concluding observations of the committee echoed the many major challenges and necessary reforms pointed out by the civil society groups.

B. 2013 treaty body review

Pakistan submitted its next periodic report in late 2011, covering the period between 2005 and 2009. The Ministry of Women Development at the time produced this report, consulting to some degree with civil society in the process.[82] The government report was again fairly positive, describing 'a four-pronged strategy ... to reduce the prevalence of poverty amongst women, promote gender equality, curb violence against women and enact legislation to empower Pakistani women'.[83]

Reference was made to Pakistan's initiatives to improve collection of disaggregated data, including capacity-building and sensitization measures aimed at the Federal Bureau of Statistics and Population Census and aligning the data collected with the gender database of the South Asian Association for Regional Cooperation (SAARC).[84] The report also referred to the creation of the Gender Crime Cell (GCC) within the National Police Bureau in 2006, a unit responsible for collating and analysing data on violence against women. Collaboration between police, government and civil society groups on various initiatives and issues was also

---

[80] Ibid. 5.
[81] *Concluding Comments of the CEDAW Committee: Pakistan*, CEDAW/C/PAK/CO/3 (11 June 2007).
[82] *Fourth Periodic Report of Pakistan to the CEDAW Committee*, CEDAW/C/PAK/4 (24 September 2011) 10.
[83] Ibid. 5.
[84] Ibid. 26.

highlighted, including the creation of crisis centres, data collection, fund-raising to promote awareness raising and capacity building, domestic violence, forced confinement, and anti-trafficking.[85]

While the report focused significantly on the positive steps Pakistan had taken to realize its CEDAW commitments, including the adoption of legislation governing women's rights in family law disputes and protection against harassment at work, as well as the establishment of a national human rights commission, it also discussed the challenges, many of which were the same as those identified in its 2007 report. These included deeply entrenched societal norms and practices which reinforce the subordination of women, particular problems faced by rurally-based women, deep inequality, and poverty. The tasks facing the government, in light of these challenges, were identified as including the need to do the following: ensure the proper understanding of international commitments and their integration into national policies; adequately monitor and enforce existing laws; challenge patriarchal and feudal systems and customary practices opposed to women's advancement, as well as working to change mindsets and attitudes; and improve access to justice. The government referred to a shortfall in available resources, as well as a lack of adequate legal and economic expertise and understanding of gender issues within government.

The notable rise in the number of shadow reports submitted in this second CEDAW review, coupled with the number of organizations and groups which collaborated on preparing and submitting the various reports, provides some indication of the rapid growth and intensification of civil society activity in the field of gender in Pakistan during this period. By comparison with the two shadow reports submitted for the first review in 2007, the CEDAW website lists eight shadow reports submitted for the second review in 2012, including reports by the Aurat Foundation,[86] Shirkat Gah,[87] and the Pakistan Dalit Solidarity Network which comprised over two dozen rights-based groups in Pakistan,[88] and a number of other major international NGOs working in Pakistan.[89]

By comparison with the positive tone of much of the government's report, Shirkat Gah's report focused on 'the inconsistencies between policy and practice that create glaring disparities between de jure and de facto gender equality due to weak implementation of otherwise adequate policies', intersecting with cultural

---

[85] Ibid. 26–28.

[86] Aurat Foundation, *Pakistan NGO Alternative Report on CEDAW* (2012).

[87] Shirkat Gah, *Obstructing Progress: Growing Talibanisation and Poor Governance in Pakistan* (2012).

[88] Pakistan Dalit Solidarity Network, *Scheduled Caste Women in Pakistan: Denied a Life in Dignity and Respect—Alternative Report to the CEDAW committee submitted in collaboration with the International Dalit Solidarity Network* (2013).

[89] The International Disability Alliance, Human Rights Watch, Equality Now, the Center for Reproductive Rights and the Global Initiative to End Corporal Punishment of Children submitted shadow reports, which are available with all other documentation on the OHCRH website: http://tbinternet.ohchr.org/SitePages/Home.aspx.

factors, and also with the aftermath of a number of devastating natural disasters (including two earthquakes) that had afflicted Pakistan during the period in question.[90]

The Aurat Foundation in preparing its shadow report engaged in a four-year consultative process, from 2008 to 2012.[91] Four provincial 'CEDAW committees' and one national 'CEDAW committee' including representatives of organizations which had prior experience of the CEDAW process were formed, and these committees held meetings with local civil society representatives, legal experts, and female parliamentarians. They debated relevant issues, developed and disseminated questionnaires to gather information on the implementation of various CEDAW provisions in Pakistan, and shared drafts of the shadow report as it developed.[92] The final report was endorsed by 24 civil society organizations, the large majority of which were domestic NGOs and groups. The Aurat report, like that of Shirkat Gah, noted that gender issues had taken a backseat to other major challenges facing the country during the reporting period, particularly the devastating earthquakes, poverty and the 'war on terror'.[93] Particular criticism was made of the government's continued unwillingness to ratify the Optional Protocol to the Convention (which gives a right of individual complaint/communication), and of the refusal to provide a constitutional or statutory definition of 'discrimination'.[94] The report noted that despite the increase in women parliamentarians[95] and urban workers, discrimination continued to increase in other and mainly rural parts of the country due in part to rising extremism and militancy. It drew attention to the role of the Council of Islamic Ideology, a body with constitutional status in Pakistan charged with advising on the compatibility of legislation with Islam, in thwarting a number of important pro-women initiatives, and particularly the proposed legislation on domestic violence in 2009.[96] The report further criticized the government's bureaucratic inertia concerning social protection of women, pointing out that amending existing laws would undoubtedly affect the traditional setup of the family unit, and would therefore be likely to upset political alliances within the government. Despite the government's assertions about improvements in education, the shadow report pointed to the low female literacy rate and the urban-rural discrepancy, the poor quality of education received, and the high dropout rates for girls compared

---

[90] Aurat Foundation (Second Shadow Report) (n. 86).

[91] Ibid. 2.

[92] Ibid. 2–3.

[93] Ibid. 1.

[94] The government report had emphasized court decisions which had ruled in favour of women and gender equality as an adequate substitute to a constitutional or statutory definition, something which Aurat strongly contested. Aurat Report (n. 86) at 9.

[95] The shadow report did push back on the GOP's claims that women's political participation had improved significantly. Although greater numbers of women had been elected to public office, the report discussed the continued dearth of women's decision-making power. Further, women remained predominantly absent from the judiciary.

[96] Aurat Report (n. 86) at 11.

with boys.[97] Overall, the report concluded that 'the major impediments to gender equality and the elimination of discrimination are an ambivalent political will on the part of the State, and resultantly its institutions; the absence of a firm commitment to the inherent principles; and a reluctance to own the State's obligations under the CEDAW Convention.'[98]

The CEDAW committee's concluding observations following the review process closely tracked the focus and sentiments of the shadow reports, emphasizing systemic issues such as: Pakistan's failure to withdraw its declaration or to ratify the Optional Protocol; the lack of legislation prohibiting both direct and indirect discrimination; the failure to repeal discriminatory laws such as the Hudood Ordinances or to curb domestic violence; and the inadequacy of resources dedicated to the National Council on the Status of Women, or to enhance women's political participation, health, education, and employment opportunities, or to increase capacity building and training. The Committee also warned that the government should ensure that the devolution of powers from the centre to the provinces following the 18th Constitutional Amendment would not adversely affect women's advancement,[99] and it called on the government to adopt legislation for religious minorities, revise discriminatory legislation on the dissolution of Muslim marriages, and raise the minimum age of marriage for girls to 18.

In preparation for the third CEDAW review in 2020, Pakistan submitted its fifth periodic report to the Committee in late 2018.[100] In this report, Pakistan has drawn attention again to a range of legal as well as policy reforms introduced, as well as defending some of the areas in which it failed to comply with the Committee's prior recommendations. Amongst the reforms towards which the government pointed were: the proposed changes to the *Jirga* tribal justice system; new complaints and redress mechanisms for women established by the NCSW; redress procedures in relation to workplace harassment; an acid crimes campaign; new women's helplines and dedicated desks in Punjab police stations; better data-gathering and awareness raising; and a variety of educational, electoral, marital and inheritance law reforms. No less than 18 civil society submissions or 'shadow reports' were brought to the CEDAW committee during this latest review cycle, with many dozens more organizations participating in the preparation of one or more of these reports, demonstrating the increasing degree of NGO mobilization and engagement with CEDAW and related international human rights processes over time.

---

[97] Ibid. 12.
[98] Ibid. 1.
[99] *Concluding Observations of the Committee*, CEDAW/C/PAK/CO/4 (1 March 2013).
[100] *Fifth periodic report submitted by Pakistan under article 18 of the Convention*, CEDAW/C/PAK/5 (9 October 2018).

C. Pakistan's Universal Periodic Reviews 2012 and 2017

In addition to the CEDAW reviews, Pakistan's overall human rights performance has also been reviewed twice in the context of the more political and less legalized Universal Periodic Review (UPR) by the UN Human Rights Council.[101] The first took place in 2012, shortly after Pakistan had submitted its initial report to CEDAW, and the second in late 2017. The UPR was introduced in 2006 as a form of peer review by UN member states of one another's performance. While there is no expert or independent committee of the kind that oversees the monitoring of treaties such as CEDAW and the Convention on the Rights of the Child (CRC), the Human Rights Council appoints a working group composed of the 47 members of the Council to undertake the review, headed by a three-person committee which prepares and organizes the work. Each state under review presents a report on its performance to the Council, and this information is generally supplemented by other stakeholder (mainly civil society) submissions, and an interactive dialogue takes place before recommendations are formulated and addressed to the state.[102] The reviews take place on a regular basis before working groups of the Human Rights Council, and approximately 40 states are reviewed each year in a number of interactive sessions. Whatever the undoubted weaknesses of a negotiated and political process like the UPR, some synergy has developed between this review process and the workings of other human rights treaty bodies, including CEDAW, with states in the UPR regularly drawing on and reinforcing the recommendations made by the other treaty bodies and procedures, thereby increasing the external political pressure on the state to comply and providing further internal leverage for domestic actors and groups.[103]

The two sets of reports and recommendations that emerged from the Human Rights Council reviews of Pakistan, while ranging beyond questions of gender to consider a broad spectrum of human rights issues, reinforced the conclusions and observations of the CEDAW committee and in turn of the civil society groups which had brought the issues before the committee.[104] As the UPR process allows for the submission of information by civil society groups, national human rights

---

[101] See Collister, 'Rituals and Implementation in the Universal Periodic Review and the UN Treaty Bodies', in H. Charlesworth and E. Larking (eds), *Human Rights and the Universal Periodic Review: Rituals and Ritualism* (2015). See also Carraro, 'Promoting Compliance with Human Rights: The Performance of the United Nations' Universal Periodic Review and Treaty Bodies', *International Studies Quarterly* (2019) 1.

[102] On the role of civil society in the UPR process, see Schokman and Lynch, 'Effective NGO Engagement with the Universal Periodic Review', in Charlesworth and Larking (n. 101) 126.

[103] For discussion of the relationship between treaty-body monitoring and the UPR, and the risk of tensions as well as synergies, see Schokman and Lynch (n. 102) 135–138, Also Collister (n. 101), and Carraro, 'Promoting Compliance with Human Rights: The Performance of the United Nations' Universal Periodic Review and Treaty Bodies', *International Studies Quarterly* (2019) 1.

[104] *Report of the Working Group on the Universal Periodic Review: Pakistan*, A/HRC/22/12 (26 December 2012).

institutions and others, a series of such submissions was made on the occasion of each of the two reviews of Pakistan.[105] The array of recommendations made in the UPR reviews included: safeguarding women's rights; following up on the CEDAW committee's recommendations (including withdrawing the declaration and ratifying the Optional Protocol); punishing perpetrators of violence against women; promoting gender equality in education and employment; and creating training and awareness programmes for law enforcement officials on violence and sexual assault against women. These issues and recommendations again mirrored those discussed in the NGO shadow reports to CEDAW. The government of Pakistan accepted most of these recommendations from the Human Rights Council, but did not accept the recommendations to decriminalize adultery and non-marital consensual sex. It also merely 'noted' rather than 'accepted' the recommendations on ratifying the optional protocol to CEDAW, repealing the Hudood Ordinances, abolishing *jirgas*, and repealing other laws that discriminate against women in the legal process, such as the evidentiary value of women's testimony.[106]

6. Pakistan's response to the human rights monitoring processes

While these international processes of review have clearly created opportunities for interested actors and civil society groups to draw attention to the range of issues facing women in Pakistan, commentators have questioned whether the UPR amounts to much more than ritualism,[107] and there has been an ongoing scholarly debate about the impact and value of treaty-body procedures.[108] The core question is whether the treaty review process and international human rights reporting have had any impact in bringing about domestic change in relation to women's rights.[109] The answer in the case of Pakistan appears to be that these processes have played quite an important role in pressing for, and helping to catalyse, a range of significant legal and institutional changes in the area of gender.

---

[105] The submissions of civil society, as well as a summary of the main points, are available on the website of the Office of the High Commissioner for Human Rights: http://www.ohchr.org/EN/HRBodies/UPR/Pages/UPRPakistanStakeholderInfoS14.aspx.

[106] A list of all recommendations and the government's responses are available online at https://www.upr-info.org/.

[107] H. Charlesworth and E. Larking (eds), *Human Rights and the Universal Periodic Review: Rituals and Ritualism* (2015).

[108] Amongst a growing literature, see E. Posner, *The Twilight of Human Rights* (2014), particularly Chs 2 and 4 and Simmons and Creamer, 'Do Self-Reporting Regimes Matter? Evidence from the Convention against Torture', *Faculty Scholarship at Penn Law* (2019) 2057.

[109] On women's rights in particular, see Simmons and Creamer, 'The Dynamic Impact of Periodic Review on Women's Rights', 81 *Law and Contemporary Problems* (2018) 31, and S. Zwingel, *How do International Women's Rights become Effective Domestic Norms? An Analysis of the Convention on the Elimination of all Forms of Discrimination against Women* (2005) PhD thesis, Ruhr-Universität Bochum, Bochum.

Between the time when Pakistan ratified CEDAW in 1996 and the end of 2017, several important legislative and policy measures were adopted to implement the state's obligations under CEDAW. While a range of other political and economic factors were undoubtedly relevant, and pressure from donors and other actors are likely to have contributed to the changes in question, the government's intention to comply with CEDAW was presented as an explicit part of the reason for a number of key reforms. Nevertheless, a prominent lawyer and women's rights activist in Pakistan has suggested that the government does not usually like to acknowledge CEDAW or international human rights law when it introduces reforms, preferring to minimize or conceal the appearance that international law or international pressure influenced its action.[110] In her view, the government generally ignores the recommendations of human rights treaty bodies such as CEDAW until the reporting process comes around, and has enacted reforms based on those recommendations only when domestic advocacy groups have followed up on these processes and maintained pressure on the government through a range of activist strategies over time.

In 2004, the Criminal Law (Amendment) Act was adopted, which for the first time identified and defined so-called honour killing as a crime, and set a minimum punishment of 10 years. This took place eight years after Pakistan had ratified CEDAW, and during the period when it should have submitted periodic reports to the CEDAW committee on its compliance with the Convention, but failed to do so. Not long before Pakistan submitted its first report to the committee, the 'Gender Reform Action Plan' was adopted in 2005. More significantly, the Protection of Women Act 2006 was passed, which—despite substantial opposition from conservative religious forces—reformed some of the more grotesque aspects of the Hudood Ordinances, including the conflation of adultery with rape, and introduced evidentiary and procedural reforms for dealing with rape cases.

Following the first CEDAW review process in 2007, a series of further important reforms were introduced. In 2010, the Protection Against Harassment of Women at the Workplace Act 2010 was adopted.[111] This legislation introduced a code of conduct prohibiting harassment in the workplace and requiring the establishment of complaints procedures, as well as establishing an Ombudsperson for the protection of woman against harassment in the workplace at the Federal as well as Provincial level. The legislation explicitly states in its 'Statement of objectives and reasons' that it adheres to the provisions of CEDAW and other international human rights instruments.[112] Following the adoption of the legislation, NGOs have provided workshops to train and sensitize representatives from the private sector

---

[110] Correspondence with Hina Jilani, Advocate of the Supreme Court of Pakistan and long-time human rights activist, May 2018.

[111] Available online at https://qau.edu.pk/pdfs/ha.pdf.

[112] For analysis of the legislation see Khan and Ahmed, 'The Protection against Harassment of Women at the Workplace Act 2010: A Legislative Review', 3 *Lums Law Journal* (2016).

and civil society organizations on how to deal with sexual harassment in the work-place.[113] Local firms and NGOs have created harassment boards within their of-fices to handle complaints. The NCSW has created complaints procedures, and has sent senior project managers to attend international training workshops dealing with workplace discrimination and harassment,[114] with local workshops based on the international training being subsequently organized within Pakistan.[115]

In 2011, several major pieces of legislation addressing a range of abuses and violence against women were adopted. The first, the Prevention of Anti-Women Practices Act, which was enacted after a five-year struggle for adoption by women's advocates, prohibits various anti-woman customary practices including forced marriages, 'bartered' marriages as compensation, and inheritance deprivation.[116] The very brief statement of objects and reasons at the end of the legislative text declares that it has been adopted because 'there are several practices and customs in vogue in the country which are not only against human dignity, but also violate human rights'.[117] A second piece of reform legislation is the Criminal Law (Third Amendment) Act 2011 which criminalizes a practice known as 'marriage with the Quran' which was a way of forcing women to remain unmarried for life in order to retain within the family and under control of male relatives the share of property which might otherwise be paid as dowry to a spouse outside the family.[118]

The third, the Acid Control and Acid Crime (Criminal Law—Second Amendment) Act was adopted the same year to include acid attacks on women as part of the criminal law and to specify penalties, as well as introducing provisions on compensation and rehabilitation of victims.[119] The legislation expressly outlaws acid attacks and broadens the definition of the attack to include 'disfigur[ing] or defac[ing]' victims, as well as including two new sections for voluntarily causing harm by dangerous means or substances.

One year later, in 2012, the Domestic Violence (Prevention and Protection) Act 2012 was adopted.[120] This was a major piece of legislation which, like the

---

[113] See Jafar (n. 18) 102.

[114] National Commission on the Status of Women, Government of Pakistan, *Impact Assessment Report: Public-Private Partnership to End 'Honour Crimes' in Pakistan Through the Implementation of Criminal Law (Amendment) Act 2004* (2010) 20.

[115] Ibid. 20.

[116] See https://pcsw.punjab.gov.pk/prevention_of_anti_women_practices. For a critical appraisal of the extent to which this law has been implemented in parts of Pakistan, see S. Zaman, *Forced Marriages and Inheritance Deprivation* (2014), available online at https://www.af.org.pk/pub_files/1416847483.pdf.

[117] Available online at http://bolobhi.org/wp-content/uploads/2012/02/Prevention-of-Anti-Women-Practices-Criminal-Law-Amendment-Act-2008.pdf.

[118] See Pianta, 'The Life of Slavery of Pakistani Women Who Are Forced To "Marry" the Quran', *La Stampa*, 30 July 2013.

[119] For a critical review of the Act and the need for longer-term preventive and protective measures, see Werlhof, 'Scarred for Life: The Impact of the Acid Control and Acid Crime Prevention Act Of 2010 on Addressing Violence Against Women in Pakistan', 3 *International Review of Law* (2014) 1, 3, available online at http://dx.doi.org/10.5339/irl.2013.dv.3.

[120] For the text of the legislation, see http://www.af.org.pk/Important%20Courts'%20judgement/Women%20protection%20against%20domestic%20violence%20bil%2013pages.pdf.

Prevention of Anti-Women Practices Act, was the outcome of a lengthy struggle to get it enacted by the national assembly, after it failed to be adopted on a previous attempt in 2009.[121] As in the case of the harassment legislation enacted in 2010, the Domestic Violence Act 2012 makes clear that it was adopted, amongst other reasons, in order to comply with CEDAW, listing in its statement of objectives and reasons that it 'responds to the Convention for the Elimination of All Forms of Discrimination Against Women of adopting zero tolerance for violence against women and introducing positive legislation on domestic violence'.[122] The Act defines and criminalizes 'domestic violence', sets minimum penalties, and requires courts to set a date for hearing within seven days of receiving a petition from a complainant, and to deal with the petition within 90 days.[123]

The Domestic Violence Act, however, was adopted following a constitutional amendment which devolved authority for domestic affairs from the central government to the four provinces and hence the legislation is applicable only in federal territory.[124] The devolution has also had an effect on efforts to promote women's rights in Pakistan in other ways. One important consequence was the dissolution of a number of federal ministries, which included the Ministry for Women Development which had previously been responsible for much of the implementation of CEDAW.[125] There has also been significant concern about the gender impact of the devolution due to the fact that the area of health policy, which has major implications for women, was devolved to the Provinces, meaning that the standards of protection and service are likely to be far from uniform across the country. To give one other relevant example of provincial disparities which can significantly affect women and girls, while the province of Sindh treats girls as reaching the age of majority at 18, the other three provinces set the age at 16. Many, including the CEDAW committee in its concluding observations following the second review of Pakistan, were concerned that efforts on behalf of gender equality would

---

[121] Wasim, 'Domestic Violence No More a Private Affair', *Dawn*, 21 February 2012, available online at https://www.dawn.com/news/697039. Interviews with leading women's NGOs such as the Aurat Foundation, Human Rights Commission of Pakistan, and National Commission for Human Rights and activists also confirmed that NGO lobbying played a heavy role in the passing of this bill.

[122] Ibid.

[123] For appraisal and critique of this measure and of the various other legislative reforms, see Zia, Aurat Foundation, 'Legislative Initiatives on Women in Pakistan—Need for Self-Critique and Reassessment', 43 *Legislative Watch* (2014) 1, 1–2, available online at https://www.af.org.pk/newsl/1402998220.pdf.

[124] For an analysis of the devolution and its consequences, see *Devolution in Pakistan: Overview of the ADB/DfID/World Bank study* (2004), available online at http://fdsindh.gov.pk/site/userfiles/DevolutioninPakistanJuly04-ADB.pdf and Cheema, Khwaja, and Qadir, 'Local Government Reforms in Pakistan: Context, Content and Causes', in D. Mookherjee and P. Bardhan (eds), *Decentralization and Local Governance in Developing Countries: A Comparative Perspective* (2006).

[125] Rukhsana Shah in 'Pakistan's Growing Gender Gap', *Dawn*, 24 August 2015, lists various important initiatives that the Ministry of Women's Development had taken in the area of women's rights and gender, and warns that 'the provinces do not appear to have the capacity or political will to develop an alternative narrative to the rampant obscurantism proliferating throughout the country', available online at https://www.dawn.com/news/1202397.

be negatively affected by the new provincial autonomy, fearing that the provinces would be less likely to undertake the major reforms needed.

Some of the developments which have taken place since the devolution, however, suggest that the change may not have been altogether negative for gender equality issues and for the implementation of CEDAW. In the first place, the abolition of the Ministry for Women's Development prompted the government to enhance the status and functions of the NCSW which had been created in 2000. Civil society groups in their submissions to the CEDAW review in 2007 had argued for the status and functions of the NCSW to be enhanced,[126] and the government took the occasion of devolution of power to the provinces to do this. The NCSW was granted financial and administrative autonomy and the seniority of a state minister was conferred on the Chairperson, giving the Chairperson the important power to make recommendations directly to the national cabinet.[127] Among the significant initiatives adopted by the NCSW in recent years have been: the establishment of a complaints mechanism for electoral complaints and monitoring elections; agreeing a procedure with the Acid Survivors Foundation to track acid crimes and advocating for a comprehensive acid attack law; piloting the Pakistan Women Media Complaints Cell to promote gender sensitivity and gender responsiveness in the media; and helping to develop a system to monitor the implementation of the Child Marriage Restraint Act (2014) in Sindh. The NCSW has also been developing indicators for CEDAW reporting, together with provisional women's ministries and the provincial Commissions on the Status of Women, prompted in part by the Concluding Observations of the CEDAW Committee on Pakistan in 2013.[128]

The move towards decentralization and provincial autonomy also potentially presents an opportunity for the promotion of gender issues at a more local political level, where local women's groups and activists may have a better chance of influence. Thus far, some of the provinces have been active and have adopted significant reforms, in particular the Punjab. The Punjab government in 2016 enacted the Protection of Women Against Violence Act, despite strong opposition from the religious clergy and others.[129] Notably, by comparison with some of the other gender reforms which lack crucial enforcement mechanisms, this legislation also provides for enforcement mechanisms including the expedition of civil remedies, and for the establishment of Violence against Women Centers.[130] One such centre opened

---

[126] See Shirkat Gah (n. 65) 2–3, 14.

[127] *Historic Gain for Women in Pakistan as Women's Commission Gains Autonomous Status*, 7 February 2012, available online at http://www.unwomen.org/en/news/stories/2012/2/historic-gain-for-women-in-pakistan-as-women-s-commission-gains-autonomous-status.

[128] Interview with Parveen Qadir Agha, Behbud, and Director of the Female Campus at International Islamic University, April 2018. See *Concluding Observations of the CEDAW Committee on the 4th periodic report of Pakistan* (2013), CEDAW/C/PAK/CO/4.

[129] Jatoi, 'The Punjab Protection of Women Against Violence Act 2016: A Critique', 15 *Legislative Watch* (2016), available online at https://www.af.org.pk/newsl/1486547583.pdf.

[130] For an analysis of the new legislation alongside a number of other institutional reforms and social incentives introduced in the Punjab to proactively address violence against women, see Tanwir

in Multan in 2017, with others to open in each division in the Punjab province, along with a range of other initiatives including a hotline for complaints and the provision of additional shelters and transitional housing for women.[131] The Punjab government also adopted the Commission on the Status of Women Act 2014 which established a provincial Commission for the Punjab. This Commission has a broad mandate, including review of laws and policies, and monitoring the implementation of law and policies to achieve gender equality and eliminate discrimination against women, including monitoring the implementation of international instruments to which Pakistan is a signatory.[132] Thus far, it appears that the Punjab Commission has been active in promoting gender equality and was described by a critic of Pakistan's progress on gender as engaged in 'path-breaking work'.[133] In 2017, the Punjab government also adopted the Punjab Women Empowerment Package, mandating the establishment of a coherent policy to address a wide range of gender concerns including gender-based violence, education, maternal health, economic opportunity, and political participation.[134]

The province of Sindh, following a two-year delay, activated the establishment of a Sindh Commission on the Status of Women which had been provided for by law since 2015.[135] Sindh also enacted the Domestic Violence (Prevention and Protection) Act in 2013.[136] Further, the Sindh Child Marriage Restraint Act 2014, which was repeatedly recommended by the NGO shadow reports to the CEDAW Committee and by the Committee itself, criminalizes marriage to any 'person male or female who is under eighteen years of age' and punishes the male contracting party (if above 18), the individual solemnizing the marriage, and the parents or guardians concerned.

A Commission on the Status of Women was also created by the province of Khyber Pakhtunkhwa in 2009, and a similar Commission was eventually created

---

et al., 'Not Accepting Abuse as the Norm: Local Forms of Institutional Reform to Improve Reporting on Domestic Violence in Punjab', 20 *Journal of International Women's Studies* (2019) 129.

[131] Rehman, 'More Centres of Violence Against Women to be set up: CM', *Business Recorder* (2017), available online at https://www.brecorder.com/2017/10/06/373347/more-centres-of-violence-against-women-to-be-set-up-cm/.

[132] See http://pcsw.punjab.gov.pk/intro. For the legislation establishing the Commission see http://punjablaws.gov.pk/laws/2555.html.

[133] Khan, 'The Global Gender Gap Report and Pakistan', *The Daily Times*, Pakistan, 7 November 2017, available online at https://dailytimes.com.pk/135301/global-gender-gap-report-pakistan/.

[134] See Malik, 'Punjab set to unveil women development policy', *Dawn*, 7 March 2018, available online at https://www.dawn.com/news/1393584.

[135] 'Members of Sindh Commission on Status of Women appointed', *Pakistan Point* (2017), available online at https://www.pakistanpoint.com/en/pakistan/news/members-of-sindh-commission-on-status-of-wome-188315.html. Sindh has been described in a leading Pakistan newspaper as one of the worst in practice for women: 'Sindh the worst province for gender equality: PHRO chief', *Daily Times* (2018), available online at https://dailytimes.com.pk/172959/sindh-worst-province-gender-equality-phro-chief/.

[136] Available online at http://www.pas.gov.pk/index.php/acts/details/en/19/215.

in 2017 by Balochistan.[137] Balochistan is one of the provinces which has been described as having a traditionally highly patriarchal society and in which the situation for women is particularly repressive. And in Khyber Pakhtunkhwa in 2019, following years without the appointment of an Ombudsperson for Protection against Harassment to hear complaints arising from the Protection Against Harassment of Women in the Workplace Act 2010, the government finally appointed a prominent human rights activist to this position.[138] Other reforms in Khyber Pakhtunkhwa include the adoption of legislation to eliminate repressive cultural practices such as forced marriage (*ghag*).[139]

Few of the major legislative reforms described above were brought about rapidly or without extensive struggle, and many efforts which have not yet been successful are still ongoing. A prominent example includes the move to prohibit child marriage at the federal level by raising the marriageable age to 18, which has encountered strong resistance from religious forces. The Child Marriage Restraint (Amendment) Bill, 2017 has been the subject of continuous contestation. It was characterized as 'un-Islamic' by a Senate Standing committee in 2017, and, despite having been passed by the Senate, it was rejected again in 2019 by the National Assembly.[140] Further, the Acid and Burn Crime Bill (initially proposed in 2012 as a follow-up to the 2010 Acid Control and Crime Prevention Bill), which includes important practical provisions such as free medical care and rehabilitation for acid burn victims, as well as a duty on medical practitioners to inform police and to photograph injuries, was eventually passed by the National Assembly in 2018 after a lengthy campaign. However, since it was not passed by the senate before the National Assembly was dissolved, it remains (at the time of writing) to be retabled.[141] The statement of reasons attached to this Bill provide that acid throwing and burn crimes are a 'heinous violation of human rights' and that the law should ensure 'protection and dignified life of Pakistani citizens within the spirit of the international Conventions signed and ratified by the Pakistan state. These include UDHR, CEDAW, CRC and ICCPR'. A similar law has been pending for the province of Khyber Pakhtunkhwa, and a major civil society and stakeholder

---

[137] See http://pabalochistan.gov.pk/pab/pab/tables/alldocuments/actdocx/2018-10-23%20 11:09:05act-no-5-women-status.pdf.

[138] 'KP gets first anti-harassment ombudsperson', *Dawn*, 3 January 2019, available online at https:// www.dawn.com/news/1455134.

[139] See the Elimination of Custom of Ghag Act 2013, Khyber Pakhtunkhwa, available online at https:// www.af.org.pk/Acts_Fed_Provincial/KP_Bill%20_Acts_since%202002/KP%202013/Elimination%20 of%20Custom%20of%20Ghag%20Act,%202013.pdf.

[140] 'pakistani parliamentarian again oppose the Child Marriage Prohibition Bill', *Gulf News*, 1 May 2019. For the 2017 debate, see 'senate body okays Child Marriage Bill 2017', *Pakistan Gender News* (2017), available online at https://www.pakistangendernews.org/senate-body-okays-child-marriage-bill-2017/.

[141] 'legal flaws hamper efforts to control acid and burn crimes', Dawn Newspaper, August 5, 2019 available online at https://www.dawn.com/news/1498114.

consultation effort in 2019 pressed for its adoption.[142] More positively, data produced by the Acid Survivors Foundation in 2019 indicated that acid burning incidents across the country had decreased by more than 50 per cent over a three-year
period, providing some hope that legislative and policy reforms are beginning to
have a social impact.[143]

Some progress has been made on another of the issues that has been the subject of persistent advocacy on the part of women's groups both within the CEDAW
process and domestically, namely, the participation of women in civic and political
life.[144] One of the 2012 CEDAW shadow reports noted that the enhanced parliamentary participation of women and, importantly, the formation of the Women's
Parliamentary Caucus in the National Assembly had helped 'to mainstream
women in national life'.[145] Another of the shadow reports in the same review commended Pakistan for the progress made on women's election participation.[146] This
is an issue on which NGOs have mobilized extensively to build capacity, holding
workshops to explain the technicalities of elections, rallying large numbers of
women to polling stations through networks of volunteers working door-to-door,
and ensuring that women receive national identity cards and domiciles enabling
them to register to vote and exercise their rights.[147] At the provincial level too, the
enactment of legislation such as the Punjab Fair Representation of Women Act
2014 has helped increase participation by women in the political sphere.[148] As the
number of women legislators elected has increased, and several women have been
made cabinet ministers in federal and provincial cabinets, it has been noted that
the increased female political participation has had a positive effect in terms of legislative issues, since female parliamentarians have been responsible for the introduction of almost 60 per cent of bills in the national assembly.[149] Predictably, too,
female parliamentarians have been a driving force behind much of the legislation

---

[142] 'Consultation on 'Khyber Pakhtunkhwa Comprehensive Acid and Burn Crime Bill 2019', available online at http://news.pakngos.com.pk/consultation-on-khyber-pakhtunkhwa-comprehensive-
acid-and-burn-crime-bill-2019/.

[143] 'Pakistan: Cases of acid attacks on women drop by half', *Gulf News*, 4 August 2019, available
online at https://gulfnews.com/world/asia/pakistan/pakistan-cases-of-acid-attacks-on-women-
drop-by-half-1.65626299.

[144] Aurat Foundation, *Legislative Quotas for Women: A Global and South Asian Overview of Types and
Numbers* (2012) 31–32.

[145] Aurat Foundation, *Pakistan NGO Alternative Report on CEDAW* 2 (2012) 11. For discussion of
the importance of the Women's Parliamentary Caucus to women's empowerment and effectiveness in
political life, see Naqvi and Syed, 'Critical mass: protection women's rights', *Dawn*, 1 June 2015, available
online at https://www.dawn.com/news/1184939.

[146] Aurat Foundation, *Legislative Quotas* (n. 144) 9.

[147] See Jafar (n. 18) 80–85.

[148] For discussion see Zia, *Legislative Initiatives on Women in Pakistan—Need for Self-Critique
and Reassessment*, 43 *Legislative Watch* (2014) 1, available online at https://www.af.org.pk/newsl/
1402998220.pdf.

[149] Aurat Foundation, *Latent Transformation* (2011) 23, available online at https://www.af.org.pk/
pub_files/1366350926.pdf.

introducing gender reforms of various kinds, particularly after the formation of the Women's Parliamentary Caucus.[150]

The Election Commission of Pakistan has developed a strategic plan to pro-mote women's participation in politics, establishing a group of key stakeholders from civil society and the public sector to deliberate amongst other things on the lessons learnt from the low turn-out in the 2013 elections.[151] The Elections Act of 2017 more recently included several provisions to promote the participation of women in politics both as candidates and as voters. It provides that returns from any constituency where women's turn-out was less than or equal to 10 per cent must be nullified; it makes it a criminal offence to prevent a woman from voting or standing in an election, and it requires all political parties to list female candi-dates in at least 5 per cent of their non-reserved national and provincial assembly seats.[152]

One further set of issues which has been the subject of advocacy for reform in Pakistan, including in several shadow reports to CEDAW,[153] is those relating to transgender discrimination—a topic which has only been highlighted in recent years, by the CEDAW committee.[154] In 2018, the national assembly passed a law entitled the Transgender Persons (Protection Rights) Act 2018, prohibiting discrimination against transgender persons in access to education, employ-ment, and health, giving them the right to have their gender changed in the na-tional database, and the right (previously denied) to inherit property, as well as protection against harassment and dismissal on grounds of gender identity.[155] A proposed amendment to refer the Bill to the Council of Islamic Ideology was rejected.[156]

---

[150] Naqvi and Syed (n. 145).

[151] Information provided by Parveen Qhadir Agha, vice-president of NGO Behbud (Behbud.org) and former Federal Secretary at the Ministry for Women Development and Social Welfare, February 2018. For a critical appraisal of the work of the Election Commission in relation to women's partici-pation, see Democracy Reporting International and Aurat Foundation, 'Women's Participation in the Upcoming 2013 Elections: Pakistan's International Commitments under CEDAW', Briefing Paper 37 (2013).

[152] Available online at http://www.na.gov.pk/uploads/documents/1506961151_781.pdf.

[153] Aurat Foundation, *Alternative Report on CEDAW–2005-2009* (2012) 80–81, on the Khawaja Sarra community.

[154] See *General Recommendation No. 27 of the CEDAW Committee on Older Women and Their Rights*, CEDAW/C/2010/47/GC.1 (19 October 2010), para. 13; and *General Recommendation No. 35 of the CEDAW Committee on Gender-Based Violence against Women, Updating Recommendation No. 19*, CEDAW/C/GC/35 (14 July 2017), para. 12. See also Holtmaat and Post, 'Enhancing LGBTI Rights by Changing the Interpretation of the Convention on the Elimination of All Forms of Discrimination Against Women?', 33 *Nordic Journal of Human Rights* (2016) 319.

[155] See Redding, 'The Pakistan Transgender Persons (Protection of Rights) Act of 2018 and Its Impact on the Law of Gender in Pakistan', available online at https://papers.ssrn.com/sol3/papers.cfm?abstract_id=3490418##

[156] 'NA passes bill seeking protection of transgender persons' rights', *Daily Times*, 9 May 2018, avail-able online at https://dailytimes.com.pk/237752/na-passes-bill-seeking-protection-of-transgender-persons-rights/.

7. The limits of legal reform without implementation

Despite the many legislative and policy reforms, however, a persistent concern has been that these measures have not had sufficient impact on the reality of life for women in Pakistan, and on their status and position in practice. Pointing to Pakistan's place close to the bottom of the Global Gender Gap ranking,[157] critics have argued that many of the legislative and policy initiatives remain merely paper reforms which are not implemented in practice.[158] In some cases they are not sufficiently funded or properly enforced, and in many cases they are barely understood or known about by many of those for whose benefit they were adopted, or even by state actors and others whose cooperation is necessary for their enforcement.[159] In other cases the reforms are partial and incomplete, representing at best a first step towards dismantling deeply discriminatory and oppressive practices.[160] There is an implementation gap, as well as a lack of adequate resources, and a lack of knowledge of the reforms both amongst those for whom they are intended as well as those who need to carry them out.

A related argument is that to focus on legal rather than other kinds of reform places excessive reliance on the state system of justice, and underestimates or overlooks the inadequacies, delays, and overload characterizing Pakistan's formal justice system, and the reality that the majority of citizens do not have recourse to it.[161] In the words of one commentator: 'Giving primacy to the state as the principal guarantor of rights, the narrow legal focus of the women's movement in Pakistan overlooks the fact that citizens rarely access the state's courts, opting for more accessible traditional dispute resolution forums.'[162] Relatedly, there has been an active debate in recent years about whether the response to the inadequacies of the official justice system by donors and the international community pronouncing their support for the reform and enhancement of the informal '*jirga*' system of dispute resolution has meant entrenching the kinds of discriminatory and misogynistic practices that have so often been the output of this all-male local justice system.[163] One promising move was the establishment of an all-women *jirga* in

---

[157] See nn. 1 and 2 above.

[158] See e.g. S. Zaman, *Forced Marriages and Inheritance Deprivation: A Research Study Exploring Substantive Structural Gaps in the Implementation of the Prevention of Anti-Women Practices (Criminal Law Amendment) Act 2011* (2014), R. Butt, *Lacunas in Pro-Women Legislation in Pakistan* (2013), and Yusuf, 'Broken promises: Why women and girls are denied rights', *Dawn*, 24 September 2016.

[159] See Bhattacharya, 'Status of Women in Pakistan', 51 *Journal of the Research Society of Pakistan* (2014).

[160] See e.g. Jatoi (n. 129).

[161] For an analysis of the difficulties for women in accessing the court system and the reforms which are needed, see S. Shaheen and K. Ali, *The Justice Prelude: A Socio-legal Perspective on Women's Access to Justice* (2017).

[162] Shaheed (n. 7) 863. See also A. Weiss, *Moving Forward with the Legal Empowerment of Women in Pakistan* (2012), available online at https://www.usip.org/publications/2012/05/moving-forward-legal-empowerment-women-pakistan.

[163] This reform was adopted by the National Assembly in the Alternate Dispute Resolution Act 2017. For criticism, see Brohi (n. 3). Also Khan, 'Pakistan's Jirgas: Buying Peace at the Expense of Women's

the Swat valley.[164] More recently, the Supreme Court of Pakistan ruled that the operation of *jirgas* were in violation of the Constitution[165] and of Pakistan's international human rights commitments under the UDHR, ICCPR, and CEDAW.[166] Nevertheless, *jirgas* are very unlikely to disappear from tribal areas of Pakistan without further change and reform, and will also require social changes to attitudes and beliefs which cannot be brought about only through legislative and policy change. Indeed the Pakistan government in its 2018 periodic report to the CEDAW committee stated that 'given the fact that Jirgas and Panchayats are embedded in the socio-cultural system, these are being transformed and regulated to work as formal alternate dispute mechanisms in order to support the existing judicial system' rather than abolished.[167]

The relevant point for present purposes is that the enactment of progressive laws promoting women's rights and prohibiting discriminatory and unjust practices is only one step in a longer process of social change, and generally also requires follow-up measures of reform and enforcement. But the deeply patriarchal character of much of Pakistan's political and social life, underpinned by the power of conservative religious forces, has been the most significant barrier to social change and to the empowerment of women. The progressive legislative measures which have been adopted are a start, but they need to be accompanied by changes in social attitudes, particularly in the attitudes of men, and of state actors such as judges, police, and prosecutors who are responsible for implementation of law and policy. The Pakistan government in its most recent report to the CEDAW committee in 2018 pointed to several training and awareness initiatives set up to train key actors in this regard.[168]

Critics of the human rights regime may point to Pakistan's dismal global gender rankings and to the ongoing discrimination faced by women in the country as evidence for the claim that human rights law is ineffective. Yet the fact that legal change by itself is insufficient to bring about social change in the short term is not evidence of the ineffectiveness of human rights law. In a country facing challenges which include entrenched poverty, extremist religious forces, terrorism, and natural disasters, social change is slow to occur and requires the interaction of a range

---

Rights?', *Open Democracy*, 30 June 2017, available online at https://www.opendemocracy.net/5050/ayesha-khan/pakistan-jirgas-womens-rights, and 'Pakistan is Mainstreaming Misogynist Tribal Justice', *The Economist Magazine*, 13 October 2017.

[164] 'Women defy local traditions in Pakistan's Swat Valley', *DW*, 29 April 2017, available online at https://www.dw.com/en/women-defy-local-traditions-in-pakistans-swat-valley/a-38609291.

[165] 'Functioning of Jirgas violative of Constitution, observes SC', *The News*, 1 August 2019, available online at https://www.thenews.com.pk/print/506513-functioning-of-jirgas-violative-of-constitution-observes-sc.

[166] 'SC Declares Jirgas/Panchayats illegal', *Pakistan Today*, 16 January 2019, available online at https://www.pakistantoday.com.pk/2019/01/16/sc-declares-jirgas-panchayats-illegal/.

[167] *Fifth periodic report of Pakistan to CEDAW*, CEDAW/C/PAK/5 (23 October 2018), at para. 32.

[168] Ibid.

of different elements which include not only legal change but also effective political leadership, investment in education, and economic development. And, indeed,
there is some evidence that Pakistan's low ranking on the global gender index (albeit an unofficial index) is not without effect on the country's leadership or concerns about its international reputation.[169]

A significant catalyst for change can sometimes come from public reaction to, or
outrage at, specific examples of gender injustice such as a *jirga*-ordered rape[170] or a
particularly notorious or graphic 'honour' killing.[171] Revulsion at particular incidents of this kind sometimes translates into social mobilization and helps to move
public opinion in favour of reform, as was the case for the reform to the Penal Code
which followed the high-profile murder of a social media star, Qandeel Baloch, in
2016.[172] Yet legislative and policy measures are also crucial steps—even if insufficient alone—to show leadership, signal reform, and establish a framework which
legitimizes and encourages social change, and can help to counter religious and cultural pressures.[173] The enactment of laws which unequivocally outlaw and prohibit
acts of violence, repression, and discrimination against women, and which address
longstanding religious and social practices which subordinate women are a crucial
part of the gradual process of change. But legislative reforms also need to be backed
up by genuine political commitment to their implementation, and resources need
to be invested in the new institutions and policies which have been created, including the national and provincial Commissions on the Status of Women.

Some signs of greater commitment and investment can be seen in a range of
recent initiatives that point to a recognition of the need for measures of implementation of the various legal reforms which have been adopted. For example,
the Women in Distress and Detention Fund Act was enacted in 2006 (and later
amended in 2011) to provide legal and financial assistance to women in detention, in order to provide jobs, books, rehabilitation, and medical attention, shelter

---

[169] Kazmi, 'Gender equality situation worst in Pakistan: WEF Report', *Pakistan Tribune*, December
2018, reports Pakistan President Arif Alvi lamenting the low rankings and posting on social media as
follows: 'Pakistan is among the worst performers on gender equality. We rank 148th out of 149 countries. This is alarming. I urge the Executive, Legislature and the Judiciary to please take note.' See https://
tribune.com.pk/story/1870520/1-gender-equality-situation-worst-pakistan-wef-report/.

[170] 'Pakistan Council orders revenge rape of 16-year-old girl', *Reuters*, 27 July 2017.

[171] Examples include the murder of Samia Sarwar in her lawyer's office in 1999, which became the
subject of a BBC documentary *Licence to Kill* (2000), or the murder of a social media star by her brother,
'Qandeel Baloch: Social media celebrity killed by brother', *BBC News*, 16 July 2016, or the murder of a
15-year-old girl and an 18-year-old boy by their parents: 'Teenage couple electrocuted in Pakistan in
Honor Killing', *Reuters*, 11 September 2017.

[172] This was the Criminal Law (Amendment) (Offences in the name or pretext of Honour) Act 2016.
See http://www.na.gov.pk/uploads/documents/1475762285_283.pdf.

[173] See Zakaria, 'It will take more than laws to end honor killings in Pakistan': available online at
https://www.cnn.com/2019/03/28/opinions/pakistan-honor-killings-afzal-kohistani-zakaria/
index.html. See also the *Guardian* report on the rise in honour killings despite the amendment to
the criminal code in 2016 following the murder of Qandeel Baloch: https://www.theguardian.com/
global-development/2019/may/17/pakistan-authorities-record-a-dozen-cases-of-honour-killing-in-
a-fortnight?CMP=Share_iOSApp_Other.

for children and legal assistance. But for reasons of official neglect and a lack of interest, the Fund was never established or operationalized, and hence no assistance was provided to women under the legislation.[174] In December 2017, however, a law to establish the Fund and provide for its effective operation through a reformed procedure was eventually adopted by the National Assembly.[175] According to the government of Pakistan in its 2018 report to the CEDAW committee, the fund has now been established and 46 million PKR was made available for disbursement to women in need. The Acid Burns and Crimes Bill 2017, discussed above, is another example of the proposed adoption of more practical measures to supplement and help with the enforcement of earlier legislation on Acid Control and Crime Prevention.[176] A prominent human rights lawyer and women's rights activist has suggested that amongst the most important and promising reforms in recent years, going beyond formal legislation and paper policies, are the actions which were taken by the Punjab government in relation to violence against women. As noted earlier, these actions include better complaint and enforcement mechanisms for legislation concerning violence against women, and the establishment of Violence against Women shelters and transitional housing for women who have been abused.[177]

Another example of an increased focus on implementation is the system of 'Treaty implementation cells' (TICs) which have been established at national and provincial level to monitor and report on the implementation of a range of international human rights treaties including CEDAW.[178] This system was adopted in part as a governmental response to the European Union's system of 'General Standardized Preferences' (GSP Plus) which grants preferential trade treatment to Pakistan conditional on its progress in relation to human rights and particularly human rights treaty implementation. While it is hard to assess to what extent these have yet been—or may become—helpful in keeping pressure on to implement provisions of CEDAW in practice, according to an EU Commission report in 2018, these TICs 'provide a useful forum for discussion and coordination which did not exist before'.[179]

---

[174] Ahmadani, 'Women in distress and Detention Act Fails to help women', *Pakistan Today*, 30 April 2017, available online at https://www.pakistantoday.com.pk/2017/04/30/women-in-distress-and-detention-fund-fails-to-help-women-2/.

[175] See http://www.na.gov.pk/uploads/documents/1513247333_242.pdf and 'National Assembly passed five bills on women, children and minorities in 2017', *Associated Press of Pakistan*, 15 January 2018, available online at http://www.app.com.pk/national-assembly-passed-five-bills-women-children-minorities-2017/.

[176] See n. 142 above and text.

[177] See nn. 129–130 above and text.

[178] See https://democracy-reporting.org/treaty-implementation-cells-next-step-for-human-rights-compliance-in-pakistan/ and https://tribune.com.pk/story/1175102/implementing-27-un-conventions-road-map-developed-reduce-gender-wage-gap/.

[179] See *The EU Special Incentive Arrangement for Sustainable Development and Good Governance ('GSP+') assessment of Pakistan covering the period 2016 - 2017*, SWD(2018) 29 final, available online at http://trade.ec.europa.eu/doclib/docs/2018/january/tradoc_156544.pdf, at 2–3.

As far as knowledge of gender reforms amongst the relevant communities is concerned, a range of initiatives has been taken, including by civil society organizations and often with funding from international donors, to address entrenched gender discrimination and subordination of women. NGOs have conducted training workshops for law enforcement with the purpose of sensitizing officials to domestic violence issues and to the provisions of CEDAW, and with a view to facilitating better police-victim interaction.[180] A range of organizations provide workshops for lawyers and law enforcement personnel on gender discrimination,[181] including workshops with police officers focused specifically on police response to violence against women and on gender awareness more generally.[182] Further, while women make up apparently only 2 per cent of police in Pakistan,[183] the first female head of an all-male police station was appointed in 2017 in Khyber Pakhtunkhwa (often considered one of the most conservative provinces, particularly from the point of view of the status of women).[184]

The first ever court to deal specifically with gender-based violence cases was established in 2017 in the Punjab, involving special procedures to avoid the lengthy procedures and slow pace of proceedings in civil and family courts, and with an explicit acknowledgement on the part of the Lahore High Court chief justice that the traditional courts have failed to dispense justice for women.[185] Plans to establish further special courts across the Punjab province dedicated to hearing cases concerning violence against women were to follow, to be presided over by women judges and prosecutors.[186] Following the Lahore pilot scheme, it was announced in 2019 that over 1000 specialized courts would be established across Pakistan to deal with violence against women.[187]

Nevertheless, only a tiny minority of senior judges in Pakistan are women, although they represent apparently one-third of the family court judges in the country,[188] and despite previous proposals for the introduction of quotas for the

---

[180] Interview with Palvasha Shahab, Human Rights Commission of Pakistan (12 January 2017).

[181] See http://www.af.org.pk/gep/index.php/grant-cycles/item/82-training-women-men-lawyers-to-provide-legal-services-to-women-including-minority-women-islamabad-rawalpindi. See also the *Report of Pakistan to the CEDAW committee*, CEDAW/C/PAK/4 (24 September 2011), at 16.

[182] Ibid. 25–26.

[183] 'Women make up less than 2pc of country's police force: report', *Dawn*, 26 April 2017, available online at https://www.dawn.com/news/1329292.

[184] 'Women play vital role in Khyber Pakhtunkhwa police', *Pakistan Forward*, 26 July 2017, available online at https://pakistan.asia-news.com/en_GB/articles/cnmi_pf/features/2017/07/26/feature-02.

[185] 'Court to deal with gender-based violence cases opens in Lahore', *Dawn*, 24 October 2017, available online at https://www.dawn.com/news/1365866.

[186] Hanif, 'Courts for women complainants, with women judges in the offing', *Dawn*, 6 October 2017, available online at https://www.dawn.com/news/1361987.

[187] 'Pakistan to set up special courts to tackle violence against women', *Reuters*, 19 June 2019, available online at https://www.reuters.com/article/us-pakistan-women-court/pakistan-to-set-up-special-courts-to-tackle-violence-against-women-idUSKCN1TK2X2.

[188] Holden, 'Women Judges and Women's Rights in Pakistan', 7 *Onati Socio-legal Series* (2017) 752, available online at http://ssrn.com/abstract=3034280.

appointment of women judges,[189] little has been done to address this imbalance.[190] At the time of writing, there has never been a female judge on the Supreme Court of Pakistan, and the High Court of Islamabad saw its first ever female judge appointed only in December 2019. In terms of the attitude of the senior courts in Pakistan towards gender reforms, it seems that while the Council of Islamic Ideology—as described earlier in relation to its blocking of attempted gender reforms—has remained staunchly opposed,[191] the Federal Shariat Court (which was established under the Constitution with the power to determine whether laws adopted are compatible with Islamic law) has been reasonably supportive in 'tackling the traditionally illiberal interpretation and application of Muslim laws' in areas of family life and gender equality.[192] Actions were twice brought to the Federal Shariat Court to challenge the proposed appointment of women, but these were rejected by the Court, which has supported the appointment of women to the judiciary.[193]

This array of initiatives towards implementing gender reforms in practice and making them more effective, while as yet only partial, is nonetheless significant in beginning to move beyond legislative reforms on the books towards tackling some of the less tractable social and cultural change that is needed.

8. Conclusion

None of the reforms in the field of gender and women's rights which have been achieved in Pakistan have come about easily or smoothly. On the contrary, they have been the result of continuous and intense political and social struggle on the part of women's groups and others working to challenge the deep social, cultural, and religious roots of gender discrimination and women's subordination in Pakistan. Yet despite these profound obstacles and persistent inertia at governmental level, significant changes have nonetheless been introduced at the legislative and policy level over the decades since CEDAW was ratified.

While legal and policy change has progressed slowly and incrementally, mobilization on the part of women's groups and NGOs focused on gender issues has clearly played a crucial role in the process. Civil society groups have been continuously involved in the processes of reform, ranging from the early stages of pressing the government to ratify CEDAW, to collaborating with women's groups to prepare and challenge the government's account of its actions on gender discrimination

---

[189] Malik, 'Gender and Judging in Pakistan', *The Nation*, 15 November 2016, available online at https://nation.com.pk/15-Nov-2016/gender-and-judging-in-pakistan.

[190] Ranja, 'Women in the Superior Judiciary', available online at https://tribune.com.pk/story/1681459/6-women-superior-judiciary/.

[191] Holden (n. 188) 757–758.

[192] Yilmaz, 'Pakistan Federal Shariat Court's Collective Ijtihād on Gender Equality, Women's Rights and the Right to Family Life', 25 *Islam and Christian–Muslim Relations* (2014) 181.

[193] Holden (n. 188) at 761–762.

by presenting detailed shadow reports to the CEDAW committee, to following up on the CEDAW and UPR processes and constantly advocating and pressing for change, as well as engaging in activities which directly implement the Convention's obligations by providing training and assisting women to get registered to vote and to actually exercise their vote.

The eventual successful adoption of most of the reforms so far has depended heavily on ongoing domestic advocacy campaigns, helped by diplomatic pressure as well as the external accountability-forcing and information-generating roles of the international human rights bodies. None of the policy reforms were introduced as a consequence of a single-issue or one-shot campaign, but as a result of repeated interactions between domestic advocates, international human rights institutions and networks, and governmental actors and bodies, taking place over sometimes lengthy periods of time. The issues of concern were repeatedly raised by an array of advocacy groups, many of which were heard and taken up by international human rights bodies in light of the state's human rights commitments, and subsequently reacted to by government and other national relevant actors and institutions. Engagement has been periodic and ongoing, and the pressure on the state has been maintained not just by the interventions of national and local advocacy groups and networks and international human rights bodies, but also by other external and internal actors such as donors, trade partners (such as the EU using its Generalised Standardised Preferences incentive[194]), and by national courts, national and provincial human rights commissions, and the media. This is not to suggest that progress has been in any sense smooth or linear, or that there has been an invariable and steady progression towards more positive outcomes for women in Pakistan. On the contrary, the iterative processes described here have involved multiple setbacks and disappointments along the way, as is evident from the lengthy and often tortuous process of getting laws such as the Acid Crimes laws or the Child Marriage Ban through the legislative process. Nonetheless the overall process, looked at over a period of decades, has resulted in a series of major achievements of significant consequence for women, including those outlined earlier.

Similarly, the example described in this chapter of women's rights groups in Pakistan mobilizing around CEDAW supports the argument that the ways in which international human rights and domestic actors and institutions engage in producing change are more complex and interactive than is implied by models of top-down versus bottom-up change. It also reveals the kind of contestation and debate that accompanies campaigns for human rights reform even amongst activists and those advocating for similar kinds of change. Mobilization for human rights reform is rarely a smooth or consensual process, even within robustly democratic political systems. Typically it involves the assertion of different and often starkly

---

[194] See n. 179 above.

contrasting values and interests, not just as between those promoting change and those resisting it, but also as between the groups mobilizing for reform. Even when those advocating for change—be they grassroots organizations, small or large NGOs, service organizations, religious groups, or professional associations—share a common goal such as gender reform, they may well differ sharply on the best ways of pursuing that goal, and even when they agree broadly on the strategy of invoking human rights in pursuit of that goal, they may differ in their views as to what influence or role international law and international processes should have.

The processes of mobilization and iterative reform in Pakistan using the international human rights system and domestic advocacy illustrate various aspects of the experimentalist dynamic outlined in Chapter 2, and depicted in Figure 2.1. The activation of CEDAW and of international human rights law to promote gender reform in Pakistan has seen repeated engagement between three main sets of actors: domestic civil society groups and their international networks, supported at times by a widening grassroots women's movement; international human rights institutions and bodies; and domestic governmental and independent actors, including courts, commissions and ombudspersons. Domestic women's groups and related NGOs have mobilized to assert rights, demand change, advocate for reform, challenge governmental accounts, and gather and present information to support their claims in both domestic and international fora. The international human rights bodies, including the UPR but in particular the CEDAW Committee process, have provided a catalyst for information-generation and reporting by government and civil society actors, as well as a forum for engagement with the government; they have elaborated on the meaning and application of treaty norms and commitments in the factual contexts presented to them, and engaged in discussion with domestic groups and governmental officials in that process; made recommendations to the government for further action and reform; and followed up on recommendations and observations made in subsequent processes or cycles of reporting. Government officials have reported and provided information to the international bodies on what actions they have taken to meet various commitments made under the treaty; they have engaged to varying degrees in dialogue; and they have responded to some of the recommendations made. The process has been ongoing: after each cycle of reporting, civil society groups have had to maintain their advocacy and pressure to gain any concrete reforms, for example by following up on the recommendations emerging from the treaty body or Human Rights Council, bringing litigation, submitting petitions, undertaking media campaigns and training, and engaging with the government on implementation of the treaty in between the periods of reporting. Other domestic actors and officials including judges, human rights commissions, and police have also reacted to the advocacy, in some cases resisting or ignoring, but in other cases reforming practices and implementing change. And a growing women's movement as manifested in particular by the Aurat women's marches organized in March each year since 2018 has been helping to keep the issues in the forefront of public debate and to build broader social support for reform.

Contrary to some of the academic critiques of the operation of international human rights law discussed in Chapter 2, Pakistan's gradual and equivocal implementation of protection for the rights listed in CEDAW does not suggest a process of external imposition of binding or authoritative prescriptions on national actors. The issues on which domestic women's groups chose to focus and which they brought to the attention of various international human rights bodies were not determined by those international institutions, even if the process of drafting and submitting shadow reports, and selecting which issues to prioritize are shaped by many factors including bureaucratic procedures and expectations and 'expert' advice and assistance.[195] Nevertheless, the issues highlighted in much of the advocacy before the CEDAW committee were among those apparently felt to be most relevant to many of the domestic groups, reflecting the concerns and preoccupations of people working in those fields—such as barriers to electoral and political participation, family rights, discriminatory inheritance and evidentiary laws, violence against women, sexual harassment, and access to education for girls. The provisions of CEDAW which were invoked and used in domestic advocacy by the 'vernacularizing' NGOs and advocacy groups—including commitments to eliminate discrimination, to suppress exploitation, and to ensure participation on equal terms with men—are, on the whole, general and open-textured rather than precise prescriptions mandating specific solutions from above. The CEDAW provisions themselves were initially agreed and ratified by the Pakistan government, and many of them reflect in a more focused or detailed way the norms contained in other major human rights treaties also ratified by the state, such as the ICCPR and the ICESR. These provisions were certainly not enforced in any hierarchical way by the treaty body responsible for monitoring compliance. Like other human rights treaty bodies, although the CEDAW Committee issues interpretations of these provisions and the rights they express, and makes recommendations based on their interpretation to the government, it has no power to compel compliance.[196] Instead it relies for their implementation on the effectiveness of its dialogue and the persuasiveness of its output, as well as on the extent to which this output is useful to domestic actors in their mobilization and advocacy, and sometimes also

---

[195] For discussion of some of these mediating factors, see Cowan and Billaud, 'Between Learning and Schooling: The Politics of Human Rights Monitoring at the Universal Periodic Review', *Third World Quarterly* (2015) 1175; and Santos, 'Mobilizing Women's Human Rights: What/Whose Knowledge Counts for Transnational Legal Mobilization?', 10 *Journal of Human Rights Practice* (2018) 191.

[196] On the role of human rights treaty bodies more generally, see Barkholdt and Reiners, 'Pronouncements of Expert Treaty Bodies: From Black Boxes to Key Catalysts in International Law' (2019), KFG Working Paper Series, No. 40, Berlin Potsdam Research Group 'The International Rule of Law – Rise or Decline?' and Borlino and Crema, 'The Legal Status of Decisions by Human Rights Treaty Bodies: International Supervision, Authoritative Interpretations or mission éducatrice?', European Society of International law Annual Research Forum 2019, Conference paper No. 3/2019.

to external actors, donors, or trade partners who are interested in the human rights record of Pakistan.

Indeed, according to one leading activist, the pronouncements of the CEDAW committee in themselves have had little effect on the government of Pakistan, which has generally ignored them and reacted only at the time that a report is due to the treaty body.[197] However, the use of the Committee's recommendations in their advocacy by domestic groups, including in their media campaigns, litigation, parliamentary lobbying and training, and sometimes in combination with external pressure from trade partners such as the EU and others, has clearly helped to bring about a set of important legislative and policy reforms over time. Apart from the series of major legislative enactments on subjects including violence, harassment, acid crimes, and anti-women practices, provincial and national bodies such as the National Commission on the Status of Women have been empowered and resourced to promote more effect change. And the process of constitutional devolution in Pakistan, which was initially a source of concern for gender reform advocates who feared that the shift of responsibility to the provinces would result in setbacks or inaction in the area of women's rights, has yielded some important reforms at the provincial level, particularly in the Punjab and also in Islamabad, even if other concerns still remain.

One notable feature of the processes of gender reform in Pakistan to date, however, has been the leading role occupied by NGOs, which are often urban and professional organizations. Despite the broader mobilization at particular times of women across the country and in relation to particular issues—such as the time of the Zia regime with the passage of the Hudood Ordinances—there had not been a wider or sustained social movement underpinning the legal and political activism for gender reform, and little awareness of international human rights other than amongst elite advocates. However, signs of hope have appeared in quite recent times with the emergence of a more widespread grassroots energy and social mobilization behind issues of gender justice of the kind which are likely to be needed to underpin major human rights reforms, and particularly to galvanize and support significant socio-cultural change. In March 2018, 2019, and 2020, the 'Aurat' women's march took place across many parts of Pakistan, including cities in rural areas, and the scale and size of these marches apparently took supporters as well as opponents by surprise.[198] The marches have comprised a wide range of participants—working-class women and women from a broad cross-section of society; women from the older established feminist movements and much younger women—and they have been demonstrating for many things, including protesting against gender violence, demanding healthcare, and demanding better workplace

---

[197] Jilani (n. 110).
[198] Saigol, 'The past, present and future of feminist activism in Pakistan', *The Herald*, 20 July 2019.

conditions.[199] The male and conservative backlash in each case has been predictably fierce and immediate, with death threats, rape threats, stoning by counter-
protesters, and social media harassment of many of the women who took part in
the marches, as well as protests and condemnation of the marches by leading poli-
ticians, clerics, and other conservative critics.[200] Nevertheless, far from being de-
terred by the violent backlash, greater numbers of women in Pakistan seem to have
been mobilized and energized by their participation in the movement, and many
have expressed their determination to continue and strengthen their challenge to a
highly patriarchal society.[201] The marches may have generated a backlash, but their
size, scale, and inclusivity seem to point towards the beginnings of a cultural shift,
particularly one involving the younger generation, which is likely to be crucial in
supporting the ongoing work of civil society groups in Pakistan to promote gender
justice and women's human rights in practice.[202]

[199] Chugtai, 'Pakistani women hold "aurat march" for equality, gender justice', *Aljazeera*, 8 March
2019, available online at https://www.aljazeera.com/news/2019/03/pakistani-women-hold-aurat-
march-equality-gender-justice-190308115740534.html.
[200] Azeem, 'Women marched for their rights. Then the backlash came', *The Diplomat*, 20 March 2019.
On the previous backlash to the 2018 march, see Shah, 'In Pakistan, a Women's March Comes With a
Price', *New Internationalist*, 28 March 2019. On the 2020 march, see Reuters, 'Islamists hurl stones and
shoes at Women's Day marchers in Pakistan', *World News*, 8 March 2020.
[201] Shahid, 'Women Will March on Despite Public Backlash', *Asia Times*, 13 March 2019; and
Shugtai, 'Pakistan Women's march: Shaking patriarchy to its core', *Aljazeera*, 8 March 2020, available
at   https://www.aljazeera.com/indepth/features/pakistan-women-march-shaking-patriarchy-core-
200308095635489.html.
[202] Shah, 'The real enemy of Pakistan's women is not men: It is society's acceptance of patriarchy',
New York Times, 14 April 2019.

4

The activation of the Convention on the Rights of Persons with Disabilities in Argentina

1. Introduction

This chapter examines the activation of the UN Convention on the Rights of Persons with Disabilities (CRPD) in Argentina, and in particular on the ways in which local and national disability rights organizations and movements have mobilized domestically and engaged repeatedly over time with international human rights bodies and national institutions to promote reform on a range of disability issues. While the chapter focuses primarily on disability rights advocacy on the issue of inclusive education, the experimentalist framework outlined in Chapter 2 is also used as a lens through which to view other aspects of human rights advocacy in Argentina including in the area of child rights.

To place the case study in context, the chapter begins with a very brief sketch of civil society and social movements in Argentina at present, particularly in relation to their engagement with international human rights law. The legal status of human rights treaties in Argentina and the state's ratification of the CRPD are briefly discussed, before moving on to look at some of the ways in which disability rights activists have activated CRPD norms in the area of domestic inclusive education reform. The study illustrates the way in which the decision by national-level actors in the field of disability advocacy to frame their claims in the language of human rights, and their iterative interaction with international norms and institutions as well as domestic institutions and courts, has helped to bring about important reforms over time, particularly in the area of inclusive education.

Argentina's relationship with international human rights law has been an uneven one. Throughout substantial periods of the twentieth century, the country's democracy was characterized by a tension between socialist-leaning populism and conservative military rule, oscillating between versions of these two. With the advent of the era of international institutions and the adoption of early human rights instruments following the end of World War II, the state ratified its first UN human rights treaty—the Convention on the Elimination of All Forms of Racial Discrimination—in 1968. But it was not until after the brutal period of military rule and violent state terrorism, which eventually came to an end in 1983, that the

Reframing Human Rights in a Turbulent Era. Gráinne de Búrca, Oxford University Press (2021). © G de Búrca.
DOI: 10.1093/oso/9780198299578.003.0004

state ratified the other major international human rights conventions. Following the return to democratic rule in 1983, the government at the time was keen for the country to rejoin the global community and to indicate its acceptance of international standards. The state ratified the Convention on the Elimination of All Forms of Discrimination against Women in 1985 and three further UN human rights treaties in 1986: the Convention against Torture and the two international covenants, namely the Covenant on Civil and Political Rights and the Covenant on Economic Social and Cultural Rights. Argentina ratified the Convention on the Rights of the Child in 1991, and the CRPD in 2008, not long after its initial entry into force.

Yet despite the return to democracy and this general embrace of international human rights since 1983, Argentina has struggled with major political challenges since that time. The most severe has been the devastating economic crisis of the early 2000s, during which the state defaulted on its international debt and the population endured a period of significant austerity, unemployment, social unrest, and greatly increased poverty. Since then the country has experienced several major political changes, including an electoral shift to the centre-right under Macri in 2015, which saw the country return to international markets the following year, and a further backlash against that economically conservative turn and against biting economic hardship in 2019. Despite this, the state's basic commitment to constitutional democracy and to the protection of human rights has remained relatively stable since the dictatorship, and civil society has remained active and vibrant throughout.

The relationship of Argentine civil society to the international human rights system will briefly be described in the next sections, before the disability rights movement is introduced.

2. Civil society and the emergence of a human rights movement in Argentina

While liberal and democratic institutions were introduced into Argentina during the nineteenth century, it has been suggested that the populist style of democracy which characterized the country throughout much of the twentieth century was unsympathetic to the liberal idea of an autonomous civil society distinct from government, or to the notion of governmental accountability.[1] While Argentina has a long history of political and social mobilization, collective action and protest, the relationship of civil society groups to the state at least during the second half of the

---

[1] For a discussion of the changing nature of Argentinian democracy and the gradual emergence of an autonomous civil society, see Peruzzotti, 'Towards a New Politics: Citizenship and Rights in Contemporary Argentina', 6 *Citizenship Studies* (2002) 77.

twentieth century has been described as falling broadly into two categories: either supporting political opposition against an authoritarian government, or serving the military government by delivering social welfare.[2] Further, the effect of the long period of authoritarian rule in Argentina from 1955 to 1983 had what has been described as a corrosive effect on civic culture and life, which 'driven by indifference and self-preservation, sank under the culture of fear'.[3]

Paradoxically, however, it was at the climax of this period of authoritarian rule, during the violently repressive and brutal military regime, that a range of distinctive and powerful social and human rights movements emerged within Argentina. One of the most prominent of these was the movement known as the Madres de Plaza de Mayo, led by the mothers and grandmothers of the disappeared.[4] During this period a broad and diverse set of human rights actors organized and established themselves, including family groups such as the Madres de Plaza de Mayo, but also an active range of religious groups and civil libertarian groups that mobilized to challenge the regime and its atrocities.[5] This movement was not unique to Argentina, but emerged across a range of states in Latin America including Chile, Paraguay, Ecuador, Peru, Nicaragua, and El Salvador in which similar authoritarian dictatorships—with extensive help from the United States under its Operations 'Condor' and 'Charly—were using violently repressive means including disappearances and killings of those who challenged their rule.[6]

According to Enrique Peruzzotti, the vicious and authoritarian nature of the Argentine state at the time, and the fact that the government was initially supported by a substantial part of the population, meant that the emerging human rights movement was cautious at first in its focus and activity. Although the movement was reliant on external support at the outset, it gradually grew in strength and eventually transformed important aspects of Argentinian society and political culture.[7] However, Peruzzotti has argued that the human rights movement after the transition to democracy failed to take proper advantage of its success, and chose to pursue a predominantly past-oriented agenda focused on punishment for the atrocities of the prior regime. Nevertheless, a longer-term effect of the movement

---

[2] Jacobs and Maldonado, 'Civil Society in Argentina: Opportunities and Challenges for National and Transnational Organisation', 37 *Journal of Latin American Studies* (2005) 141.

[3] Ibid.

[4] See Jelin, 'The Politics of Memory: The Human Rights Movement and the Construction of Democracy in Argentina', 21 *Latin American Perspectives* (1994) 38, and Bosco, 'The Madres de Plaza de Mayo and Three Decades of Human Rights' Activism: Embeddedness, Emotions, and Social Movements', 96 *Annals of the Association of American Geographers* (2006) 242. For the broader implications for the UN human rights system of Argentina's domestic campaign of terror, see I. Guest, *Behind the Disappearances: Argentina's Dirty War against Human Rights and the United Nations* (1990).

[5] A. Brysk, *The Politics of Human Rights in Argentina: Protest, Change and Democratization* (1994).

[6] See J. P. McSherry, *Predatory States: Operation Condor and Covert War in Latin America* (2005); and P. W. Kelly, *Sovereign Emergencies: Latin America and the Making of Global Human Rights Politics* (2018).

[7] Peruzzotti (n. 1) 84–85.

was a shift towards a more constitutional politics aimed at establishing 'a system of protective rights that could institutionalize an autonomous and pluralistic civil society'.[8] At the same time, the character of the new democracy, even while marking a break from the immediate authoritarian past and from the strongly populist phases that preceded it, has been described as retaining a majoritarian or 'delegative' character influenced by that populist past, with civil society initially relegated to a mobilizational role.[9]

Brysk has similarly argued that the transition to democracy was a complex process for the human rights movement, and for civil society more generally.[10] Argentina's return to democracy did not ensure the kind of responsiveness to domestic human rights pressures that was hoped for,[11] and the transnational support and alliances developed by domestic human rights groups during the military regime gradually weakened, with international attention focused mainly on regime change and turning elsewhere once Argentina was a democracy.[12] Nonetheless, it seems clear that the emergence of strong domestic human rights movements during the military dictatorship helped lead in the longer term to a new period of civic engagement in Argentina, and eventually to a 'new democratic political culture organized around a concern for rights and constitutionalism', and for improved governmental accountability.[13]

Civil society groups subsequently entered an active and turbulent new phase with broad underlying social support following the onset of Argentina's dramatic economic crisis in the early 2000s. This period saw an uprising against governmental and economic elites, and major public protests and collective action staged by workers, *piqueteros* (the 'unemployed workers movement' or MTD),[14] and other grassroots groups.[15] The 1990s had brought major changes within Argentinian politics and society, as elsewhere around the world, with openness to international political and security institutions being accompanied by regional trade integration through Mercosur, and an extensive programme of domestic economic liberalization and transformation of the public sphere. New movements came together during this period of neoliberal economic government, using various tactics

[8] Ibid. 86. See also Abregú, 'Human Rights after the Dictatorship: Lessons from Argentina', 34 *NACLA Report on the Americas* 12.

[9] See Abregú, ibid. On the theory of delegative democracy more generally, see O'Donnell, 'Delegative Democracy', 5 *Journal of Democracy* (1994) 55.

[10] Brysk, 'From Above and Below: Social Movements, the International System and Human Rights in Argentina', 26 *Comparative Political Studies* (1993) 259.

[11] Jelin (n. 4) 46–49.

[12] Brysk, 'From Above and Below' (n. 10).

[13] Peruzzotti, 'Accountability Struggles in Democratic Argentina: Civic Engagement from the Human Rights Movement to the Nestor Kirchner Administration', 2 *Laboratorium* (2010) 65, 67.

[14] See e.g. Bulkstein, 'A Time of Opportunities: The Piquetero Movement and Democratization in Argentina', in C. Raventos (ed.), *Democratic Innovation in the South: Participation and Representation in Asia, Africa and Latin America* (2008).

[15] Risley, 'The Power of Persuasion: Issue Framing and Advocacy in Argentina', 43 *Journal of Latin American Studies* (2011) 663.

including human rights law and language to challenge corruption, impunity, and economic and social injustices.[16] At the same time, even as many civil society groups during this period moved towards occupying an oppositional role and fundamentally challenging political and economic elites, others chose to interact with the 'discredited political class' and to find common ground in advancing their goals, including specific human rights agendas in the aftermath of the crisis.[17]

Civil society participation in policymaking has more recently been described as an emergent area of inquiry within Argentina in particular and within Latin American politics more generally.[18] A range of empirical studies have pointed to the fact that civil society groups are actively involved 'in policy domains as varied as judicial reform, poverty alleviation and reproductive rights', often using international human rights norms and conventions to help them advocate for policy reforms.[19] NGOs, associations, and non-profit groups are currently recognized by the state as 'significant social and political actors', with growing strategic relevance in the policy process.[20] While some political leaders sought to concentrate executive power and to undermine civil society attempts to promote greater governmental accountability,[21] there has nonetheless been a reasonably stable degree of political support for a human rights agenda in the country since the end of the dictatorship.

Recent years have seen a renewal of more urgent mobilizations for reform, backed by wider social support. Following a further period of economic turbulence and recession after the election of Macri's centre-right government in 2015, which led the government to seek another large loan from the International Monetary Fund, social protests began again in earnest. The protests have seen large numbers of people taking to the streets and invoking the language of human rights to challenge social hardships and to demand change, as well as to commemorate the human rights atrocities during the dictatorship. These protests have brought together the human rights struggles of the past with those of the present, and swelled the normal ranks of NGOs and organized civil society groups with more widespread and powerful popular support. The renewed movement

[16] See K. A. Faulk, *In the Wake of Neoliberalism: Citizenship and Human Rights in Argentina* (2012), examines two social movements using human rights strategies in Argentina during this time: Memoria Activa which was established to seek justice following the devastating bombing of a Jewish cultural centre in Buenos Aires in 1984, and Cooperativa Bauen, a worker-run collective enterprise set up by employees of a bankrupt hotel following the economic crisis. See also M. Sitrin, *Everyday Revolutions: Horizontalism and Autonomy in Argentina* (2012).

[17] Ibid.

[18] See generally A. Risley, *Civil Society Organizations, Advocacy and Policy-Making in Latin American Democracies* (2015).

[19] Risley, 'The Power of Persuasion' (n. 15).

[20] See Jacobs and Maldonado (n. 2).

[21] See Peruzzotti (n. 13) on how Néstor Kirchner's government sought to undermine and divide the network of human rights movements, despite his use of human rights discourse to promote a progressive image and generate support from the left.

has included women's marches beginning in 2016 under the heading 'Ni Una Menos' to protest violence against women and femicide, and these marches have gradually merged with wider protests focusing on economic injustice and austerity cuts, as well as abortion law reform.[22] The protests have used the language of human rights alongside other strategies, and have brought together demands for labour rights and socio-economic rights alongside gender justice.[23] The scale and intensity of the protests in 2018 and 2019 were successful in pressing for the adoption of an emergency food law.[24] However, although a bill to decriminalize abortion in the first trimester failed at the last hurdle, the movement for abortion law reform attracted widespread support,[25] and legislation legalizing abortion was introduced in 2020.[26]

The relationship between organized civil society and wider social mobilization will be returned to further below.

3. Interaction between domestic civil society and international human rights norms and institutions

Given how repressive the domestic environment was during the military dictatorship, the human rights movement that emerged at that time initially gained traction primarily through the network of external support it developed, generating international attention and placing pressure on the government from a range of other states as well as from international institutions and actors.[27] Brysk has described how transnational networks helped domestic advocates to challenge the regime even in the face of such repression by mobilizing resources, protection, information, and pressure, and how they also helped in the establishment of democratic structures and institutions in the transitional phase after the regime was defeated.[28]

---

[22] Nowell, 'Argentina's Ni Una Menos Turns Focus to Economic Crisis, Abortion', *Aljazeera*, 3 June 2019, available online at https://www.aljazeera.com/news/2019/06/argentina-ni-una-menos-turns-focus-economic-crisis-abortion-190603203634026.html. For discussion of the 'human rights' resignification of gender crimes which occurred with the *Ni Una Menos* movement, see Luengo, 'Gender Violence: The Media, Civil Society, and the Struggle for Human Rights in Argentina', 40 *Media Culture and Society* (2018) 397.

[23] 'Massive Mobilization Against the Socioeconomic Crisis in Argentina', *Newsclick*, 30 August 2019, available online at https://www.newsclick.in/massive-mobilization-against-socio-economic-crisis-argentina.

[24] Alcoba, 'Argentine Senate approves emergency food law after mass protests', *Aljazeera*, 18 September 2019, available online at https://www.aljazeera.com/news/2019/09/argentine-senate-approves-emergency-food-law-mass-protests-190918222010371.html.

[25] Henao, 'Abortion rights activists renew battle in Argentina', *AP News*, 28 May 2019.

[26] Goñi, 'Argentina set to become first major Latin American country to legalise abortion', *The Guardian*, 1 March 2020, in Buenos Aires, available online at https://www.theguardian.com/world/2020/mar/01/argentina-set-to-become-first-major-latin-american-country-to-legalise-abortion.

[27] Brysk, 'From Above and Below' (n. 10).

[28] Brysk, *The Politics of Human Rights in Argentina* (n. 5).

As outlined in Chapter 2, the mechanism by which domestic human rights actors within despotic or authoritarian states generate and join transnational advocacy networks to leverage the influence of external actors and institutions over domestic governmental actors was famously depicted by Keck and Sikkink as a 'boomerang' effect.[29] The authors described a process of strategic mobilization of information, whereby domestic actors bring to wider attention the wrongs being committed by framing issues in such a way as to persuade other powerful actors, who in turn have the capacity—whether economic, political, or other—to bring pressure on the state to change. Keck and Sikkink pointed to domestic activists such as those within Argentina and other Latin American states whose ability to promote change was blocked by a repressive government, who then reached out to international allies and NGOs in other states to mobilize their governments to bring pressure on the repressive state, whether bilaterally or through international organizations or mechanisms. They cited the example of the Mothers and Grandmothers of the Plaza de Mayo, who lobbied the US and other governments to cut off military and economic aid to Argentina, and asked the UN and the Inter-American Commission on Human Rights to condemn Argentina's abuses.[30] And while Keck and Sikkink emphasized the important originating role of domestic civil society actors in bringing forth information, and in framing the issues as human rights abuses, the focus of their account moved then to the enforcement by external actors such as powerful states or international organizations, which had the economic and material leverage to prod the offending state to comply. The boomerang metaphor in this way encompassed a two-stage process—the original action of domestic groups sending information out to external actors, and the response from those external actors in the form of international economic and political pressure on the state to change its practices. This kind of short-term and powerful external pressure on the Argentine regime undoubtedly played an important part in bringing an end to the period of state terrorism, and eventually the electoral defeat of the regime.

However, the boomerang metaphor did not capture other important elements of the ways in which domestic civil society actors and international human rights institutions interact to bring about domestic change, particularly once a democratic system has been established or re-established. Later research by Beth Simmons and others built on the insight that ongoing domestic advocacy can be crucial,[31] and Sikkink's own subsequent work went on to study what she described

---

[29] M. Keck and K. Sikkink, *Activists Beyond Borders: Advocacy Networks in International Politics* (1999).

[30] Ibid. 92–94 and 104–110.

[31] See B. Simmons, *Mobilizing for Human Rights: International Law in Domestic Politics* (2009). See also, for further analysis of the role of domestic actors in ongoing implementation of international human rights, chapters 3 and 5 of T. Risse, S. C. Ropp, and K. Sikkink, *The Persistent Power of Human Rights* (2013): Simmons, 'From Ratification to Compliance: Quantitative Evidence on the Spiral Model' and Dai, 'The Compliance Gap and the Efficacy of International Human Rights Institutions'.

as 'insider-outsider coalitions', namely the kind of interactions between domestic and international actors that occur when there is a sufficient degree of openness at both the domestic and the transnational level.[32] This insight is at the heart of the experimentalist account of human rights law and advocacy that was advanced in Chapter 2, which proposes that the effectiveness of human rights treaties in promoting reform within a broadly democratic state hinges on an ongoing, iterative role for domestic activists and other actors. Domestic advocates are more effective agents of change when their role is not just one of drawing attention to human rights abuses and calling in the support of transnational allies and international actors, but an ongoing one engaging in different ways over time at both domestic and international level, including building support, proposing reforms, and leveraging the standards articulated by international institutions to advocate, mobilize, litigate, challenge, and pressurize national-level actors and institutions to bring about change. The role of international human rights institutions and actors in this process—perhaps unlike the role of external actors vis-a-vis a highly repressive regime such as Argentina during the dictatorship—is less one of coercion or top-down enforcement than the provision of a focal point for information-generation, discussion and contestation, norm elaboration, and accountability-enhancement.

Before moving on to the study of disability rights activism, a recent example of this kind of iterative engagement of domestic advocacy groups with international human rights norms to promote policy reform in Argentina will briefly be described. The example concerns the child rights movement. The UN Convention on the Rights of the Child was first ratified by Argentina in 1990, and was integrated into the Constitution in 1994.[33] Immediately following its ratification, a new civil society alliance, the CSACIDN, was created from the assembly of various existing groups concerned with child welfare, specifically in order to monitor the implementation of the Convention.[34] This included preparing shadow reports for the purposes of Argentina's appearances before the Committee on the Rights of the Child. The first round of reporting began in 1993, with the Committee issuing its concluding observations in 1995.[35] A second alliance of children's rights organizations was created in 2001—the Colectivo de Derechos de Infancia & Adolescencia.[36] Amy Risley has described how these civil society alliances mobilized domestically and made use of the international human rights treaty body system to draw

---

[32] Sikkink, 'Patterns of Dynamic Multilevel Governance and the Insider Outsider Coalition', in D. Della Porta and S. Tarrow (eds), *Transnational Protest and Global Activism* (2005) 151.

[33] Article 75, para. 22 of the Argentine Constitution. This provision gives the Argentine Congress the power to approve treaties, and declares that treaties have higher standing than ordinary laws. It also lists the treaties which 'stand on the same level as the Constitution', and these now include the Convention on the Rights of the Child.

[34] This acronym is translated as 'Argentine Committee for the Monitoring and Application of the International Convention on the Rights of the Child'. See https://www.casacidn.org.ar/.

[35] See the OHCHR Treaty Body website for details and documentation: http://tbinternet.ohchr.org/_layouts/TreatyBodyExternal/countries.aspx?CountryCode=ARG&Lang=EN.

[36] See http://www.colectivoinfancia.org.ar/V3/.

attention to child rights issues, to frame their demands and concerns, and to bring pressure to bear domestically for reform, making 'frequent and impassioned appeals to global norms concerning children's rights'.[37] She argues that they used the process of shadow-report preparation to 'carve out a space from which to generate policy alternatives'; articulating a strong critique of the existing social and political system as regards its effects on young people (including in relation to poverty, social exclusion, school drop-out rates, domestic abuse, the juvenile justice system, and institutionalization) as well as generating practical proposals and policy reforms to advance child rights in a positive way.[38] Risley notes that the organizations of NGOs and non-profit groups did not simply make use of existing opportunity structures but also created their own opportunities.

Grugel and Peruzzotti have also described the central role played by the Convention on the Rights of the Child (CRC) and the international treaty-body monitoring system in the rise of the children's rights movement in Argentina.[39] On their account, the ratification and more particularly the constitutional incorporation of the CRC was a catalysing event that brought together a group of existing domestic actors and NGOs who had not previously collaborated. They point out that the Convention was crucial in fostering a domestic advocacy coalition which then took inspiration from the framing of children's issues under the CRC to pursue a 'rights-oriented politics aimed at introducing concrete legislative and institutional reforms'.[40] They suggest that the ratification of the CRC came about not just because of a pre-existing domestic child rights constituency in Argentina but as part of a regional trend and because of the state's ongoing interest in signalling its re-entry into the international system. But once the treaty was ratified and domestically incorporated, it had the effect of galvanizing domestic groups and bringing them together into a rights-based coalition. The authors point out that the new coalition of hitherto disparate organizations interested in different aspects of children's welfare not only shifted their advocacy to coalesce around a rights-based agenda but also, with the help of international organizations such as UNICEF, established a national network to generate information and to evaluate the state's progress in relation to the provisions of the Convention. They argue that the effect of coming together and the new roles undertaken by the coalition had the result of transforming the children's NGO and civil society sector from 'a disparate and

---

[37] Risley, 'The Power of Persuasion' (n. 15).

[38] Ibid. 681–686.

[39] Grugel and Peruzzotti, 'Grounding Global Norms in Domestic Politics: Advocacy Coalitions and the CRC in Argentina', 42 *Journal of Latin American Studies* (2010) 29. See also the authors' comparison of the implementation of the CRC in Argentina and two other South American jurisdictions in Grugel and Peruzzotti, 'The Domestic Politics of International Human Rights Law: Implementing the Convention on the Rights of the Child in Ecuador, Chile and Argentina', 34 *Human Rights Quarterly* (2012) 178.

[40] Grugel and Peruzzotti, 'Grounding Global Norms' (n. 39) 32.

weak set of organisations with little capacity for independent mobilization' into an effective network with the concept of rights at its centre.[41]

The significance of the Child Rights Convention and of the interaction with its monitoring body for the domestic child rights coalition is underscored by Grugel and Peruzzotti's description of tensions which arose within the network, causing a group to break away and form a separate alliance. This took place during the years between the two cycles of treaty reporting when the coalition lacked 'the glue of having to report to the UN'.[42] Nevertheless, despite their differences and tensions, the two coalitions managed to work together again when the time came to report a second time to the UN treaty body in 2002. Afterwards, it seems that the momentum did not dissipate when the reporting cycle had finished but continued thereafter, and a subsequent joint campaign for legislative reform and the introduction of a Children's Code was mounted. This resulted, after several years of collective efforts and advocacy, in the adoption in 2005 of the relevant reform, the *Ley de Protección Integral de los Derechos del Niño*.[43]

On the one hand, just as with the legislative and policy reforms in relation to women's rights in Pakistan discussed in Chapter 3, the enactment of such laws is only one step in a longer process of political and social change. At the same time, the existence of a child rights coalition and a collection of actors mobilized and equipped—including through their continuous interaction with international norms and institutions—to advocate, promote, challenge, and undertake domestic reform was an important part of that ongoing process. There have been two further cycles of reporting to the Committee on the Rights of the Child, as well as two cycles of reporting to the UN Human Rights Council under the Universal Periodic Review since the enactment of the reform legislation in 2005.[44] Each of these cycles brought extensive reporting and advocacy by the two child rights coalitions and by a range of other civil society actors, keeping pressure on the Argentine government to sustain the commitment to reform in relation to children's welfare and rights. The ongoing engagement between international and the domestic actors—including treaty bodies and other international organizations, civil society groups, national governmental actors, and courts—has created a dynamic that has helped to drive and maintain a continuing process of domestic reform.[45] It has been pointed out that the advocacy challenging policies of austerity which undercut all socio-economic rights needs to be integrated with advocacy specifically in relation

---

[41]   Ibid. 47.

[42]   Ibid. 48.

[43]   Ibid. 51.

[44]   For a compilation of relevant extracts from the Universal Periodic Review of Argentina in 2013 which focus on children's rights, see the website of the Child Rights International Network: https://www.crin.org/en/library/publications/argentina-childrens-rights-universal-periodic-review-second-cycle.

[45]   For a study of the impact of a class action to enforce children's right to early education in Buenos Aires, see F. Basch, *Children's Right to Early Education in the City of Buenos Aires: A Case Study on ACIJ's Class Action*, International Budget Partnership Impact Case Study, Study No. 5 (August 2011).

to children's rights, if real and progressive reform is to be brought about in that sector.[46] And, indeed, in the 2018 consideration by the Committee on the Rights of the Child of Argentina's periodic report on its compliance with the Convention, the government was questioned on the impact of austerity measures, and the implications of its economic crisis and the IMF program on its commitment to reducing socio-economic inequality,[47] and specific recommendations to the government on the need for adequate public budgeting to realize children's rights even in situations of economic crisis were included in its concluding observations.[48]

The remainder of this chapter examines a number of recent disability rights campaigns in Argentina, with particular focus on inclusive education, through the lens of the experimentalist account of human rights law and advocacy set out in Chapter 2.

4. The emergence of disability rights activism in Argentina

By the time Argentina ratified the CRPD in 2008 there was, as described above, an active domestic civil society focused on the promotion of human rights. Amongst these domestic movements was a set of actors and groups focused specifically on promoting and advocating for the rights of persons with disabilities.

While many organizations concerned with the welfare of persons with disabilities existed in Argentina throughout the twentieth century, most of these were focused on the practical task of providing services and later helping people with disabilities to deal with the bureaucracy of the welfare state, rather than rights-based organizations focused on empowerment and advocacy.[49] Bregain has described the early stages of the international disability rights movement towards the end of the 1960s and the way in which domestic disability rights mobilization took place in different countries, including Argentina.[50] Led initially by religiously inspired 'fraternities' of individuals with disabilities seeking to emancipate themselves, and gradually becoming more radical and focused on protest, the Argentinian movement got underway in the early 1970s. While some joined the Marxist-inspired *Frente de Lisiados Peronistas* (literally translated as the Peronist

---

[46] See Risley, 'From "Perverse" to "Progressive"?: Advocating for the Rights and Well-Being of Argentina's Children', 19 *International Journal of Children's Rights* (2011) 72.

[47] 'Committee on the Rights of the Child Considers Report of Argentina', 15 May 2018, available online at https://www.ohchr.org/EN/NewsEvents/Pages/DisplayNews.aspx?NewsID=23088&LangID=E.

[48] See the Committee on the Rights of the Child, Concluding Observations on the combined fifth and sixth periodic reports of Argentina, paras 10, 35, and 36, 1 October 2018.

[49] M. Chudnovsky and Dal Masetto, 'Luces y Sombras de Las Organizaciones Sociales y Su Relación con el Estado', in C. H. Acuña and L. G. Bulit Goñi (eds), *Políticas Sobre la Discapacidad en la Argentina* (2010).

[50] Bregain, 'An Entangled Perspective on Disability History: The Disability Protests in Argentina, Brazil and Spain, 1968-1982', in S. Barsch, A. Klein, and P. Verstraeten (eds), *The Imperfect Historian: Disability Histories in Europe* (2013) 133.

Front of the Crippled) and became involved in resisting the military dictatorship after 1976, a broader alliance including some of the more traditional groups and associations of persons with disabilities was also created, focusing on drafting legislation concerning work for people with disabilities.[51] A key piece of legislation, the Integral Protection System for Disabled People, was adopted during the period of the military dictatorship in 1981, following a sustained and ultimately successful campaign.[52] The broader issue of access and accessibility, which has become a cornerstone of the disability rights movement in more recent times, first began to gain greater attention in Argentina when the *Asociación Argentina pro Hogares y Promoción del Discapacidado* (HODIF) was created in 1983 after the end of the dictatorship.[53]

The paradigm-shifting transformation from a medical model to a social model of disability, with groups and organizations comprised of and led by persons with disabilities at the forefront, took hold in Argentina over time, as it did elsewhere.[54] The growing movement for disability rights increasingly placed issues of access and inclusion at its centre. By 1998, a collection of organizations in Argentina had come together to form the radical and influential Disability Rights Network (REDI).[55] The REDI network began by campaigning for legislative reform focused on the need for wheelchair access to buildings, and then on to labour and employment, emphasizing the right to work and arguing for the rights of persons with disabilities to earn a proper income.[56] However, with the onset of the economic crisis in the early 2000s, REDI joined forces with other human rights, protest, and campaigning groups and shifted its attention to a range of other issues including access to justice and sexuality, as well as the relationship between poverty and disability, making itself the 'voice of the conjoined human rights and disability movement'.[57] Nevertheless, despite these alliances, many different strands and differences of approach continued, with some arguing that the disability rights movement should

---

[51] Bregain (ibid.) describes the creation of the *Unión Nacional Socioéconomico del Lisiado* (National Socioeconomic Union of the Disabled) in 1974, which worked on the introduction of the legislation in parliament.

[52] Ley 22431-81, *Sistema de protección integral de los discapacitados*. For an account of the campaign to have it adopted see R. Sbriller, *La Revolución de los Rengos: Origen del Derecho a Trabajo de las personas con discapacidad en la Argentina* (2016), available online at http://servicios.infoleg. gob.ar/infolegInternet/anexos/20000-24999/20620/norma.htm#:~:text=Art%C3%ADculo%20 1%C2%B0%20%2D%20Instit%C3%BAyese%20por,neutralizar%20la%20desventaja%20que%20la.

[53] See http://www.hodif.org.ar/. The website of the organization now begins by declaring that it adheres to the conception of human rights, based on the social model of disability, promoting the active participation of all its members in all areas of daily life.

[54] For an overview of the social model of disability, see Shakespeare, 'The Social Model of Disability', in L. Davies (ed.), *The Disability Studies Reader* (2017) 195.

[55] See Schrader and Chavez Penillas, 'Crisis, Class and Disability in Argentina; Red por los Derechos de las Personas con Discapacidad (REDI)', 32 *Disability Studies Quarterly* (2012), available online at http://dsq-sds.org/article/view/3274/3107.

[56] Joly, 'Disability and Employment in Argentina: The Right to Be Exploited?', 42(2) *NACLA Report on the Americas* (2009) 5–10.

[57] Schrader and Chavez Penillas (n. 55).

be articulating a more fundamental critique of the capitalist system and not just an argument for the fuller inclusion of persons with disabilities into that system.[58]

Chudnovsky and Potenza dal Masetto describe a high level of heterogeneity amongst the civil society organizations in Argentina today which are focused on disability.[59] Their study, carried out in 2010 and based on two different databases— one a governmental registry and the other from an NGO[60]—identified 1,453 and 2,357 organizations respectively focused on the welfare of persons with disabilities.[61] While most of these organizations are described by the authors as engaging primarily in service-provision, they also focus on rights promotion in their work,[62] hence suggesting that, today, less of a division exists between the different kinds of civil society organizations in the disability field as far as the rights-based approach is concerned.

5. The legal status of the Convention on the Rights of Persons with Disabilities in Argentina

A. Ratification of the CRPD

When the CRPD was first adopted and opened for signature in 2007, Argentina was one of the earliest states to join. In 2008 it signed up to the Convention and its Optional Protocol, which permitted the bringing of individual and group communications (complaints) from victims. The state had been active in the negotiation and drafting of the Convention too, issuing a statement at the time of adoption to point out Argentina's support for the Convention and support for the input of civil society and disabled persons organizations in the process of adoption.[63] Domestically, there was significant political support for its ratification, and the Convention was unanimously approved by both houses of the Congress.[64]

In speeches made to the Parliament at the time of ratification of the Convention, the integral role of civil society and of disabled persons organizations and representatives was emphasized, as was the typical governmental assurance that the Convention did not really introduce any new rights or entitlements, since these were said to be already protected within domestic law, but rather would help with

---

[58] Di Stefano, 'Disability and Latin American Cultural Studies: A Critique of Corporeal Difference, Identity and Social Exclusion', 4 *Canadian Journal of Disability Studies* (2015) 49.

[59] Chudnovsky and Dal Masetto (n. 49).

[60] Fundación Par, *Quiénes Somos*, available online at https://www.fundacionpar.org.ar/quienes-somos.

[61] Chudnovsky and Dal Masetto (n. 49) 259 and 262.

[62] Ibid. 264.

[63] See http://www.un.org/esa/socdev/enable/convstatementgov.htm#ar.

[64] Cámara de Diputados de la Nación Argentina, Versión Taquigráfica, 10ma Reunión, 5ta sesión ordinaria, 12 May 2008.

enforcement and realization of these legal rights in practice.[65] As occurred with the Convention on the Rights of the Child some years after its ratification, the main text of the Convention on the Rights of Persons with Disabilities—though not the Optional Protocol—was granted constitutional status in 2014.[66] A number of significant legal reforms were undertaken following the ratification of the CRPD, including a reform of the Civil Code in 2014, in particular with regard to the system of guardianship or wardship and the exercise of legal capacity by persons with disabilities.[67] Notably, this was an issue on which the government of Argentina had been questioned and pressed by the Committee on the Rights of Persons with Disabilities during the state's first cycle of reporting to the treaty body on its compliance with the provisions of the Convention in 2012.[68]

B. Individual complaints under the Optional Protocol

At the time of writing, there has been just one individual communication submitted by an Argentine national to the CRPD Committee and decided on by the Committee in October 2014. The case concerned the imprisonment of an officer of the Buenos Aires police who had been convicted of crimes against humanity committed during the dictatorship, and who had since suffered a stroke and claimed that the conditions of his detention and lack of access to rehabilitation violated his rights. Without commenting on the state's reference to the nature of the offences for which the author of the communication had been imprisoned, the Committee found a number of violations on the part of Argentina including a failure to provide reasonable accommodation in the circumstances for a person with a disability, and made a set of recommendations to the state to provide appropriate measures and reasonable accommodation to persons with disabilities in the circumstances of detention.[69] After several exchanges during the follow-up procedure between the state, the complainant, and the CRPD Committee, the Committee in 2016 agreed

---

[65] See the speech by Claudio Morgado, Cámara de Diputados de la Nación Argentina, Versión Taquigráfica, 10ma Reunión, 5ta sesión ordinaria, 21 May 2008, available online at http://www1.hcdn.gob.ar/sesionesxml/reunion.asp?p=126&r=10.

[66] This was done by Law 27.044, of September 19, 2014, which declares that it grants constitutional hierarchy to the provisions of the CRPD in accordance with Article 75 para. 22 of the Constitution. See n. 33 above on Article 75 para. 22.

[67] See Ley 26/994, available online at http://servicios.infoleg.gob.ar/infolegInternet/anexos/235000-239999/235975/norma.htm.

[68] See the questions in relation to the compatibility of the Civil Code which were put to the government representatives during the 8th Session of the Committee on the Rights of Persons with Disabilities on 3 December 2012: UN Doc. CRPD/C/SR.79.

[69] See Views adopted by the Committee at its eleventh session (31 March–11 April 2014) on Communication no 8/2012, X v Argentina, UN CRPD/C/11/D/8/2012

that the steps taken by Argentina since 2014 to correct the violations were satisfactory and discontinued the communication.[70]

C. The reporting procedure under the CRPD

If the individual complaints procedure has been little used, the reporting procedure, by contrast, has proven to be a major focal point for civil society advocacy, and for mobilization for reform. The first CRPD reporting cycle for Argentina began in 2010 when the government presented its initial report to the Committee[71] pursuant to Article 35 of the Convention.[72] Similar to the procedure governing other UN human rights treaty bodies, Article 36 provides that the Committee, following a dialogue with the state, should make such suggestions and general recommendations on the report as it deems appropriate, and Article 33(3)—uniquely as yet among UN human rights treaties—expressly provides that '[c]ivil society, in particular persons with disabilities and their representative organizations, shall be involved and participate fully in the monitoring process'.

In this first cycle, two shadow reports were submitted to the Committee by domestic civil society organizations. The first was presented by the *Movimiento por los Derechos Ciudadanos* and focused on four principal issues: first, the lack of effective participation of persons with disabilities in the relevant institutional settings responsible for implementation of the CRPD particularly in light of Argentina's federal system; second, a criticism of the operation of a government committee charged with working on issues of accessibility; third, the question of inclusive education for persons with disabilities; and, finally, a question about the impact of the use of agrochemicals/pesticides on the origin and incidence of particular disabilities.[73] The second and wide-ranging shadow report was a collective submission by five leading NGOs including the REDI network discussed above,[74] as well as the *Centro de Estudios Legales y Sociales* (CELS, a leading Argentine civil and human rights strategic litigation-focused organization founded during the military dictatorship), the *Asociación por los Derechos Civiles* (ADC), *Federación Argentina de Instituciones Ciegos y Ambliopes* (FAICA, focused on blindness), and

---

[70] See the *Annual Report of the Committee on the Rights of Persons with Disabilities to the General Assembly*, UN Doc. A 72/55.

[71] *Initial report submitted by Argentina under Article 35 of the Convention*, UN Doc. CRPD/C/ARG/1 (28 June 2011).

[72] Article 35 of the CRPD provides that state parties must submit to the Committee 'a comprehensive report on measures taken to give effect to its obligations under the present Convention and on the progress made in that regard'.

[73] Shadow Report to the UN Committee on the Rights of Persons with Disabilities by the *Movimiento por los Derechos Ciudadanos*, INT_CRPD_NGO_ARG_14806_S.

[74] See n 55 above and text.

Federación Argentina de Entidades Pro Atención por las Personal con Discapacidad Intelectual (FENDIM, focused on persons with mental disabilities).[75]

The second reporting cycle began in August 2017, during which seven shadow reports were submitted to the CRPD committee, including a collective report prepared by 28 different civil society organizations including, once again. REDI, FAICA, and CELS.[76] With the caveat that it is early to try detecting a trend after just two cycles, the scale and intensity of the mobilization of domestic disability-rights-focused NGOs around the reporting process of the CRPD appears to be growing with each cycle.[77]

Simultaneously, Argentina's general human rights performance has been twice reviewed by the Human Rights Council within the framework of the Universal Periodic Review since its ratification of the CRPD: once in 2012 and once in 2017. At least 34 civil society organizations submitted information to the review process in 2012. Ten of these were joint submissions or coalitions, with several focusing in whole or in part on issues of disability.[78] In 2017 there were 35 civil society submissions, including 22 coalitions or joint submissions, and a broad range of disability issues was raised by at least six of the submissions. Amongst the recommendations made by at least five other governments to Argentina following the review were to fully implement the provisions of the CRPD including promoting inclusive education and moving away from the special school system. In its response to the review, the government of Argentina in 2018 accepted each of these recommendations, and specifically mentioned its acceptance of the need for a system of inclusive education, making reference to recent work done to implement this.[79]

D. The Argentine Supreme Court and the CRPD

In 1994, a major set of amendments to the Constitution of Argentina was adopted, including a provision which grants priority to international treaties over ordinary laws (without however granting constitutional status to treaties), and a further provision granting constitutional status to a specified range of regional and international human rights treaties signed by the state.[80] Following these

---

[75] Shadow Joint Report to the Committee on the Rights of Persons with Disabilities by REDI, CELS, ADS, FAICA, and FENDIM, INT_CRPD_NGO_ARG_14809_S.

[76] See the website of the Office of the High Commissioner on Human Rights, available online at http://tbinternet.ohchr.org/_layouts/TreatyBodyExternal/Countries.aspx?CountryCode=ARG&Lang=EN.

[77] The Argentine government submitted its report to the CRPD committee in March 2019, and the report will next be considered by the committee which will issue concluding observations.

[78] All documentation relevant to the UPR, including the submissions of civil society which are linked, can be found via the OHCHR website, available online at http://www.ohchr.org/EN/HRBodies/UPR/Pages/UPRArgentinaStakeholderInfoS14.aspx.

[79] 37th Session of the UN Human Rights Council 2018, A/HRC/37/5/Add.1.

[80] Article 75 para. 22 (in English translation) provides: 'The Congress shall have power … to approve or reject treaties entered with other nations and with international organizations, and concordats

amendments, the Supreme Court in a 1998 ruling indicated a judicial openness towards the enforcement of international law by declaring that judges are bound to comply with the state's obligations deriving from treaties and other sources of international law.[81]

Further, and at least until recently, the Supreme Court has also treated the output of international courts and treaty-bodies as relevant sources of law. In the case of *Giroldi* concerning the American Convention on Human Rights in 1995, the Court ruled that the reference to the 'conditions under which treaties were in force' in Article 75 para. 22 meant that the courts should particularly consider the application of these treaties by the tribunals which are competent for their interpretation and application.[82] Drawing on this formulation in later cases, the Supreme Court has regularly cited a range of international bodies and legal instruments, including non-binding instruments, in order to interpret the international obligations of the state.[83] In a perhaps surprising deviation from this embrace of the jurisprudence of human rights bodies, however, the Supreme Court in February 2017 in the *Fontevecchia* case rejected the suggestion that it must overturn an earlier decision it had given on freedom of expression,[84] in order to comply with a ruling of the Inter-American Court of Human Rights which found that earlier decision to be in violation of the provisions of the American Convention on Human Rights.[85] The Supreme Court did not reject the authority or rulings of the Inter-American Court more generally, but took the view that the regional human rights court in this instance had exceeded its jurisdiction and its remedial powers by purporting to order the revocation of an earlier decision of the Argentine Supreme Court. It remains to be seen whether this case was an unusual departure, in reliance on notions of remedial complementarity or subsidiarity, from the otherwise consistent openness

with the Holy See. Treaties and concordats have higher standing than laws. The following international instruments, under the conditions under which they are in force, stand on the same level as the Constitution, but do not repeal any article in the First Part of this Constitution, and must be understood as complementary of the rights and guarantees recognized therein.' See also n. 33.

[81] Corte Suprema de Justicia de la Nación, *Acosta, Claudia*, 321: 3555 (1998), para. 15.

[82] Corte Suprema de Justicia de la Nación, *Giroldi, Horacio*, 318: 514 (1995), para. 11.

[83] See for a review of this jurisprudence, Pinto and Maisley, 'From Affirmative Avoidance to Soaring Alignment: The Engagement of Argentina's Supreme Court with International Law', available online at https://www.academia.edu/20225843/From_Affirmative_Avoidance_to_Soaring_Alignment_The_Engagement_of_Argentina_s_Supreme_Court_with_International_Law.

[84] See the Resolution of the Supreme Court of 14 February 2017, in Ministerio de Relaciones Exteriores y Cultos, informe sentencia dictada en el caso 'Fontevecchia y D'Amico vs. Argentina' por la Corte Interamericana de Derechos Humanos, CSJ 368/1998 (34-M)/CS1; and its original ruling on 25 September 2001 upholding the imposition of a fine on journalists for publishing an apparently libellous story about former president Carlos Menem.

[85] The judgment of the Inter-American Court of Human Rights finding that the Supreme Court ruling upholding the penalty was incompatible with freedom of expression as protected under the American Convention on Human Rights was given in *Fontevecchia and D'Amico v. Argentina*. Judgment of 29 November 2011, and the later order (supervision of execution of the initial judgment) by the Inter American court that the Supreme Court decision should be revoked was given in *Fontevecchia y D'Amico vs. Argentina* No. 12.525, on 18 October 2017.

of the Supreme Court towards international law and to the output of international human rights tribunals in particular, or whether it represents the beginning of a more restrictive trend.

At the time of writing, the Supreme Court has cited the output of the Committee on the Rights of Persons with Disabilities on one occasion,[86] and as will be discussed below, it has dismissed appeals in cases in which the lower courts made their decisions in reliance on standards set by the CRPD Committee, thereby indirectly affirming those standards.[87] Further and notably, the Supreme Court has cited the provisions of the CRPD itself in over two dozen decisions, including a judgment in 2012 when the Court relied on Articles 3, 7, and 28 of the Convention on the Rights of Persons with Disabilities, along with provisions of the UN Convention on Economic, Social and Cultural Rights, to rule that the state must take action to help a disabled child and her mother to find housing.[88] The CRPD has also been cited on numerous occasions by other courts in Argentina.[89]

E. Domestic visibility and public salience of the CRPD

One particular issue which recently brought the Convention to the centre of public debate in the country was the availability of pensions for persons with disabilities. In May 1997, the government passed a decree adopting new implementation measures for a longstanding disability pension law.[90] The decree was adopted as part of the government's Washington-consensus-oriented agenda under President Carlos Menem at the time, and it introduced a range of new restrictions on access to pensions for persons with disabilities. However, this decree was not implemented until May 2017, when the government of President Mauricio Macri invoked it to exclude a large number of recipients from the pension programme. While the exact number was contested, it seems to have affected between 50,000 and 170,000 persons.[91] According to news reports, those affected were not notified of the policy

---

[86] This is the *Alespeiti* case, which was also the subject of an (unsuccessful) individual petition to the CRPD Committee, see nn. 69–70 above and text. For the Supreme Court case, see CFP 14216/2003/TO1/6/1/CS1, Felipe Jorge, Alespeitti, Incidente de Recurso Extraordinario, 18 April 2017.

[87] See below nn. 120 and text.

[88] Corte Suprema de Justicia de la Nación, Q.C.S.Y., 335:452 (2012), III pp. 11–12.

[89] See Aiello, 'Argentina', in A. Lawson and L. Waddington (eds), *The UN Convention on the Rights of Persons with Disabilities in Practice: A Comparative Analysis of the Role of Courts* (2018) 13.

[90] Executive Decree 432/97, available online at https://www.desarrollosocial.gob.ar/wp-content/uploads/2015/07/Decreto-432-1997-Reglamentacion-de-la-Ley-de-Pensiones-a-la-vejez-y-por-invalidez-actualizado.pdf.

[91] The government claimed the lower number, while others cited the higher: compare G. Morini, *Fallo obliga a Gobierno a reponer pensiones por discapacidad y lo vuelve causa colectiva*, 7 September 2017, available online at http://www.ambito.com/896344-fallo-obliga-a-gobierno-a-reponer-pensiones-por-discapacidad-y-lo-vuelve-causa-colectiva, with Carillo, 'Batalla judicial por las pensiones por invalidez', *El País*, 14 June 2017, available online at https://www.pagina12.com.ar/44010-batalla-judicial-por-las-pensiones-por-invalidez.

change, and found out about the decision only when their pension payments did not appear in their bank accounts.[92]

The public response was immediate and angry, with protests taking place in Buenos Aires and other cities across the country. A number of judicial complaints were filed throughout the country against the decision, some brought by people affected by the measure or by political parties or civil society organizations,[93] as well as by public prosecutors.[94] In a lawsuit suit filed by the NGO REDI in September 2017, the judge handed down an interlocutory ruling which ordered the government to restore all pensions in the country with immediate effect.[95] The judge made reference to the CRPD, including the right to dignity and to live independently.[96] By this stage, the government, under the additional pressure of public opinion and protest, had announced that it would reverse its original measure and restore the pensions for persons with disabilities.[97]

While the litigation itself was not the trigger for reversal of the restrictive measure, the broader public protest and debate on the issue, including the various legal actions which were initiated, brought widespread popular attention to the Convention and its provisions on the rights of persons with disabilities. The government's attempt to cut pensions for persons with disabilities was a front-page story in the main national newspaper for days and frequent reference was made to the CRPD and its impact in Argentina. Lawyers from REDI, the *Asociación Civil por la Igualdad y la Justicia* (ACIJ) and other organizations were interviewed in prominent media outlets, and they emphasized the likely incompatibility of the measure with Article 19 of the CRPD, which protects the rights of persons with disabilities to live independently and in the community.[98] Senators and members of Congress also accused the government of violating the Convention,[99] and

---

[92] See https://www.telesurtv.net/english/news/Macri-Govt-Axes-Pensions-for-83000-People-with-Disabilities-20170613-0024.html.

[93] See Carillo (n. 91).

[94] 'Fiscal Asegura Que Las Pensiones Por Discapacidad Son Un Derecho Adquirido', *Minuto Uno*, 14 June 2017, available online at https://www.minutouno.com/notas/1556641-fiscal-asegura-que-las-pensiones-discapacidad-son-un-derecho-adquirido.

[95] See 'Amparo por pensiones no contributivas', *REDI*, 17 July 2017, available online at www.redi.org.ar/index.php?file=Prensa/Comunicados/2017/17-07-17_Amparo-por-pensiones-no-contributivas.html.

[96] Juzgado Federal de la Seguridad Social 8, *Asociación REDI c/ Estado Nacional – Ministerio de Desarrollo Social s/Amparos y Sumarísimos*, case 39031/2017 (5 September 2017), available online at http://www.fiscales.gob.ar/wp-content/uploads/2017/09/Sentencia.pdf.

[97] 'Argentina Govt backtracks on plan to cut Disability Pensions', available online at https://www.telesurenglish.net/news/Argentina-Govt-Backtracks-on-Plan-to-Cut-Disability-Pensions-20170616-0009.html.

[98] Rafele, 'Para ONGs, El Recorte En Las Pensiones Por Discapacidad Es Inconstitucional y Provocará Una Ola de Amparos', *Todo Noticias*, 13 June 2017, available online at http://tn.com.ar/economia/para-ongs-el-recorte-en-las-pensiones-por-discapacidad-es-inconstitucional-y-provocara-una-ola-de_799671.

[99] See e.g. 'Sergio Massa Pidió "Volver Atrás" La Medida Que Afectó La Distribución de Las Pensiones Por Discapacidad', *Infobae*, 14 June 2017, available online at https://www.infobae.com/politica/2017/06/14/sergio-massa-pidio-volver-atras-la-medida-que-afecto-la-distribucion-de-las-pensiones-por-

the second largest party within the government coalition introduced a proposed amendment to reverse the implementation of the decree, arguing that any other measure would be in violation of the CRPD.[100] Several days later the government announced that it would restore the pensions to persons with disabilities which had been cut 'by mistake'.[101] However, the fact that the 1997 decree was nonetheless left in place has been criticized by human rights organizations for creating a situation of uncertainty and unjustified administrative discretion.[102]

While the issue of pensions was perhaps predictably one which touched on the interests and economic welfare of many people, and aroused particular indignation due to its impact on elderly persons with disabilities as some of the most vulnerable in society, the salience and impact of the CRPD on policy reform in Argentina can also be seen in a series of other recent initiatives. The next section describes a number of these initiatives taken by disability rights organizations and actors on the issue of inclusive education, which illustrate how the use by domestic activists of the CRPD, and the consequent engagement between civil society, government and other domestic actors, and the Committee on the Rights of Persons with Disabilities, have influenced policy change in Argentina.

6. Inclusive education: civil society activation of the CRPD to catalyse disability rights reform

The issue of inclusive education has been a central one in contemporary discussions around the world on disability reform, with the focus being primarily— although not without active debate and disagreement—on ending segregated or 'special' education for persons with disabilities, and promoting inclusion within educational programs and facilities for all students, with and without disabilities.[103] While at the time when the Convention was being drafted there were initially differences of view as to whether a commitment to special education should

---

discapacidad/; de Alonso, 'Para Stanley, Las Personas Con Discapacidad Son Descartables', *argnoticias. com*, 19 June 2017, available online at. https://www.biencuyano.com.ar/?p=6066.

[100] See https://www.grupolaprovincia.com/argentina/desde-la-ucr-quieren-flexibilizar-los-requisitos-acceder-pensiones-126520, 15 June 2017.

[101] 'El Gobierno restablecerá las pensiones por discapacidad', *La Opinion*, 16 June 2017, available online at https://diariolaopinion.com.ar/noticia/182954/el-gobierno-restablecera-las-pensiones-por-discapacidad.

[102] 'Las personas con discapacidad no son una prioridad para el Gobierno argentino', *ACIJ*, 5 June 2019, available online at https://acij.org.ar/las-personas-con-discapacidad-no-son-una-prioridad-para-el-gobierno-argentino/.

[103] See A. J. Artiles, E. B. Kozleski, and F. R. Waitoller (eds), *Inclusive Education: Examining Equity on Five Continents* (2011). For a collection of recent essays on the subject, see the special issue of *Prospects* journal on *Inclusive Education: Open Debates And The Road Ahead*, edited by Clementina Acedo, Ferran Ferrer and Jordi Pàmies, 39(3) *Prospects* (2009).

be retained and whether a right to choose between inclusive or special education should be included, the final text opted clearly in favour of inclusive education.[104]

Article 24 of the CRPD is a detailed provision which begins by recognizing the right of persons with disabilities to education, and moves on to state that: 'With a view to realizing this right without discrimination and on the basis of equal opportunity, States Parties shall ensure an inclusive education system at all levels and lifelong learning'.

Article 24(2) continues by requiring State Parties to ensure that 'persons with disabilities are not excluded from the general education system on the basis of disability', that 'reasonable accommodation of the individual's requirement is provided', that 'persons with disabilities receive the support required within the general education system to facilitate their effective education' and Article 24(5) provides that States Parties shall ensure 'that persons with disabilities are able to access general tertiary education, vocational training, adult education and lifelong learning without discrimination and on an equal basis with others'. And while the CRPD itself does not define the concept of inclusive education, the Committee on the Rights of Persons with Disabilities has described it broadly as 'a process that transforms culture, policy and practice in all educational environments to accommodate the differing needs of individual students, together with a commitment to remove the barriers that impede that possibility'.[105]

In Argentina, as elsewhere, there is a spectrum of views as to the meaning of inclusive education, and there has been a debate about the desirability or otherwise of maintaining specialized educational facilities for students with disabilities.[106] Nevertheless, the domestic movement for inclusive education is now an active and growing one, comprised of more than 150 organizations gathered within a domestic coalition called *Grupo Artículo 24*, which has been pressing for cultural and social as well as legal change.[107] This coalition also participates in a wider Latin American regional network on inclusive education.[108]

---

[104] de Beco, 'Transition to Inclusive Education Systems According to the Convention on the Rights of Persons with Disabilities', 34 *Nordic Journal of Human Rights* (2016) 40. Also della Fina, 'Commentary on Article 24', in V. della Fina, R. Cera, and G. Palmisano (eds), *United Nations Convention on the Rights of Persons with Disabilities: A Commentary* (2017) 439.

[105] UN Committee on the Rights of Persons with Disabilities General Comment No 4 (2016) on the right to Inclusive Education, 2 September 2016, CPRD/C/GC/4, at para. 2.9.

[106] For a discussion of the resistance of teachers' unions to inclusive education in Argentina, see *Elena Dal Bó On Inclusive Education In Argentina*, Inclusive Education Canada, 14 February 2017, available online at http://inclusiveeducation.ca/2017/02/14/elena-dal-bo-on-inclusive-education-in-argentina/. For an account of the moves towards recognition of inclusion at the policy level in Argentina and its challenges in practice, see Skliar and Dussel, 'From Equity to Difference: Educational Legal Frames and Inclusive Practices in Argentina', in Artiles, Kozleski, and Waitoller (eds) (n. 103).

[107] The domestic advocacy coalition created to promote inclusive education is called the Article 24 Group: *Grupo Artículo 24*, http://www.grupoart24.org/.

[108] This is the Latin American regional network for inclusive education, *Red Regional por la Educación Inclusiva* (RREI), http://rededucacioninclusiva.org/, which is comprised of 14 coalitions and NGOs representing persons with disabilities from Brazil, Colombia, Paraguay, Peru, and Uruguay, as well as Argentina.

The following sections describe two recent initiatives for change led by individuals and NGOs supporting them who invoked the CRPD before domestic courts and drew on the output of the CRPD committee to challenge educational practices and policies which excluded people with disabilities, as well as some other CRPD-inspired collective campaigns to promote inclusive education in Argentina through the use of media and the provision of information and training sessions.

A. The Emiliano Naranjo case

Emiliano Naranjo was an avid swimmer who wanted to become a physical education teacher.[109] Having finished secondary school and obtained a bachelor's degree in physical education at the Universidad de La Matanza, his application for a further degree at the same institution to enable him to become a physical education teacher was rejected. The reason given by the university for rejecting his application was that completion of this degree necessitated the taking of practical courses that required certain physical abilities; and Naranjo could not take these courses since he had been born with a disability which impeded the coordinated movement of his legs.

During his bachelor's degree, he had been able to follow a special curriculum provided for people who were injured during their studies and could therefore avoid the required practical courses. But there was no accommodated curriculum available for the advanced degree. The Dean of the School that had rejected his application was quoted as saying that while the school had worked hard to be inclusive, the particular degree for which Naranjo had applied included practical courses requiring certain physical abilities, and that the school would be violating the principle of equality as between Emiliano Naranjo and other students if he were to be dispensed from the requirement to complete these courses.[110]

Assisted by the *Asociación por los Derechos Civiles* (ADC), a civil rights NGO which uses public interest litigation and other tactics to pursue human rights causes,[111] Naranjo brought legal proceedings against the university.[112] His claim relied in part on Article 24 of the CRPD, along with various other international human rights sources including Article 13 of the International Covenant on

---

[109] Naranjo has written an autobiographical account in E. Naranjo, *Malestar de Educador* (2014).

[110] Fernando Lucan Acosta was quoted in the following terms: 'Emiliano planteó que teníamos que darle el título de profesor sin cursar ninguna. Esto quiebra el principio de igualdad con el resto de los estudiantes': Olaberria, 'Una Apuesta a la Diferencia', 12 *Página* (2015), available online at https://www.pagina12.com.ar/diario/sociedad/3-264761-2015-01-26.html.

[111] See http://adc.org.ar/causes/educacion-inclusiva/ for the organization's focus on the issue of inclusive education.

[112] See Juzgado Federal en lo Civil y Com. y Cont. Adm. de San Martín 2, *N., E. P. c/ Universidad Nacional de la Matanza (UNLAM) s/Amparo Ley 16.986*, Nro. 18040126/2011 (22 November 2013), at 3–11.

Economic Social and Cultural Rights and the observations of the Committee on Economic, Social and Cultural Rights which monitors that Covenant, as well as a report of the UN Special Rapporteur on the right to education who had advocated for the right to education of persons with disabilities.[113] Notably, this particular report of the UN Special Rapporteur had been prepared with input from civil society organizations in many jurisdictions, including from Argentina.[114]

In November 2013, the judge at first instance ruled in favour of Naranjo's claim, and much of the judicial reasoning relied on the requirement of 'reasonable accommodation' which is a central concept in the CRPD.[115] Citing the CRPD as well as the report of the Special Rapporteur, the judge stated that the denial of reasonable accommodation has now been recognized as a form of discrimination.[116] She pointed to the importance of judges adopting and applying the perspective of disability in their interpretation and application of the law, noting that this could bring about change for the lives and circumstances of persons with disabilities.[117] The judge ultimately ruled that the university should admit Emiliano Naranjo and allow him to sit only the theoretical components of the exams in the courses needed to obtain the teaching degree.[118] The university's appeal against the decision was rejected by the Court of Appeals, which again cited extensively from the report of the Special Rapporteur on the Right to Education, and upheld the order of the instance below to admit him to the degree course he wanted to pursue.[119]

This decision was subject to a further appeal to the National Supreme Court, which rejected the appeal in a single-paragraph ruling and made reference only to the opinion presented to the court by the Office of the Advocate General (*Procuradora General*).[120] The Advocate General in her opinion argued that the CRPD had introduced a new paradigm on matters concerning persons with disabilities, and referred also to the *Furlan v. Argentina* case of the Inter-American Court of Human Rights concerning a child who had been disabled in an accident for which the state was partly responsible.[121] The Advocate General's Opinion also

[113] Report of the UN Special Rapporteur on the right to education, V. Muñoz, *The right to education of persons with disabilities*, UN Doc. A/HRC/4/29 (19 February 2007.

[114] Ibid. para. 47 for a list of the sources and jurisdictions from which the Special Rapporteur sought information in the preparation of the report.

[115] Juzgado Federal en lo Civil y Com. y Cont. Adm. de San Martín 2, *N., E. P. c/ Universidad Nacional de la Matanza (UNLAM) s/Amparo Ley 16.986*, Nro. 18040126/2011 (22 November 2013) 21.

[116] Ibid. 27.

[117] Ibid. 21.

[118] Ibid. 28.

[119] Cámara Federal de San Martín, Sala II, Causa 18040126/2011 – Orden 11.056 – Reg. no. 16/14 Fº73/84, *Naranjo, Emiliano Pablo c/ Universidad Nacional de la Matanza (UNLAM) s/Amparo Ley 16.986* (17 March 2014).

[120] Decision of the Supreme Court of 19 November 2019, Recurso de Hecho, Naranjo, Emiliano Pablo el Universidad Nacional de La Matanza si amparo ley 16.986, available online at http://public.diariojudicial.com/documentos/000/065/635/000065635.pdf. For the Opinion of the Advocate General of 1 June 2015, see http://www.fiscales.gob.ar/wp-content/uploads/2015/06/CSJ-94-2014-Naranjo.pdf.

[121] *Furlan v. Argentina*, judgment of the Inter-American Court of Human Rights (31 August 2012).

cited a range of other international law sources in its discussion of article 24 of the CRPD, including notably the Concluding Observations of the Committee on the Rights of Persons with Disabilities on Argentina's first report to the treaty body.[122] Article 37 of the Committee's Concluding Observations on Argentina, which was cited by the Advocate General in her opinion in the *Naranjo* case, referred to the risk that the principle of inclusive education would be limited or undermined by a failure to tailor programs and curricula to the needs of pupils with disabilities.[123]

Notably, the process leading up to the adoption by the CRPD Committee of these Concluding Observations on Argentina in 2012 involved the participation of domestic civil society organizations promoting the issue of inclusive education. In fact, Emiliano Naranjo himself collaborated on the drafting of one of the shadow reports, as did the organizations REDI and *Asociación por los Derechos Civiles* (ADC), which subsequently brought the litigation in his case.[124] The shadow report which they submitted to the CRPD committee pointed to the obstacles confronting inclusive education in Argentina, and to the difficulties facing students with disabilities in schools.[125] Further, when a representative of the Argentine government, in a hearing before the CRPD Committee during the reporting procedure, pointed to the fact that some states believed that inclusive education could be provided through special schools outside of the normal school system,[126] the Committee in paras 37 and 38 of its Concluding Observations made clear that it did not consider special schools to constitute inclusive education and emphasized the need to tailor programs and curricula to the needs of students with disabilities.

A second relevant source cited by the Advocate General in her opinion to the Supreme Court in Emiliano Naranjo's case was a thematic study on the right of persons with disabilities to education prepared by the Office of the UN High Commissioner for Human Rights in 2013.[127] The report was prepared at the request of—and subsequently approved by—the Human Rights Council,[128] in consultation with a wide range of stakeholders, including international and regional

---

[122] Committee on the Rights of Persons with Disabilities, *Concluding observations on the initial report of Argentina as approved by the Committee at its eighth session (17–28 September 2012)*, UN Doc. CRPD/C/ARG/CO/1 (8 October 2012).

[123] Ibid. para. 37.

[124] Comité Sobre los Derechos de las Personas con Discapacidad, 8 Período de Sesiones, Evaluación sobre Argentina, Informe Alternativo, *Situación de la Discapacidad en Argentina - 2008/2012*. Presentado de manera conjunta por: REDI – CELS – FAICA – FENDIM – ADC. The shadow report is available on the treaty body website: http://tbinternet.ohchr.org/.

[125] Ibid. 67.

[126] Committee on the Rights of Persons with Disabilities, Eighth session, Summary record (partial) of the 80th meeting, *Consideration of reports submitted by States parties under article 35 of the Convention (continued), Initial report of Argentina (continued)*, UN Doc. CRPD/C/SR.80 (9 October 2012), para. 43. Notably, the same state representative agreed that autonomous universities, just as state universities, were required to comply with the provisions of the CRPD. See para. 50.

[127] Office of the United Nations High Commissioner for Human Rights, *Thematic study on the right of persons with disabilities to education*, UN Doc. A/HRC/25/29 (8 December 2013).

[128] See Resolution 25/20 adopted by the Human Rights Council, *The right to education of persons with disabilities*, UN Doc. A/HRC/RES/25/20 (14 April 2014).

organizations and actors, and civil society organizations, including organizations of persons with disabilities.[129] In preparing the report, the OHCHR heard the views of various organizations,[130] including the International Disabilities Alliance in which REDI participates.[131] The thematic study also drew on the concluding observations of the CRPD Committee on Argentina to emphasize the need for inclusive education, 'ensuring that pupils with disabilities who attend special schools are enrolled in inclusive schools'.[132]

Further, the opinion of the Advocate General which the Supreme Court followed in the *Emiliano Naranjo* case has continued to be influential after the case, and has been widely cited by NGOs in other judicial and administrative claims concerning inclusive education.[133] The *Naranjo* case has in turn become an important and influential one not only domestically, but also at the international level, with the International Disabilities Alliance citing it as an example of the requirement of reasonable accommodation in its submission to the treaty body monitoring the UN Convention on Elimination of All Forms of Discrimination against Women.[134]

The *Naranjo* case seems at first glance to be an instance of a single individual with a disability challenging a barrier he has encountered in order to be able to complete his education, but it provides an interesting window into of the work of the local, national, and regional disability rights movement at both the domestic and the international level. While Naranjo himself used the litigation to contest an obstacle he had personally encountered, he was already active in the broader disability rights movement and had participated in the drafting of one of the earlier shadow reports to the CRPD Committee during the period of Argentina's reporting in 2012. Hence the CRPD Committee at that time was presented with evidence from Naranjo and from coalitions of disability activists in Argentina about the challenges facing persons with disabilities there, including barriers to inclusive education. The reverse strategy was then subsequently used by Naranjo, with the backing of the civil rights and disability rights organizations REDI and ADC, when he brought his own domestic challenge before the local courts. On this occasion, rather than presenting information to an international authority and

---

[129] Office of the United Nations High Commissioner for Human Rights, *Thematic study on the right of persons with disabilities to education*, UN Doc. A/HRC/25/29 (18 December 2013), para. 1.

[130] See http://www.ohchr.org/EN/Issues/Disability/Pages/SubmissionStudyEducation.aspx.

[131] See http://www.redi.org.ar/index.php?file=Quienes-somos/English-presentation.html.

[132] Office of the United Nations High Commissioner for Human Rights, *Thematic study on the right of persons with disabilities to education*, UN Doc. A/HRC/25/29 (18 December 2013), see in particular footnote 29 of the Study, and also footnotes 2, 24, and 28.

[133] See e.g. in the case of Alan Rodríguez discussed in Section 6.B (the *Naranjo* case is cited in the *Amparo* (i.e. the legal action) of Alan Rodríguez, at 35).

[134] 'An Argentinean federal court granted access to higher education to a person with physical disabilities to be eligible to become a gym professor and ordered the university to provide reasonable accommodation ... this decision was confirmed by the higher federal court', IDA submission to the CEDAW Committee's General Discussion on Girls'/Women's Right to Education 58th session, 7 July 2014, at 11.

audience about the realities of life for persons with disabilities in Argentina and the barriers they face, he presented information about the provisions and principles of the CRPD and the emerging international jurisprudence on the right to inclusive education to a domestic authority and audience, in the context of his specific challenge to the university's refusal to admit him to a degree course. The pressure for reform, in other words, came neither primarily from above, from an international authority, nor primarily from below, through the demands of domestic advocates, but from ongoing engagement between these and other actors at both the international and the domestic levels about the meaning and applicability of the commitments agreed by the state under the CRPD in the particular factual context of university admissions.

B. The Alan Rodríguez case

Alan Rodríguez was a student who finished his primary and secondary school education in 2013 at the age of 17, having successfully completed all of the courses offered to him at secondary school.[135] As he had Down syndrome, he had graduated under a personalized education project, passed all classes within this project, and completed five years of secondary school.[136] He was informed by the school that unlike his classmates, he would not be given an official certificate to indicate that he had completed his education, since he had not satisfied certain minimum requirements set by local regulation for the general school population.

Assisted by the *Asociación Civil por la Igualdad y la Justicia* (ACIJ), an NGO dedicated to 'promoting compliance with laws that protect disadvantaged groups and eliminate discriminatory practices',[137] Rodríguez brought legal action against the city of Buenos Aires, claiming that to apply the requirements of this regulation to him was discriminatory and impeded his right to education. The first instance judge ruled in his favour, declaring that the local regulation concerning minimum requirements was unconstitutional, and ordering that the school should provide him with the requisite certificate, and that the City of Buenos Aires should confirm

---

[135] Alan Rodríguez gives an account of his story in a petition published on Change.org, available online at https://www.change.org/p/soledad-acunia-por-mi-discapacidad-me-niegan-mi-t%C3%ADtulo. For various media accounts of his story, see T. Zolezzi, *No tan incluidos: los chicos con discapacidad, lejos del título oficial*, 27 September 2019, available online at https://www.lanacion.com.ar/1880367-no-tan-incluidos-los-chicos-con-discapacidad-lejos-del-titulo-oficial and F. Massa, *Un colegio privado deberá darle apoyo especial a una estudiante con discapacidad*, 9 May 2017, available online at https://www.lanacion.com.ar/2021943-un-colegio-privado-debera-darle-apoyo-especial-a-una-estudiante-con-discapacidad.

[136] See the summary of the case provided by the Right to Education project, an international human rights NGO focused on the right to education, available online at http://www.right-to-education.org/sites/right-to-education.org/files/resource-attachments/RTE_C%C3%A9sar_Alan%20_Rodr%C3%ADguez_2016_En.pdf.

[137] See https://acij.org.ar/asociacion-civil-por-la-igualdad-y-la-justicia/.

it.[138] The judge's reasoning relied significantly on Article 24 of the Convention on the Rights of Persons with Disabilities, and also on the interpretation of this Article by the CRPD Committee, particularly in the Committee's General Comment No 4 on the Right to Inclusive Education.[139]

General Comments are a form of soft law guidance issued by human rights treaty bodies outside the regular state reporting context, and their impact and influence depends in large part on their quality and persuasiveness.[140] The General Comment on the Right to Inclusive Education was being drafted by the CRPD Committee during the time Alan Rodríguez's case was being heard domestically, and the process by which it was adopted was a broadly participatory one in which submissions were received from many civil society organizations.[141] Amongst the organizations making submissions to the Committee was the coalition of NGOs for inclusive education, *Grupo Artículo 24*, mentioned above,[142] of which the NGO *Asociación Civil por la Igualdad y la Justicia* which brought proceedings on behalf of Rodríguez was a member.[143] The submission of the coalition—in a section which closely matches the issues as they arose in the *Rodríguez* case—specifically raised the problem of the lack of certification of the studies of persons with disabilities, which had not been addressed by the Committee in its earlier version of the draft General Comment which had been made publicly available.[144] Following the advocacy of *Grupo Artículo 24* on the issue of certification,[145] however, the final version of the General Comment included express reference to this issue. Paragraph 12(g) of the General Comment asserts that 'effective transitions', including transitions

---

[138] *Rodriguez, Cesar Alan contra GCBA y Otros*, sobre Amparo Número: A47249 2015/0, judgment of 24 October 2016, available online at http://public.diariojudicial.com/documentos/000/071/280/000071280.pdf.

[139] Ibid. For General Comment No. 4 of the CRPD, see UN Doc. CRPC/C/GC/4 (26 August 2016), available on the website of the OHCHR.

[140] See e.g. Keller and Grover, 'General Comments of the Human Rights Committee and their legitimacy', in H. Keller and G. Ulfstein (eds), *UN Human Rights Treaty Bodies: Law and Legitimacy* (2012) 116, and Mechlem, 'Treaty Bodies and the Interpretation of Human Rights', 42 *Vanderbilt Journal of Transnational Law* (2009) 905.

[141] For a list of the submissions made to the CRDP Committee on the drafting of the General Comment, see http://www.ohchr.org/EN/HRBodies/CRPD/Pages/GCRightEducation.aspx.

[142] See n. 107 above.

[143] For the *Grupo Artículo 24* submission, see the list at http://www.ohchr.org/EN/HRBodies/CRPD/Pages/GCRightEducation.aspx.

[144] The Draft is still available online at http://www.ohchr.org/EN/HRBodies/CRPD/Pages/GCRightEducation.aspx.

[145] *Grupo Artículo 24* argued in its submission, available ibid., that 'incluso en los casos excepcionales en los que se admitió la flexibilización de la currícula, sólo se otorga el título o certificado de la educación básica a quienes acreditan ciertos aprendizajes considerados mínimos, definidos en base a criterios de normalidad (y no en base al plan pedagógico individual), y que no responden a los fines que de acuerdo a CDPD y otros tratados debe orientarse la educación' (translated as 'even in those exceptional cases in which flexibilization of the curriculum was granted, the degree or certification of basic education was only granted to those who accredited certain learnings which are considered minimum, defined on the basis of criteria of normalcy (and not on the basis of the individual pedagogical project), and which do not respond to the goals to which education must be oriented, according to the CRPD and other treaties').

from school to tertiary education and to work, are a core feature of the right to inclusive education, and that along with a range of other guarantees including reasonable accommodation they require the 'capacities and attainments' of persons with disabilities to be 'certified on an equal basis with others'.[146]

This provision of the General Comment was then cited, presumably in response to advocacy by Alan Rodríguez's lawyers, by the first instance judge in his case, who used Article 12(g) to dismiss the suggestion made by the school and by the city that it would be sufficient if the document provided to the student indicated that he had completed courses at the school over a certain number of years. The judge ruled that, on the contrary, a merely descriptive record of that kind would indicate that the student was 'integrated, but not included'.[147] What was required in order to satisfy the rights of the student was 'an acknowledgment that he finished his educational process: not merely that he was in a class, but that he incorporated the knowledge that was offered and taught to him, taking into account his constitutionally acknowledged right to inclusive education'.[148] An appeal against the first instance decision was brought by the school and the city, but it was upheld in a brief ruling by the Court of Appeals in 2017.[149] Alan Rodríguez eventually received his certificate in December 2017, four years after his initial complaint.[150] Apart from the importance of the legal victory in itself, the case also gained significant public attention and support due to extensive coverage of its attractive and sympathetic applicant in the popular media, including in leading national newspapers.[151]

The civil society organizations that had supported and worked on the *Rodríguez* case then decided to try building on its success by seeking the adoption of a national

---

[146] Committee on the Rights of Persons with Disabilities, *General Comment No. 4 (2016) on the right to inclusive education*, UN Doc. CRPD/C/GC/4 (25 November 2016), para. 12(g).

[147] *Rodriguez, Cesar Alan contra GCBA y Otros*, sobre Amparo Número: A47249 2015/0, judgment of 24 October 2016, available online at http://public.diariojudicial.com/documentos/000/071/280/000071280.pdf: ('parecería implicar la emisión de una constancia que acredita que el actor pasó por la escuela, que estuvo allí una cantidad de años, que fue integrado pero no incluido').

[148] Ibid. ('El título que requiere el amparista es el equivalente al reconocimiento que certifique que ha culminado su proceso educativo, no meramente que estuvo en un aula, sino que incorporó los conocimientos que le fueron ofrecidos y enseñados, teniendo en cuenta su derecho constitucionalmente reconocido a la educación inclusiva.')

[149] Cámara en lo Contencioso Administrativo de la Ciudad Autónoma de Buenos Aires, *Rodríguez Cesar Alan contra GCBA y otros sobre amparo*, case A47249-2015/0 (17 March 2017).

[150] See http://acij.org.ar/despues-de-4-anos-alan-rodriguez-recibe-su-titulo-secundario/.

[151] See e.g. Zolezzi, 'No Tan Incluidos: Los Chicos Con Discapacidad, Lejos Del Título Oficial', *La Nación*, 17 March 2016, available online at http://www.lanacion.com.ar/1880367-no-tan-incluidos-los-chicos-con-discapacidad-lejos-del-titulo-oficial; 'La Justicia Ordenó Darle El Título a Un Chico Con Síndrome de Down', *La Nación*, 27 October 2016, available online at http://www.lanacion.com.ar/1950738-la-justicia-ordeno-darle-el-titulo-a-un-chico-con-sindrome-de-down; 'El Caso de Alan Reaviva La Polémica Por La Educación Inclusiva', *La Nación*, 29 March 2016, available online at http://www.lanacion.com.ar/1884127-el-caso-de-alan-reaviva-la-polemica-por-la-educacion-inclusiva; 'Después de 3 Años de Lucha, Un Joven Con Síndrome de Down Obtuvo Su Título Secundario Por Un Fallo Judicial', *La Nación*, 25 October 2016, available online at http://www.lanacion.com.ar/1950490-despues-de-3-anos-de-lucha-un-joven-con-sindrome-de-down-obtuvo-su-titulo-secundario-por-un-fallo-judicial; 'Por Una Educación Inclusiva', *La Nación*, 30 October 2016, available online at http://www.lanacion.com.ar/1951667-por-una-educacion-inclusiva.

regulation governing the conferral of titles for students with disabilities.[152] An initial degree of success was achieved with the adoption by the Federal Council of Education (CFE) of Resolution 311/16 on the Promotion, Accreditation, Certification and Titling of Students with Disabilities.[153] The Resolution opens by citing the CRPD, and Article 24 in particular, and imposes on the provinces responsible for lower and middle schools a range of obligations deriving from the principle of inclusive education. While *Grupo Artículo 24*, in its subsequent shadow report to the CRPD Committee as part of Argentina's 2017 reporting cycle, criticized certain aspects of the Resolution for not going sufficiently far in eradicating discriminatory practices,[154] other NGOs, including REDI, CELS, and FAICA in their joint shadow report, were more critical still, arguing that the Resolution continues to reflect a segregationist paradigm by requiring provinces to continue providing special education, and that it is incompatible with the CRPD.[155] In the meantime, *Grupo Artículo 24* and others are continuing to advocate publicly for the interpretation and application of Resolution 311/16 in conformity with the principles and provisions of the CRPD.[156]

The situation was exacerbated in May 2017 when the Ministry of Education adopted a further Resolution 2509 to complement Resolution 311/16, establishing guidelines for the application of its principles with the explicit goal of ensuring the effectiveness of the CRPD.[157] Five NGOs led by the *Grupo Artículo 24* and the *Asociación Civil por la Igualdad y la Justicia* brought administrative proceedings before the Ministry arguing that this second resolution was clearly incompatible with the CRPD. They argued that Resolution 2509, by acknowledging that 'those students who could not complete all their curricular studies in the general secondary education school will have to complete their school trajectory in special schools', was in breach of the state's obligation—based on Article 24 CRPD and elaborated by the CRPD Committee in General Comment 4—to establish a single school system rather than a specialized system alongside the general one.[158] They emphasized the significance of the CRPD Committee's interpretation of the Convention's obligations, and they were highly critical of the failure—which itself constituted a

---

[152] In its shadow report to the CRPD Committee in 2017, *Grupo Artículo 24* attributes the adoption of a regulation in late 2016 by the Federal Council of Education (CFE Resolution 311/16) in part to the extensive media coverage of Alan Rodriguez's case. See *Grupo Artículo 24 Report*, INT_CRPD_ICS_ARG_28478_S, at 15.

[153] Resolución CFE No 311/16 (15 December 2016), available online at https://www.argentina.gob.ar/sites/default/files/res-311-cfe-58add7585fbc4.pdf.

[154] *Grupo Artículo 24 Report*, INT_CRPD_ICS_ARG_28478_S, at 15.

[155] *Joint Report of various Argentine CSOs to the Session of the CRPD*, INT_CRPD_ICS_ARG_28578_E, at 21.

[156] See 'En Buenos Aires, los alumnos con discapacidad podrán tener su título oficial', *La Nación*, 26 February 2018, available online at https://www.lanacion.com.ar/2112102-en-buenos-aires-los-alumnos-con-discapacidad-podran-tener-su-titulo-oficial.

[157] Resolución 2509/17 del Ministerio de Educación de la Nación (31 May 2017).

[158] Note of Grupo Artículo 24 and others to the Minister of Education, Alejandro Finocchiaro (18 July 2017). 2.

breach of Article 4(3) CRPD—to consult with organizations of persons with disabilities in the drafting and adoption of Resolution 2509.[159] Notably too, in relation to the issue decided in the *Rodríguez* case, they argued that Resolution 2509 had wrongly removed from the earlier Resolution 311 the wording which required the conferral of titles on students with disabilities at all levels. In its shadow report to the CRPD Committee in August 2017 concerning Argentina's compliance with the Convention, *Grupo Artículo 24* specifically raised the issue of Resolution 2509, summarizing the claims from its complaint to the Ministry, and requesting the Committee to raise the issue with state representatives.[160] In addition, in its 'list of issues' identified for the dialogue with the state the Committee asked about the implementation of Resolution 311 to ensure inclusive education.[161] The state in its report to the Committee in 2019, however, referred only in passing to Resolution 2509 as one of the resources for implementing Resolution 311, and at the time of writing the CRPD Committee had not yet responded to the report.[162]

The *Rodríguez* case illustrates both the capacity for success of specific initiatives, given the eventually positive outcome of the litigation for his personal circumstances, but also the ongoing struggle to translate particular successes into broader policy change. It also demonstrates the breadth of activities and strategies at domestic and international level used by different parts of the disability rights movement, including participating in transnational discussions on the meaning of norms; advocating before international bodies for the applicability of these developing norms to factual contexts in Argentina. lobbying for legislative measures to implement them at the domestic level; litigating particular cases which exemplify important issues; and moving activities back and forth between the national and the international levels seeking clarification and external pressure when domestic actors are resistant to arguments for change. Ultimately, and without strong external incentives to comply, these international norms and recommendations can become effective in promoting reform when used and advocated in a way that is made persuasive to relevant domestic actors such as courts, prosecutors, public officials, parliamentarians, and others who can effect change. At times, and for particular initiatives such as the certification of education for students with disabilities, it seems this can be done without wider underlying social support, but when more extensive—and expensive—change is called for, as in the case of the pension reform, the generation of broader public support to underpin the human rights

---

[159] Ibid. 8. Article 4(3) CRPD provides: 'In the development and implementation of legislation and policies to implement the present Convention, and in other decision-making processes concerning issues relating to persons with disabilities, States Parties shall closely consult with and actively involve persons with disabilities, including children with disabilities, through their representative organizations.'

[160] *Grupo Artículo 24 Report*, INT_CRPD_ICS_ARG_28478_S, at 16.

[161] UN CRPD Committee, List of issues prior to the submission of the combined second and third periodic report of Argentina, CRPD/C/ARG/QPR/2 (8 September 2017), para. 29.

[162] Second and Third Combined Periodic Report of Argentina Under Article 35 of the Convention on the Rights of Persons With Disabilities, UN CRPD/C/ARG/2-3 (5 March 2019), Annex.

campaign seems important, if not essential. Even in the case of the issue of inclusive versus specialized education, it may have been strategically wise for *Grupo Artículo 24* to concentrate on public advocacy and on building a more extensive support base to underpin their legal and policy reform initiatives, so as to have wider resources to draw on in the case of setbacks such as Resolution 2509 discussed above.

C. The collection of information on inclusive education

In addition to campaigns and litigation on specific issues and cases such as the award of certificates and titles, or reasonable accommodation in admission to degree programmes, domestic disability advocacy groups have successfully mobilized around a broader range of issues pertaining to inclusive education, including the fundamental need for the collection and availability of adequate data on the subject in order for any serious policy reforms to be effectively pursued. Article 31 of the CRPD provides that states have an obligation 'to collect appropriate information, including statistical and research data, to enable them to formulate and implement policies to give effect to the present Convention'.

In 2013, five of the most active domestic organizations advocating for disability rights, *Grupo Artículo 24*, REDI, ACIJ, ADC, and the *Asociación Sindrom de Downe de la República de Argentina* (ASDRA), filed a request with the Ministry of Education for access to information seeking basic statistics on persons with disabilities in both special and regular schools. When the Ministry acknowledged that it did not gather such data, the organizations brought legal proceedings to demand that the government gather and present basic statistical data on the educational trajectory of those attending special schools, as well as appropriate and reliable data on the attendance of persons with disabilities at regular schools. They referred to the basis of this obligation in the CRPD and pointed to the recommendation made by the CRPD Committee to Argentina to take the necessary measures to ensure that students enrolled in special schools be incorporated into inclusive schools.[163] The CRPD Committee had previously made these recommendations to the state in response to the shadow report submitted by a group of Argentine NGOs to the Committee in 2012,[164] urging the state both to ensure the inclusion of students enrolled in special schools into the general education system with reasonable accommodation, and to 'systematize its collection, analysis and dissemination of statistics and data' on the situation of persons with disabilities.[165] The petition of

---

[163] Memorial of CSOs concerning Article 31 CRPD, at 17–18 (on file with the author).

[164] Joint Shadow Report (2017) to the CRPD Committee of various CSOs, INT_CRPD_NGO_ARG_14809_S.

[165] Committee on the Rights of Persons with Disabilities, *Concluding observations on the initial report of Argentina as approved by the Committee at its eighth session (17–28 September 2012)*, UN Doc. CRPD/C/ARG/CO/1 (8 October 2012), paras. 38 and 50.

the NGOs to the Ministry in 2013 emphasized the relationship between this lack of information on the one hand, and the substantive violation of the right to inclusive education on the other,[166] and noted the recognition of that relationship in the concluding observations of the CRPD Committee in 2012.[167]

The first instance judge hearing the legal proceedings rejected the case on procedural grounds based on the lack of urgency and manifest illegality, and the organizations appealed.[168] The prosecutor before the Court of Appeals agreed with the organizations, basing his opinion on Article 31 of the CRPD, as well as Article 13 of the American Convention on Human Rights concerning the right of access to information.[169] The appeal court also agreed and ordered the Ministry of Education in a brief ruling to take the necessary steps to collect the relevant information.[170] The Ministry's appeal against this ruling was rejected by the Supreme Court.[171]

In parallel with the domestic proceedings which invoked and relied on both the provisions of the CRPD and the Committee's observations, the NGOs also pursued the issue internationally in a range of fora before the CRPD Committee. The first such forum was in the context of a 'Day of General Discussion on the right to education for persons with disabilities' held in 2015.[172] *Grupo Artículo 24* and the ACIJ submitted two documents for discussion to the Committee on this occasion, one concerning inclusive schools and mentioning the importance of data in that respect,[173] and the other specifically on Article 31 of the Convention and the obligation to collect and make available data.[174] The exchange of information produced on the occasion of the Discussion Day was then referred to in the context of the 2017–18 reporting cycle of the Argentine Government to the CRPD Committee. The shadow report submitted for the 2017–18 cycle by *Grupo Artículo 24* made extensive reference to the issue and criticized the continuing failure of the state

---

[166] Memorial of CSOs concerning Article 31 CRPD, at 55.

[167] Ibid. para. 38: 'The Committee recommends that the State party develop a comprehensive State education policy that guarantees the right to inclusive education…'

[168] See the summary of the decision in the opinion of the prosecutor before the Court of Appeals: Fiscal General en lo Civil y Comercial Federal y en lo Contencioso Administrativo Federal, Sala en lo Cont. Adm. Fed. I, *Expte. 26.701/2015, ACIJ y otros c/Estado Nacional – Ministerio de Educación s/Amparo Ley 16.986* (28 September 2016) 1–2.

[169] Fiscal General en lo Civil y Comercial Federal y en lo Contencioso Administrativo Federal, Sala en lo Cont. Adm. Fed. I, *Expte. 26.701/2015, ACIJ y otros c/Estado Nacional – Ministerio de Educación s/ Amparo Ley 16.986* (28 September 2016) 11–12.

[170] Cámara Nacional de Apelaciones en lo Contencioso Administrativo Federal, *Expte. 26.701/2015, ACIJ y otros c/Estado Nacional – Ministerio de Educación s/Amparo Ley 16.986* (3 November 2016).

[171] Corte Suprema de Justicia de la Nación, *Asociación Civil por la Igualdad y la Justicia y otros c/ EN – MO Educación s/ amparo ley 16.986* (3 October 2017).

[172] See http://www.ohchr.org/EN/HRBodies/CRPD/Pages/DGDontherighttoeducationforpersonsw ithdisabilities.aspx.

[173] See https://acij.org.ar/wp-content/uploads/2015/03/Submission-CRPD-Grupo-Art-24-on-right-to-inclusive-education.doc.

[174] See https://acij.org.ar/wp-content/uploads/2015/03/Submission-CRPD-ACIJ-art-24-on-data-production.docx.

at the time (which was before the conclusion of the case by the Supreme Court) to produce the relevant data.[175] Subsequently, the government in 2018 responded to the court that it had included the information requested by ACIJ in its Annual Survey of Statistical Information on Education,[176] and responded to the CRPD Committee in 2019 that the Annual Survey was being improved.[177]

D. Training Public Servants on Inclusive Education

In addition to public mobilization, media campaigns, litigation strategies, and policy advocacy, disability rights advocates in Argentina have also pursued more targeted educational mechanisms such as the provision of training workshops for public servants[178]. As in Chapter 3 in relation to education on the UN Convention on the Elimination of All Forms of Discrimination against Women (CEDAW) in Pakistan, these workshops have been provided for officials in a range of different government branches, including the executive (particularly the Ministry of Education), but also the judiciary, public defenders, and prosecutors. The workshops have tried to reach officials beyond the major cities, and in parts of the country where access to NGO resources, research, and training are likely to be scarce.

The workshops organized have followed a three-part structure, the first part comprising the provision of information and the second and third parts being more participatory. They begin with a presentation by the lawyers from the relevant NGOs explaining the principles of the Convention, the standards established by the CRPD and the Committee, and the recommendations made by the treaty body to the state. The second part involves a discussion of the various barriers which impede implementation of the Convention, ranging from legal barriers such as the absence of adequate regulation or gaps in the law, to social, cultural, and attitudinal barriers within communities and government. The final part involves discussion of the more specific obstacles to the enforcement of Convention principles encountered by these officials in their daily activities. Those providing the training use the interactive sessions not only to help officials find ways of addressing such obstacles but also to gather relevant local information from those officials about the implementation process and its problems. This information is then used by the

---

[175] See https://tbinternet.ohchr.org/_layouts/15/treatybodyexternal/Download.aspx?symbolno=IN T%2fCRPD%2fICS%2fARG%2f28478&Lang=en.

[176] Note from the Government of 5 July 2018, in Asociación Civil por la Igualdad y la Justicia y otros v Estado Nacional—Ministerio de Educación s./ Amparo Ley 16986, Expediente N. 26701/2015.

[177] Second and Third Combined Periodic Report of Argentina Under Article 35 of the Convention on the Rights of Persons With Disabilities, UN CRPD/C/ARG/2-3 (5 March 2019), para. 290.

[178] The information on which section (iv) and (v) are based was provided in an interview with two staff members of the Asociación Civil por la Igualdad y la Justicia: Celeste Fernández, Coordinator of the Disabilities and Human Rights Division, and Pamela Smith Castro.

NGOs in their advocacy and lobbying at federal level, as well as in their strategic litigation agenda and in the planning of public campaigns, and for the purposes of international presentations before the CRPD Committee, the OHCHR, or the Human Rights Council.

While many of the training workshops are targeted at local officials and executives at various levels, others are provided directly to teachers and school directors. With the consent of provincial authorities, the NGOs provide interdisciplinary training sessions involving, for example, legal, educational, and psychology specialists, aimed at challenging and transforming the paradigm of disabilities which informed prior practice, and introducing the newer paradigm reflected in the CRPD. Online as well as in-person outreach is used.[179]

Perhaps surprisingly, it seems that teachers' unions have objected to the provision and success of these workshops, although this may be due to the normal resistance on the part of practitioners to change, or to a specific resistance to being told how to carry out their profession by 'experts' from the capital city.[180] More importantly and immediately, there is also an understandable fear that the implementation of inclusive education, through its inclusion of students with disabilities in regular schools, could lead to significant redundancies among special education teachers or loss of benefits that they currently enjoy.

Another source of resistance to training efforts comes from some communities of persons with disabilities themselves, reflecting the range of different views and contestation within the disability communities. Some disability rights activists interviewed for this chapter mentioned that people with hearing disabilities, for example, are wary of the inclusive education approach. Their concern is that since socialization takes place initially through language, it is extremely challenging to generate a truly inclusive environment for very young children with hearing disabilities or deafness. And since they are sceptical about the commitment of the state to date to providing such an inclusive environment, they prefer for now to maintain the special school model, and thus they challenge the inclusive education agenda.

E. Generating support and awareness through public campaigns

Another of the strategies of Argentine civil society organizations working on inclusive education has been to appeal directly to the general public through popular campaigns, seeking to widen the degree of popular support underpinning their cause. And it seems they have found that the issue of inclusive education—as

---

[179] See e.g. the 'Moodle' set up by *Grupo Artículo 24*: http://moodle.grupoart24.org/.

[180] See the interview at n. 106 above, for reference to the resistance of teachers' unions to the changing paradigm of disability rights and its implications for education.

evident in the case of Alan Rodríguez—is one that generates empathy and interest on the part of the public and in the media. Argentina's pride in public education, and the centrality of children to the issue may explain some of the receptivity of the public to the cause of inclusive education. During the course of the *Rodríguez* case, the lead NGOs not only encouraged discussion of the CRPD in media outlets, but also used social media actively and conducted a successful petition to the Minister of Education on Change.org.[181] The platform was used to post updates on the case, and to lobby authorities towards the eventual adoption of CFE Resolution 311/16 on the conferral of educational certificates and titles.[182]

The NGOs *Asociación por los Derechos Civiles* and *Grupo Artículo 24* also set up a website to make available materials and information for various stakeholders on the issue.[183] The CPRD features centrally in the website, which includes a section aimed at gathering complaints and information from people affected by possible violations of the Convention. The *Asociación Civil por la Igualdad y la Justicia* also launched a recent web project to provide detailed information about what schools can and cannot do in relation to children with disabilities, in order to inform and empower families and their children.[184] Amongst the reasons for launching the website—which provides information and model forms for people to use to challenge school or Ministry of Education decisions—was the experience of *ACIJ* and *Grupo Artículo 24* in meeting families of children with disabilities who had encountered great difficulty in finding a school that would accept their child.[185]

7. Conclusion

With an active civil society involved in aspects of both advocacy and policymaking, Argentina's ratification and incorporation of international human rights treaties since the dictatorship has in different ways catalysed and enhanced domestic mobilization for change on a range of fronts. The main examples on which this chapter has focused are different in kind from the atrocities such as disappearances and torture which first gave rise to the modern Argentine human rights movement in the 1970s. The disability rights movement today is a broad and plural one focused on a wide range of social, political, and economic injustices facing persons with disabilities, including access to public services and welfare, the right to work, inclusive education, and personal autonomy.

---

[181] See n. 135 above.
[182] See n. 153 above.
[183] See http://www.educacion-inclusiva.com.ar/.
[184] See https://www.porunaeducacioninclusiva.org/.
[185] One case involved a mother who had been rejected by 42 schools before finding one which would accept her child who had been diagnosed with mild autism.

The initial commitment made by states that adopted the UN Convention on the Rights of Persons with Disabilities to accept certain broad obligations, including the procedural and participatory provisions of the CRPD which mandate the integral involvement of persons with disabilities and their representative associations at all stages of the policy and implementation process, seems to have unleashed a powerful dynamic in the disability rights field. And while some of that dynamism may be present in other human rights issue areas where there was no such explicit participatory commitment in the relevant treaty—as evident from the child rights movement in Argentina—it is nonetheless the case that the paradigm introduced by the CRPD has been particularly successful in galvanizing and strengthening the role of relevant civil society organizations and has had a notable impact on mobilization, advocacy, and policy reform in the disability field. The examples of advocacy around inclusive education discussed in this chapter included an ongoing process of engagement and back-and-forth between national and international levels involving domestic activists, state actors and institutions, and international human rights bodies that helped to create stronger public awareness of injustices and to promote change to economic and educational practices that harmed marginalized categories of citizens.

While a variety of organizations of persons with disabilities and their advocates was already active in relation to disability issues well before the adoption of the CRPD in Argentina, the state's ratification and constitutional incorporation of that treaty galvanized many of these groups around an explicit disability rights agenda. Activists worked to build a more collective and coordinated movement, to highlight and publicize issues including that of inclusive education, to identify and advance particular cases, and to use legal and other strategies to challenge a range of injustices both in domestic and international fora. At the national level they sought and generated information from the state as well as from affected individuals and families, and attempted to educate the public and state officials on the issues facing people with disabilities, as well as mobilizing affected constituencies and their supporters. At the international level they used the treaty-body reporting process to organize collaboration amongst themselves, draft shadow reports, highlight particular issues, and generate international attention. They worked to inform and influence the jurisprudence and output of the treaty body and other human rights actors like the UN Special Rapporteur on Education or the Office of the High Commissioner on Human Rights by participating in 'discussion days' and in the drafting of influential normative documents like General Comments and reports, and to have an input into the Concluding Observations following the state reporting process. These normative sources—General Comments, Reports, and Concluding Observations—were then later invoked and relied on in domestic litigation to advance disability rights and to influence prosecutors, judges, and advocates general, as seen in the *Emiliano Naranjo* and *Alan Rodríguez* cases, leading ultimately to reforms aimed at advancing the rights of persons with disabilities in relation to access to education. The *Naranjo* and *Rodríguez* cases also highlight the fact that domestic courts can be significant institutions in supporting and promoting change, even if individual cases do not usually bring about wider reform without other sustained channels of advocacy, persuasion and pressure. The cases also highlight the fact that reform is rarely achieved through a single or discrete event, but is usually the product of an ongoing struggle and an often slow process that includes setbacks and losses rather than only successes.

Reflecting the 'nothing about us without us' motto of the disability rights movement, domestic actors such as Naranjo, Rodríguez, and their advocates have been active at the local, national, and transnational levels, invoking the ideas and principles underlying the CRPD to raise awareness and support as well as to gather information and challenge societal attitudes, policies, and practices that impede the lives of people with disabilities, or subject them to further economic and social marginalization. There is certainly no implication—contrary to what some of the critics of human rights have alleged—that an international authority or cadre of experts has imposed external rules on the state, or that a set of unaccountable actors has captured domestic institutions in order to promote special interests, or that the state was forced under powerful external pressure to comply with its treaty promises. The Argentine disability rights movement comprises a broad and diverse—though certainly not always harmonious—collection of groups which have worked in different ways to promote the rights and welfare of a significant but often neglected or excluded part of the population. Key actors within the movement have leveraged the broad international consensus around the CRPD, which had been approved and ratified by the Argentine parliament and validated further by domestic constitutional incorporation, so as to highlight injustices and to press for change. They did this by acting at both international as well as regional, national, and local levels, participating in debates about the meaning and application of the CRPD norms agreed by states through CRPD Committee observations and general comments, OHCHR studies, Special Rapporteur reports, and within other forums for normative elaboration, and by generating information and awareness at domestic level through media campaigns, political lobbying, and strategic litigation. Many of the relevant advocacy groups have been active in regional networks too, and have drawn support from other domestic and transnational NGOs and organizations working in Latin America and beyond.

The international human rights institutions and actors for their part—particularly the CRPD Committee but also other actors such as UN Special Rapporteurs and the Office of the High Commissioner for Human Rights—have provided a forum for the information and complaints brought before them by domestic advocates and constituencies, engaged in discussion and elaborated on the principles and provisions agreed under the CRPD in light of the arguments and the information brought to them through the official and shadow reporting system, and commented on and highlighted the failures and shortcomings of the state.

The third important set of actors alongside the domestic activists and their networks, and the various international institutions as well as regional and international networks, have been domestic institutions including courts, ombudspersons, parliamentarians, legislators, and media, who responded in different ways to claims and challenges brought by activists to enforce and promote these rights in various contexts. The independence and robustness of these national institutions have been important factors in the relative success of domestic disability rights mobilization strategies in promoting policy change and reform. The back-and-forth dynamic between the domestic and international and indeed regional levels cannot be characterized as mainly top-down or mainly bottom-up. There has been ongoing interaction between them, with each relying in various ways on the other. The international human rights institutions have no power of enforcement or compulsion, which means that the commitments signed onto by the states and domestically ratified and incorporated depend for their enforcement on being taken seriously by parliaments, courts, and other national institutions when activated and claimed by advocates. And the domestic advocates have been able to strengthen their arguments and the persuasiveness and traction of their claims by drawing on the normative resources of the CRPD, the widespread international consensus underpinning it, as well as the state's ratification and incorporation of that treaty. Finally, the work of domestic advocates and activists has been significantly enhanced, particularly when dealing with more contested reforms, by their cultivation of wider public support and the galvanization of a broader social movement, as occurred in the case of the pension cuts affecting persons with disabilities.

The examples described in the chapter highlight the importance of domestic advocates as well as social movements in the implementation and elaboration of human rights commitments in the Argentinian disability context and show that their actions were not confined to that of providing information and advocacy while relying primarily on external networks or institutions for enforcement. On the contrary, although international human rights institutions and actors have clearly been a significant part of the picture, the role they played can be better described as providing a focal point for information-generation and normative elaboration as well as a forum for accountability enhancement, rather than one of conventionally understood 'enforcement'. Similarly, while local and national actors within Argentina undoubtedly drew upon and mobilized international resources and networks just as the 'boomerang' model originally described, bringing issues to the attention of international monitoring bodies and preparing petitions and shadow reports to highlight problems and abuses, they have also had an important ongoing domestic role in following up on the interventions of international actors, using the outputs of international bodies at the national and local level to challenge, contest, advocate, explain, and promote change. This iterative dynamic has been evident in much of the extensive rights mobilization after the consolidation of democracy in Argentina, when the opportunities for domestic advocacy became much more expansive than they were during the period of military rule, and the opportunity to use human rights law along with other resources to press for reform was significantly enhanced. Hence, while during the 'gross phase' of human rights violations, external coercion and pressure seems to have been vital to help domestic activists in challenging abuses and bringing about change,[186] and the boomerang metaphor seems apt for this phase, once the transition to a less repressive and more democratic regime occurred, external political pressure or coercion was less prominent and less available, and the process of human rights mobilization and reform instead became a more pluralist, interactive, and long-term one involving ongoing engagement between an array of domestic, regional, and international actors and institutions.

---

[186] Brysk, 'From Above and Below' (n. 10).

5

Using international human rights law to mobilize for children's rights and reproductive rights in Ireland

1. Introduction

Drawing on the experimentalist framing of international human rights set out in Chapter 2, this chapter examines two unfolding processes of social change in Ireland over the past decades which both included the engagement of domestic advocacy groups with international human rights law as a key element of those campaigns. The first concerns the way the adoption of the Convention on the Rights of the Child catalysed social activism and transformed the treatment of child welfare policy and approaches to children's rights in Ireland. The second deals with the impact on Irish law and policy concerning reproductive rights, particularly access to abortion, of the interaction between domestic advocacy groups and a broad range of international human rights regimes and processes in their campaigns for change. The international regimes which were engaged during the reproductive rights campaign included the UN Convention on the Elimination of All Forms of Discrimination against Women (CEDAW), the International Covenant on Civil and Political Rights (ICCPR), the International Covenant on Economic Social and Cultural Rights (ICESR), the European Convention on Human Rights (ECHR), and the Council of Europe, the UN Universal Periodic Review (UPR), and the Convention against Torture (CAT), amongst others.

The two campaigns to promote children's rights and reproductive rights respectively are analysed below against the backdrop of two important features which characterized the mid-to-late twentieth century Irish constitutional system, namely, the institutionalized influence of the Catholic church on social issues including gender and the family, and Ireland's dualist approach to international law.

Ireland's modern engagement with international law began after the country achieved independence from Britain in 1922. Following a transitional period as a 'free state' and under dominion status, the current Constitution was adopted in 1937, and in 1949 the state left the British Commonwealth and formally declared itself a republic. While the Constitution was intended to mark a definitive break with Britain and to reflect the distinctiveness of the Irish state, many traces of British influence nonetheless remained; the system of common law and the dualist

Reframing Human Rights in a Turbulent Era. Gráinne de Búrca, Oxford University Press (2021). © G de Búrca.
DOI: 10.1093/oso/9780198299578.003.0005

approach to international law being two such features. Although Article 29(1) of the Constitution affirms the state's 'devotion to the ideal of peace and friendly co-operation amongst nations founded on international justice and morality', Article 29(6) provides that 'no international agreement shall be part of the domestic law of the State save as may be determined by the Oireachtas'. Hence although treaties signed by the state are binding as a matter of international law, the provisions of such treaties cannot in general be enforced in domestic courts until they are incorporated by an act of the legislature or a constitutional amendment.[1]

The 1937 Constitution also included numerous provisions that reflect the influence of the Catholic church on its drafting and on Irish society more generally.[2] This is particularly evident in the provisions governing the status and protection of the family and on the role of women and their 'life within the home'.[3] Further, while the Constitution was adopted some years before the Universal Declaration of Human Rights and does not contain a formal or separate bill of rights, Article 40 of the Constitution from the outset included protection for certain individual rights such as personal liberty and freedom of expression, assembly, and association. Article 44 protects freedom of religion and conscience, while Article 45 contains a list of non-justiciable 'guiding principles of social policy'.[4]

The combination of the influence of the church and of Catholic social thinking on provisions of the Constitution relating to women and to the family, and the dualist approach to international law—including human rights treaties—has had ongoing implications for many social issues in Ireland over the second half of the twentieth century and the beginning of the twenty-first. The influence of the Church, as also reflected in provisions of the Constitution, strongly affected societal attitudes towards the status of women, particularly as regards reproductive rights, divorce, and their role within the family. It also played an important role in the approach taken towards the position of children within the family, with a

---

[1] On the other hand, general principles of international law and customary international law can become part of Irish law through practice, although they do not have primacy over Irish law, whether statutory or constitutional. For a discussion see Symonds, 'The Incorporation of Customary International Law into Irish Law', 31 *Irish Jurist* (1996) 165. For a broad summary of the status of international law in Ireland, see the note prepared by the research service of the Irish Parliament, the Oireachtas, available online at https://www.oireachtas.ie/parliament/media/housesoftheoireachtas/libraryresearch/lrsnotes/LRSNoteInternationalLaw_121942.pdf.

[2] For an account of the drafting which includes a nuanced discussion of the role of important figures from the Catholic Church, see D. Keogh and A. McCarthy, *The Making of the Irish Constitution 1937* (2007). See also O Tuama, 'Revisiting the Irish Constitution and De Valera's Grand Vision', 2 *Irish Journal of Legal Studies* (2011) 54.

[3] Article 41.2.1 of the Irish Constitution provides: 'In particular, the State recognizes that by her life within the home, woman gives to the State a support without which the common good cannot be achieved'. For an account of opposition by Irish women to this and other aspects of the 1937 Constitution affecting women, see Luddy, 'A "Sinister and Retrogressive Proposal": Irish Women's Opposition to the 1937 Draft Constitution', 15 *Transactions of the Royal Historical Society* (2005) 175.

[4] Amongst other things, Article 45 provides that the state 'shall strive to promote the welfare of the whole people' and 'pledges itself to safeguard with especial care the economic interests of the weaker sections of the community'.

marked emphasis on the authority of parents rather than on the rights of the child. Articles 41 and 42 of the Constitution at the time of their drafting firmly established the authority and primacy of the family 'as the necessary basis of social order', and emphasized the 'inalienable right' of parents to educate their children.[5] Overall, and despite a general provision referring to the imprescriptible rights of the child and a specific provision referring to the right of children to a public education free of religious instruction, the emphasis of the constitutional provisions as adopted, and also the pre-existing social reality that they reflected and enshrined, was firmly on the autonomy of the family unit and on the authority of parents, rather than on finding ways to protect the rights of children.

While it might be assumed that a children's rights agenda, particularly today, is less likely to be socially controversial or highly politicized in the way reproductive rights often are, advocacy for children's rights nonetheless remains a socially divisive topic in various contexts. The Bulgarian government in 2019, for example, under strong pressure from a conservative social movement campaigning for 'traditional family values', withdrew its rights-based National Child Strategy 2019–2030.[6] Religious and conservative groups argued that parents should have the right to physically discipline their children, alleging that the Strategy aimed to diminish the rights of parents, and rather than rebutting these claims, the government chose to withdraw the Strategy.[7] This is one instance of a wider backlash in various parts of the world against what is depicted as 'gender ideology' and which has visible implications for laws against domestic violence, promoting child welfare, governing reproductive rights, the situation of transgender persons, and much more, across Europe and elsewhere.[8]

It is certainly true that both children's rights and reproductive rights have, in different ways, been the site of social and political contestation in Ireland over the past three decades or more. The case studies described below illustrate the changes that have come about in these two issue areas, and the role that an array of international human rights norms, institutions, and processes has played in supporting and reinforcing the campaigns for political and legal change waged by domestic activists. While the initial impetus for change came from domestic groups with a strong interest or stake in the outcome, ongoing pressure from and engagement with

---

[5] Article 41.1 provides: 'The State recognizes the Family as the natural primary and fundamental unit group of Society, and as a moral institution possessing inalienable and imprescriptible rights, antecedent and superior to all positive law'.

[6] See D. Petrova, *Being BOLD in difficult times: Bulgarians organizing for liberal democracy'*, Open Global Rights, 3 April 2020, available online at https://www.openglobalrights.org/being-bold-in-difficult-times-bulgarians-organizing-for-democracy/.

[7] For criticism of these allegations as factually inaccurate and distorted, see the NGO Eurochild, *Child Rights under Attack in Bulgaria*, 27 May 2019.

[8] See *Anti Gender Movements on the Rise? Strategizing for gender equality in Central and Eastern Europe*, Heinrich Boll Stiftung, Publication Series on Democracy No. 38 (2015). Also Corredor, 'Unpacking "Gender Ideology" and the Global Right's Antigender Countermovement', 44 *Signs: Journal of Women in Culture and Society* (2019) 613.

international human rights institutions and actors has helped to bolster domestic activists and their advocacy. In some instances—as was seen also in relation to the coalition of child rights advocacy groups in Argentina described in Chapter 4[9]—the initial formation or coalescence of such groups was catalysed by the enactment of a human rights treaty, and by the opportunity offered by human rights treaty review to generate input into domestic reform processes.

Treaty bodies such as the Convention on the Rights of the Child (CRC), CEDAW, ICESR, and ICCPR committees, as well as Special Rapporteurs, Commissioners of the Council of Europe, and the European Court of Human Rights were amongst the international bodies called on both by individuals and by NGOs and others to respond to a range of incidents and claims. In the case of reproductive rights, a series of dramatic and distressing individual cases which were brought to international human rights bodies helped to generate public awareness and build a wider social movement as well as enhancing domestic political pressure. In the case of children's rights, on the other hand, ongoing advocacy and repeated engagement with one particular international human rights treaty body by a coalition of committed NGOs helped over time to bring about a series of important policy reforms. The various international bodies and actors, in addition to generating publicity and placing an onus on the state to respond, also articulated and reinforced the standards set by international human rights norms, interpreting these in the context of the issues and claims brought before them by individuals, NGOs, and state actors. Their statements and outputs in their turn were used and leveraged domestically by activists to build social support, to increase political pressure, and to litigate, advocate, and mobilize further for change.

2. Ireland and international human rights law

While the 1937 Constitution enshrines a number of specific individual rights, and the Irish courts at various stages added further 'unenumerated' rights to these,[10] Ireland's integration of international human rights instruments was initially less than fulsome. The Universal Declaration on Human Rights was adopted in 1948, and Ireland was an early ratifier of the European Convention on Human Rights (ECHR) upon its adoption in 1950. In terms of implementing the rulings of the Court of Human Rights, which found it to be in violation of the Convention,

---

[9] See Chapter 4 and the analysis provided by Grugel and Peruzzotti, 'Grounding Global Norms in Domestic Politics: Advocacy Coalitions and the CRC in Argentina', 42 *Journal of Latin American Studies* (2010) 29.

[10] The famous early case in which a doctrine of unenumerated rights was originally articulated was *Ryan v. Attorney General* [1965] Irish Reports 294. Following a series of other expansive judgments, later cases indicated a more cautious approach See e.g. *TD v. Minister for Education* [2000] 3 Irish Reports 66. For a recent analysis see O Mahony, 'Unenumerated Rights? Possible Future Directions after NHV', 41 *Dublin University Law Journal* (2019) available at SSRN: https://ssrn.com/abstract=3084619.

Ireland has been reasonably compliant,[11] with the exception of a number of high-profile cases where the process of compliance was long drawn out or only partial.[12] Nevertheless, despite prompt ratification and a general inclination to comply with specific rulings against it, Ireland waited a full 50 years before incorporating the ECHR into domestic law, which it did by adopting the European Convention on Human Rights Act of 2003. In so doing, Ireland became the last member state of the Council of Europe to incorporate the Convention into domestic law, and hence to render its provisions justiciable before domestic courts, rather than merely binding on the international plane.[13]

As far as the major UN human rights treaties are concerned, Ireland has by now signed and ratified most of these, including the two Covenants on Civil and Political Rights and on Economic, Social and Cultural Rights, as well as CEDAW, the Convention on the Elimination of Racism (CERD), the Convention on the Rights of the Child (CRC), and most recently the Convention on the Rights of Persons with Disabilities (CRPD). Nevertheless, the state was far from being one of the early ratifiers of these international instruments. The two Covenants, adopted by the UN in 1976, were not ratified by Ireland until 13 years later in 1989. CERD, adopted by the UN in 1969, was not ratified by Ireland until 31 years later in 2000. The Convention against Torture, adopted by the UN in 1987, was not ratified by Ireland until 15 years later in 2002. The two international human rights treaties most rapidly ratified by the state were CEDAW in 1985, four years after its adoption, and the Convention on the Rights of the Child in 1992, three years after its adoption. The Convention on the Rights of Persons with Disabilities was ratified by Ireland in 2018, 10 years after its adoption by the UN, making Ireland the very last of the 28 EU member states at the time (including the UK) to ratify it.

Further, none of the UN human rights treaties has been incorporated into Irish law, thus formally limiting the extent to which they can be relied on domestically, particularly before national courts. In the words of one close observer, Ireland's approach to international human rights treaties has been at best respectable, but reveals:

an air of official complacency, demonstrated by . . . the relatively slow pace of ratification of most of the treaties and reluctance to do so in respect of others; the almost blanket refusal to incorporate UN treaties into domestic law; delays in

---

[11] Suzanne Egan and Adrian Forde characterize Ireland's response as 'obedient albeit often slow and reluctant'. See Egan and Forde, 'From Judgment to Compliance: Domestic Implementation of the Judgments of the Strasbourg Court', in S. Egan, L. Thornton, and J. Walsh (eds), *Ireland and the European Convention on Human Rights: 60 Years and Beyond* (2014), at 17–18.

[12] See Paris, 'The European Convention on Human Rights Act: Implementation Mechanisms and Compliance', in S. Egan (ed.), *International Human Rights: Perspectives from Ireland* (2016) 91.

[13] For a collection on the impact of the ECHR in Ireland 60 years after its adoption, see S. Egan, L. Thornton, and J. Walsh (eds), *About Ireland and the European Convention on Human Rights: 60 Years and Beyond* (2014).

submitting periodic reports; and above all, a disinclination to implement treaty body recommendations, absent a clear political incentive to do so emanating from the domestic landscape.[14]

Egan goes on to point out that Ireland's delay in ratifying treaties and its reluctance to incorporate them is the consequence of an official policy that treaties should not be ratified until domestic law is already in compliance with their terms, and of the related view that incorporation into domestic legislation becomes effectively unnecessary at that stage since domestic law is already believed to be fully compliant.[15]

Ireland's approach to international human rights treaties thus reveals a fairly static understanding of their role and function that can be summarized as follows: human rights treaties establish clear norms and domestic law should be brought into compliance with those norms in order to enable the state to ratify such treaties. Once ratified, however, the role of a human rights treaty is seen as being purely external and declaratory, serving as primarily a reminder of the standards previously set and as a buffer against regression, but without relevance for any evolution of domestic legal norms and practice.

In contrast with the static image on which the Irish state's approach to international human rights law is based, however, the case studies in this chapter point to a much more dynamic role for international human rights treaty systems in practice due to their activation by domestic actors. It is clear from developments in the field of child rights and reproductive rights that even when human rights treaties are not incorporated and hence not formally justiciable before national courts, the engagement between social movements, activists and NGOs, government officials, and human rights monitoring mechanisms and institutions as regards how a particular treaty is being implemented or not in the domestic context is, to use Robert Cover's famous term, a jurisgenerative practice. Far from being a static buffer, the human rights treaty regime offers a forum in which issues and claims are regularly raised, rights norms are asserted, debated, contested, interpreted, and applied to new and changing situations as they arise. And while the dynamism within the system is in large part a function of the energy and resources of the relevant domestic advocates and social actors and groups, their activism is at times strengthened, reinforced, and channelled by the international institutions with which they engage, and which supply a forum for accountability and pressure from above.

The children's rights case study focuses primarily on the engagement of civil society organizations with two international human rights processes: the Convention on the Rights of the Child (CRC) and the treaty body that oversees its

---

[14] Egan, 'The UN Human Rights Treaty System', in S. Egan (ed.), *International Human Rights: Perspectives from Ireland* (2015), at 77.
[15] Ibid. 81.

implementation, the Committee on the Rights of the Child, as well as the Universal Periodic Review of the UN Human Rights Council, over the decades since the CRC was signed and ratified. The reproductive rights case study on the other hand examines a highly contested and turbulent social terrain in Ireland and the change that was brought about over several decades through the gradual mobilization of domestic organizations and groups, including their engagement with a wide range of human rights institutions and forums including the ECHR, CEDAW, ICCPR, ICESR, CRC, and UPR amongst others. Unlike the children's rights arena in which a reasonable number of child advocacy organizations already existed and rapidly coalesced into a strong and effective alliance following the ratification of the CRC, reproductive rights advocacy in Ireland emerged and gained traction much more slowly, and consisted initially of a very small group of organizations. The mobilization of an anti-abortion movement for constitutional change in the 1980s had the effect of precipitating a series of incidents and cases involving 'an alphabet' of women and girls (since the most prominent were known by the initials X, Y, D, A, B, and C) who were restricted from access to abortion in circumstances that gave rise to shock and social outrage. It was mainly in response to this set of incidents that a broader and stronger reproductive rights movement gradually developed in Ireland. Both of these movements—for child rights and for reproductive rights—became central, albeit in different ways and to different degrees, in galvanizing social reform and used their ongoing engagement with the international and European human rights systems as an important part of the strategy to promote political and legal change.

3. Case study 1: children's rights reform

The UN Convention on the Rights of the Child was adopted in 1989. Perhaps reflecting the perception of the treaty at the time, before the subsequent rise of the anti-'gender ideology' movement, as a politically unobjectionable instrument underpinned by fairly broad-based and near-global consent, it rapidly became one of the most extensively ratified human rights treaties, achieving near-universal ratification with 196 parties. Ireland, as noted above, ratified the treaty just three years after its adoption. Declaring itself committed to achieving the 'maximum protection possible for the rights of all children', the state ratified the Convention without entering any reservations.[16]

While a number of groups and organizations dedicated to the welfare of children was already in existence in Ireland by this time, the adoption and ratification of the CRC catalysed the creation of a coalition of several of these under the

---

[16] Initial Report of Ireland to the Committee on the Rights of the Child of 17 June 1996, UN Doc. CRC/C/11/Add.12, at para. 3.

umbrella of the Children's Rights Alliance.[17] Founded in 1993, the year following Ireland's ratification of the Convention, the coalition initially consisted of 11 organizations which came together to explore the possibility of working collectively to promote the implementation of the Convention in Ireland. The Coalition was initially a small enterprise, funded by grants from a number of foundations and philanthropic organizations, but grew significantly over time. Currently, it comprises over 100 organizations, and has been a central and influential actor in the move to reform child policy in Ireland in the direction of a rights-based approach.

Shortly before the creation of the Children's Rights Alliance, a prominent lawyer named Catherine McGuinness (who later became a Supreme Court judge) had chaired an investigation into a case known as the Kilkenny incest case, in which a young girl had been systematically raped, abused, impregnated, and beaten by her father for over 16 years despite having multiple contacts with social and health services during that time. When her account was eventually believed and her abuser was prosecuted, he received only a short jail sentence for the years of violence and abuse he had inflicted. In response to a public outcry, the government announced an investigation into the case, to be chaired by Catherine McGuinness. In her eventual report, she pointed amongst other things to the Supreme Court's interpretation of the Constitution's provisions on the rights of children 'as a member of a family', which in her view 'seems to render it constitutionally impermissible to regard the welfare of the child as the first and paramount consideration in any dispute as to its upbringing or custody between parents and third parties such as health boards without first bringing into consideration the constitutional rights of the family'.[18] McGuinness's view was shared by many others within the children's rights movement, and it underpinned their advocacy for an amendment to the Constitution in this regard and for many related legislative and policy changes.

A. Ireland's first review before the Committee on the Rights of the Child 1998

Ireland's first report to the Committee on the Rights of the Child was made in 1996, four years after ratification of the Convention. This report, as is typical of government reports to human rights treaty bodies, presented a largely positive picture of the extent to which Ireland was in compliance with the requirements of the Convention and the steps that had been taken to implement it, even while acknowledging areas—including child abuse, homelessness, and treatment of juvenile offenders—where there was room for improvement.[19] The government

---

[17] https://www.childrensrights.ie/.

[18] Kilkenny Incest Investigation Report of May 1993, at 30-31.

[19] For a criticism of the extent to which Ireland's (second) report to the CRC Committee presented a mostly positive picture, see Kiersey and Hayes, 'Reporting the Rhetoric, Implementation of the

pointed out that while the family enjoyed special protection under the Irish Constitution, following a number of high-profile abuse cases Irish law had recently begun to move away from the view of children as the property of their parents and towards viewing them as separate persons with autonomous rights distinct from the family.[20] The report presented the 1991 Child Care Act as part of this shift, asserting that it reflected the guiding principles of the Convention and the best interests of the child, and mentioning also the recent creation of a junior ministry with special responsibility for children within the departments of health, education, and justice. Much of this first state report was taken up with the issue of child abuse and measures to counter it, given the prominence of the issue in the country at the time.

As discussed in the preceding chapters, what makes the human rights treaty body system operate as an accountability mechanism rather than an opportunity for public self-congratulation by states is the role of civil society and others in bringing alternative information to light, challenging the accounts of governments in the form of shadow reports, and proposing a clear and demanding version of what the treaty provisions require in the circumstances. However, as was also the case in relation to the first review of Pakistan by the CEDAW committee discussed in Chapter 3, and the first review of Argentina by the CRPD Committee discussed in Chapter 4, the mobilization of Irish civil society around the review process of the Convention on the Rights of the Child did not happen immediately, but rather developed gradually over time. The number of alternative reports on the occasion of Ireland's first review by the Committee on the Rights of the Child was very low, with just one shadow report being submitted. This report was submitted by the Children's Rights Alliance which, having begun as a grouping of just 11 organizations in 1993, comprised over 60 organizations by the time of submission of this report in 1997.[21]

The shadow report challenged the positive account of the government in various ways. An overarching criticism was the lack of a coordinated governmental approach to children's rights across policy areas, the lack of any national implementation plan or strategy for the Convention, and the failure to incorporate protection for children's rights into the Constitution, as had been recommended by an earlier constitutional review group. The fact that the minister for children was a junior ministry without membership of the cabinet and which remained dependent on other ministries to raise issues in cabinet, and the absence of an independent body

United Nations Convention on the Rights of the Child as Represented in Ireland's Second Report to the UN Committee on the Rights of the Child: a Critical Discourse Analysis' 16 *Child Care in Practice* (2010) 327.

[20] Initial State Report (n. 16) 7.

[21] Children's Rights Alliance, *Small Voices: Vital Rights*, Submission to the UN Committee on Rights of the Child (1997), available online at https://www.childrensrights.ie/sites/default/files/submissions_reports/files/ShadowReportSmallVoices97_0.pdf.

such as an Ombudsman to monitor implementation of the Convention and coordination across government, was also criticized. Other issues raised as matters of concern were the situation of children in poverty, the situation of children with disabilities (including the lack of inclusive education), child homelessness, the situation of children at risk and abused (including the lack of adequate statistics), the juvenile justice system and the situation of children in detention, the need to raise the age of criminal responsibility, and the need to abolish 'reformatory' and 'industrial' schools.[22]

The response of the Committee in its concluding observations at the end of the session pointed to many of the issues which had been highlighted in the shadow report's concerns and recommendations, particularly those focused on systemic issues such as integrating protection for children's rights into the Constitution, adopting a national strategy for children, establishing a single body to coordinate and protect children's rights, establishing an Ombudsman for Children office, and improving data collection.[23] Specific issues on which the concluding observations focused included the reduction of poverty, access to services for disadvantaged groups, corporal punishment and child abuse, juvenile justice, children's participation in decision making, the rights of children with disabilities, and addressing the mental health of children. It seems quite clear that the issues raised by the civil society alliance influenced many of the recommendations of the Committee to the state following the review.

B. Ireland's second review before the Committee on the Rights of the Child 2005

The second review of Ireland's implementation of the CRC took place almost a decade after the first, providing an opportunity to review and appraise any progress or positive reform which had taken place over the period since the first review, and in response to it. The government's report was submitted in 2005, a full six years after it was due.[24] It was put together by a new National Children's Office which had been established following the first CRC review, and had been made responsible for improving the coordination of children's services and for implementing a National Children's Strategy. The report came after a period of strong economic

---

[22] These institutions, now referred to as Children Detention Schools, were first established in the nineteenth century in England and Ireland. Reformatory schools were for children who had been convicted of criminal offences, while Industrial schools were supposed to be for children who were destitute or vagrant. They were notoriously strict and harsh and children were susceptible to abuse and neglect.

[23] UN Committee on the Rights of the Child, *Concluding Observations*, UN Doc. CRC/C/15/Add.85 (1998).

[24] *Second Report of Ireland to the Committee on the Rights of the Child*, UN Doc. CRC/C/IRL/2 (9 December 2005).

growth for Ireland (colloquially referred to as the 'Celtic tiger' period), and the government made reference to the fact that this had allowed for significant investment in children's services and policies. It emphasized the importance of the 10-year National Children's Strategy as a cross-governmental response adopted following consultation with a wide array of stakeholders including civil society groups, parents, children, and academics, and which included representatives of many of these stakeholder groups on its advisory council. The adoption of the strategy and the consultative process preceding it was presented by the government as a response to the concerns of the CRC committee in its first review about insufficient involvement of the non-governmental sector in the promotion and development of children's rights.

The state report went on to detail many of the functions and achievements of the newly created national Children's Office, and many of the initiatives which had followed from the adoption of a National Children's Strategy, including the decision to establish an independent Ombudsman for Children in 2002. The establishment of a Children's Ombudsman had been one of the major objectives of the Children's Rights Alliance when it was first established to promote the implementation of the CRC.[25] According to the government's report, the new Ombudsman for Children's Office was created to ensure an independent mechanism to 'vindicate the rights of children' as required under the CRC. The Ombudsman's office was given power to investigate complaints on behalf of children and to engage in children's rights awareness campaigns.[26]

Apart from these structural and institutional changes, Ireland's report also listed a range of legislative initiatives relevant to the welfare and rights of children in relation to education (including education for children with disabilities), children in conflict with the law, and children in need of special care. The report announced a reduction in child poverty, increased investment in child protection and preventative family support services, and a review which had been undertaken of the Child Abuse Guidelines to reflect the provisions of the Convention.[27] In addition to presenting positive developments, the government acknowledged continuing concern about child obesity, high rates of suicide, and harmful use of alcohol and drug abuse.

---

[25] The institution of an independent Ombudsman for children seems to have originated in Norway, which created such an office in 1981 and versions of that model have since spread to many other jurisdictions, in part under the influence of the recommendation of the Committee on the Rights of the Child in its General Comment No. 2 The Role of Independent National Human Rights Institutions, CRC/GC/2002/2. For an early discussion, see Melton, 'Lessons from Norway: The Children's Ombudsman as a Voice for Children', 23 *Case Western Reserve Journal of International Law* (1991) 197.

[26] The Office established by the Ombudsman for Children Act 2002. See https://www.oco.ie/about-us/.

[27] For the current version of these guidelines, see https://www.tusla.ie/uploads/content/Children_First_National_Guidance_2017.pdf.

Supplementing and in some respects challenging the state report, four shadow reports were submitted to the CRC committee during this second review cycle. The Children's Rights Alliance, which had submitted the sole shadow report during the first cycle, submitted two on this occasion. Comprising by this stage over 80 organizations working with and on the issue of children in Ireland, the Alliance submitted one substantial and comprehensive report covering each cluster of rights under the Convention,[28] and a second report compiled (with the support of the Alliance) by children living in Ireland.[29] Two further shadow reports were submitted by independent human rights monitoring bodies, the first by the newly established Ombudsman for Children's Office, and the second by the Irish Human Rights Commission.

The main report of the Children's Rights Alliance agreed with the government that the most significant advances in relation to children's rights were the adoption of the National Children's Strategy and the array of structural and institutional changes it introduced. But the Alliance was critical of the Strategy for being neither rights-based nor a strategy for implementing the Convention. The shadow report suggested that the government was deliberately hesitant about adopting a rights-based approach for fear of incurring excessive funding obligations,[30] and criticized the government for failure to take action on many of the recommendations made by the CRC Committee following the first review. The report was also critical of the continued fragmentation of responsibility for children's issues across government departments, and of the fact that the new Minister for Children still had no automatic right to attend cabinet meetings. While the creation of the Ombudsman for Children was welcomed, the Alliance was very critical of the fact that children in detention were excluded from making complaints to the Ombudsman. Other recommendations made in the report were—again—to include children's rights within the Irish Constitution, given that the protection afforded at the time to the family by the Constitution emphasized the authority of the family over the rights of children and limited the enactment of progressive legislation for children. The same recommendation for constitutional incorporation was made in the shadow reports of the Ombudsman for Children and the Irish Human Rights Commission to the CRC Committee. Various other recommendations made by the Alliance report included reform of the family law system including addressing the lack of representation of children in court cases affecting them, juvenile justice, and child protection. Areas of concern mentioned were vulnerable child groups including asylum seekers, migrants, and Travellers, who were particularly affected by poverty, accommodation problems, and difficulties in accessing health and

---

[28] Children's Rights Alliance, *From Rhetoric to Rights: Second Shadow Report to the United Nations Committee on the Rights of the Child* (2006).

[29] Children's Rights Alliance, *Our Voices Our Realities: A Report to the United Nations Committee on the Rights of the Child by Children Living in Ireland* (2006).

[30] *From Rhetoric to Rights* (n. 28) at 3, para. 17.

educational services. The chronic under-funding of services in the area of mental health was also noted and criticized.

The Alliance's second shadow report, compiled by children living in Ireland through workshops and consultations, raised a number of additional issues such as the need to listen to children, and like the main shadow report, gave particular emphasis to the issue of poverty and issues of access for children with disabilities. The report of the Ombudsman for Children's Office focused particularly on the limitations and exclusions placed on the Ombudsman's powers of investigation, including the provision preventing the investigation of children detained in prisons or police stations.[31] The Ombudsman was also prevented at the time, under the terms of the Act establishing the Office, from investigating the police, the Defence Forces, and 'any action taken in the administration of the law relating to asylum, immigration, naturalisation or citizenship'. The shadow report argued that these exclusions and restrictions removed some of the most vulnerable children and young people in the State from the Ombudsman's investigatory remit.[32]

The fourth of the shadow reports, submitted by the Irish Human Rights Commission, reinforced several of the issues highlighted in the Children's Rights Alliance report. It focused on children in the criminal justice system, trafficking, poverty, family reunification, and vulnerable groups, including particularly Travellers, children with disabilities, and children from religious minorities or non-religious groups.

Following the dialogue with the state, the CRC Committee in its response issued a long series of recommendations to Ireland.[33] Tracking many of the concerns identified in the shadow reports, the Committee criticized the continuing lack of a rights-based approach to child policy and practice, including in the National Children's Strategy, and recommended that the provisions limiting the scope of the Ombudsman for Children's investigative powers be reviewed. Some of the other Committee recommendations that reinforced criticisms and proposals made in the shadow reports included: integrating children's rights into the Constitution; extending privacy to all legal proceedings involving children; adopting a rights-based framework for addressing the needs of children with disabilities; recognizing the Traveller community as an ethnic group and sensitizing teachers to Travellers' issues; bringing policy and procedure on child refugees into line with international standards; developing a child abuse prevention strategy; enhancing access to reproductive and sexual health information and services; and ensuring that children with mental health difficulties could benefit from appropriate services.

---

[31] Ombudsman for Children, *Report of the Ombudsman for Children to the UN Committee on the Rights of the Child on the occasion of the examination of Ireland's Second Report to the Committee* (2006) 12.

[32] Ibid. 11.

[33] UN Committee on the Rights of the Child, *Concluding Observations: Ireland*, UN Doc. CRC/C/IRL/CO/2 (2006).

Hence the second review, characterized by the active involvement of civil society groups and independent human rights organizations interacting with state actors and the Committee members, both highlighted some of the reforms that had been introduced since the first CRC review—including major structural and institutional reforms like the introduction of a National Children's Strategy, a stronger ministry for children to coordinate child policy issues across government, and the introduction of an Ombudsman for Children Office—and also drew attention to ongoing problems across a range of specific issue areas as well as a more general reluctance to embrace the implications of a rights-based framework for child policy.

C. Ireland's third review before the Committee on the Rights of the Child 2015

Ireland's next report to the CRC Committee was a combined third and fourth report submitted in 2013, eight years after the previous one.[34] On this occasion, civil society groups, including the Children's Alliance, were consulted by the government during the drafting of the report and the report indicates that various revisions were made in response to the proposals made and comments received from the Alliance on earlier drafts.

Unlike the Celtic Tiger context of the earlier report, this time the state's submission took place following a major recession which had brought rising unemployment and widespread public expenditure cuts. The government's report acknowledged the impact of the recession and the cuts on child welfare, and particularly on the welfare of children within vulnerable families with single parents or ill or disabled parents, and the significant increase in the number of children living in poverty. Further, the state report acknowledged other 'emerging areas of concern', some of which had been identified by previous shadow reports, including child trafficking, childhood obesity, the need to address literacy and numeracy.

Nevertheless, the government led by seeking to highlight positive reforms which had taken place since the second review, as well as reforms which were pending such as the establishment of a statutory Child and Family Agency to reform the delivery of child protection services in the state.

Key amongst the reforms which had been introduced since the previous CRC review—following persistent pressure over the years from the Child Rights Alliance to enhance the status of the junior ministry—was the creation of a Department of Children and Youth Affairs, with full cabinet status. The second major initiative, which had long been advocated by civil society groups and human rights bodies, was the holding of a Constitutional referendum on children's rights in 2012. The

---

[34] Department of Children and Youth Affairs, *Ireland's Consolidated Third and Fourth Report to the UN Committee on the Rights of the Child* (2013).

referendum to introduce the amendment, which amongst other things recognized the 'natural and imprescriptible rights of children' and required the best interests of the child to be a paramount consideration in judicial and custody proceedings, passed with a vote of 58 per cent despite a relatively low turnout, and despite criticism of the government campaign by the Referendum Commission as well as by the Supreme Court following a legal challenge to the result.[35]

On the occasion of the third review, there was a further increase again in the number of alternative reports: rising from one in the first cycle in 1998, to four during the second cycle in 2005, and to nine in the combined third and fourth cycles in 2013. This points to the continuing increase in the engagement of civil society with the treaty body process over time. In this instance, six shadow reports were submitted by civil society organizations: two from the Children's Rights Alliance (one in conjunction with UNICEF, to reflect the voices of children); one from an organization representing Travellers and Roma; one from a reproductive rights organization; and two from international NGOs focusing on specific issues (one on the abolition of corporal punishment, and the other on the prohibition of non-consensual medical treatment on intersex children). Three further reports from independent human rights institutions were submitted to the CRC Committee, two by the Ombudsman for Children Office, and one by the Irish Human Rights and Equality Commission.

The most comprehensive shadow report was that submitted by the Children's Rights Alliance. Once again, while recognizing the various positive reforms that had taken place since the previous review including the amendment of the Constitution, the report was critical of the limitations of the new constitutional provision, including the delay in acting on it and the fact that many of the positive consequences to flow from it would require action by the legislature.[36] The report also commended the creation of the Department of Children and Youth Affairs and the post of minister for children and youth affairs with full cabinet status, as well as the creation of the Tulsa Child and Family Agency, while warning of the need to resource these new institutions properly. The new follow-on National Policy Framework for Children and Young People was also commended, with the Alliance report noting that 17 of the commitments of the new strategy reflected

---

[35] *McCrystal v. Minister for Children and Youth Affairs* [2012] 2 Irish Reports 726; and Referendum Commission *Report on the Referendum on the 31st Amendment to the Constitution (Children) Bill 2012* (2013).

[36] The Constitutional referendum has come in for substantial criticism on a range of grounds, including lack of clarity about what exactly it was designed to achieve, what wording would be necessary to achieve this; and the campaign that took place prior to the referendum has also been criticized. See O'Mahony, 'Falling Short of Expectations: The 2012 Children Amendment, from Drafting to Referendum', 31 *Irish Political Studies* (2016) 252, Doyle and Kenny, 'Constitutional Change and Interest Group Politics: Ireland's Children's Rights Referendum', in R. Albert, X. Contiades, and A. Fotiadou, *The Foundations and Traditions of Constitutional Amendment* (2017). See also the Referendum Commission report and Supreme Court ruling at n. 35 and text.

outstanding recommendations from the Concluding Observations of the CRC Committee in earlier reviews.

However, the Alliance report was highly critical of various other aspects of child policy and the situation of children in Ireland despite the various reforms introduced since the previous review. In particular, the situation of children living in poverty—a growing number, and with a substantial number also at risk of poverty—was emphasized, as was the treatment and situation of asylum-seeker children and especially those living in 'direct provision' (a system of state-funded accommodation initially introduced as an emergency but which became institutionalized and semi-permanent for many families). Amongst the reforms recommended was to increase the payment to such children, providing self-contained units to families with recreational space, and extending the remit of the Office of the Ombudsman for Children to include the examination of complaints from children in direct provision. The state of child and adolescent mental health services also came in for substantial criticism, in the absence of any clear legal entitlement to mental health care for children, the excessive length of waiting lists, the absence of any policy to guide the transition from child to adult mental health service, and the insufficiency of safeguards. The Alliance report recommended reforms to the Mental Health Act 2001 to address these. A range of other issues that came in for continued criticism in the report included: discrimination in school admissions; racism; infant mortality; gender recognition; children in court; backlogs in child protection referrals; domestic violence; sexual exploitation and abuse; corporal punishment; guardianship; special care; aftercare; children with disabilities; obesity; education; bullying; Traveller and Roma children; the sale, trafficking, and abduction of children; and juvenile justice.

The Children's Rights Alliance's second report was prepared in conjunction with UNICEF Ireland to present the voices of children and was compiled by holding workshops, visiting schools, creating online surveys, and collecting submissions.[37] The range of issues included the importance of listening to young people, the levels of stress experienced by children, bullying, exams, mental health, the environment, the education system, poverty, and inequality.

The two remaining specific single-issue domestic shadow reports dealt with the situation of Traveller and Roma children on the one hand, and abortion rights on the other hand. The first of these focused on the areas of greatest discrimination faced by Traveller and Roma children, mainly health, welfare and education, and noted also the lack of reliable data collection and the failure to disaggregate data according to ethnicity, thereby making it difficult to formulate policy reform.[38]

---

[37] Children's Rights Alliance, *Picture Your Rights* (2015).
[38] Pavee Point, *Irish Traveller and Roma Children Shadow Report: A Response to Ireland's Consolidated Third and Fourth Report to the UN Committee on the Rights of the Child* (2015).

The impact of cuts on the sector, including through the abolition of the National Consultative Committee on Racism, the extreme poverty faced by Roma children, the problem of racial profiling, access to social security and childcare, educational disadvantages, and the failure to recognize Travellers as a distinct minority ethnic group were also highlighted.

The Abortion Rights Alliance submitted the second of the targeted shadow reports, outlining how Ireland's highly restrictive laws criminalize abortion and do not respect the right to physical and mental health of girls and young women.[39] The report criticized the Protection of Life During Pregnancy Act 2013, arguing that it did not fulfil Ireland's obligations either under international human rights law or under the Irish Constitution as interpreted by the Supreme Court in key case law.[40] The report also pointed to the state's failure to provide comprehensive education on sexuality and relationships, and called on the state to ensure that all young women, including asylum seekers, undocumented girls, and girls with disabilities have access to reproductive health information, and that relationship and sexuality programs be delivered in all schools.

The last of the two civil society shadow reports were submitted by international non-governmental organizations. The International Intersex Human Rights NGO in its shadow report argued that the government should introduce legislation to ensure that no child or infant is subject to non-consensual and unnecessary medical or surgical treatment, and to guarantee the autonomy and self-determination of the child.[41] The Global Initiative to End All Corporal Punishment of Children submitted a one page report welcoming the abolition of the criminal law defence of 'reasonable chastisement' and recommending that all measures be taken to ensure the implementation of a prohibition on corporal punishment in Ireland.[42]

The remaining shadow reports were submitted by National Human Rights Institutions in Ireland: the Ombudsman for Children and the Irish Human Rights and Equality Commission. While these reports covered similar issues to those which had been submitted by the civil society groups, the Ombudsman for Children's report was informed primarily by information derived from statutory investigations undertaken by the Office, by trends emerging from the complaints made to it by or on behalf of children, and from the Office's direct engagement with children.[43] The report, which was full of examples from complaints and

[39] Abortion Rights Alliance, *Submission to the Committee on the Rights of the Child* (2015).

[40] For further discussion of the interaction of domestic advocacy groups with the CRC Committee and other international human rights bodies on the issue of reproductive rights, see below at nn. 190–192 and text.

[41] International Intersex Human Rights NGO, *NGO Report to the 3rd and 4th Periodic Report on the Convention on the Rights of the Child* (2015) 12.

[42] Global Alliance to End all Corporal Punishment of Children, *Submission to the Committee on the Rights of the Child* (2015).

[43] Ombudsman for Children, *Report of the Ombudsman for Children to the UN Committee on the Rights of the Child on the Occasion of the Examination of Ireland's Consolidated Third and Fourth Report to the Committee* (2015).

investigations it had undertaken over the years, covered issues such as: child-centred budget analysis (child budgeting); data collection; awareness raising; consent to medical treatment; age of criminal responsibility; the best interests of the child; birth registration; protection of privacy; family law reform; child poverty; homelessness; mental health; complaints' handling in the education sector; asylum and immigration; and minority children. The Ombudsman for Children also submitted a short second report detailing stories from children themselves and from their parents about complaints they had made to the Ombudsman for Children. The Irish Human Rights and Equality Commission shadow report focused on general measures of implementation, civil rights and freedoms, basic health and welfare, education, and special protection measures.

In its Concluding Observations in the combined third and fourth reporting session, the Committee issued 33 recommendations to Ireland, with particular emphasis on general measures of implementation, disability, basic health and welfare, and special protection measures.[44] While the Committee welcomed the range of reforms that had taken place, it pointed to its previous recommendations which had not been implemented, such as in the area of independent monitoring, children with disabilities, health services, adolescent health, juvenile justice, minority children, refugees and asylum-seeking children.

The Committee's extensive list of recommendations echoed and reflected a great many of the recommendations made by civil society in their shadow reports.[45] Amongst the many recommendations were some that had previously been made to Ireland by other international human rights treaty bodies such as the CEDAW Committee, the Human Rights Committee of the International Covenant for Civil and Political Rights and, as noted below, the Universal Period Review of the UN Human Rights Council. And while the list on first reading appears as a long and somewhat improbable laundry list, the iterative nature of the exchanges between the CRC Committee, the state, and civil society advocacy groups, not just in this particular human rights forum but also in various others at international and domestic level, has the effect of making the process a longer-term, gradual, and more deliberative one which has helped to bring about a range of policy changes over time.

D. Ireland before the Universal Periodic Review 2011 and 2016

Alongside the various human rights treaty-body reviews to which states submit themselves, the annual and more political processes of the UN Human Rights

---

[44] UN Committee on the Rights of the Child, *Concluding Observations on the Combined Third and Fourth Periodic Reports of Ireland*, UN Doc. CRC/CIRL/C0/3-4 (2015).

[45] Ibid. The Recommendations are contained in Part III of the Concluding Observations.

Council's Universal Periodic Review also take place. During the periods of scrutiny by the Committee on the Rights of the Child between 1998 and 2016 described above, Ireland was also examined twice under the Universal Periodic Review, once in 2011 and once in 2016.

Over the two cycles of review, the Human Rights Committee and its working groups issued 39 recommendations to Ireland on children rights. Many of the recommendations reinforced or supported the recommendations described above which had been made by the Committee on the Rights of the Child, including making available non-denominational schooling for all children; the provision of adequate resources for the Child and Family Agency; adequate implementation of the National Children's Strategy; the closure of a notoriously harsh and antiquated penal institution for young offenders (St. Patrick's Institution);[46] holding a constitutional referendum on children's rights; extending the remit of the Ombudsman for Children Office to include children in prison and asylum-seeking children; and prohibiting corporal punishment. Other recommendations relevant to children included conducting investigations into the so-called 'mother and baby homes', which were institutions usually run by the Catholic church where unmarried mothers had been kept in cruel and often brutal circumstances, and in which many children had died.

In response to the Human Rights Council, Ireland accepted 34 of the 39 recommendations and 'noted' (a formal euphemism to indicate that the state did not at the time expressly agree to implement them) the other five, which were the recommendations to reinstate the age of criminal responsibility to 14 years; to protect and promote reproductive rights; to issue medical cards for Traveller and Roma communities; to strengthen measures to eliminate discrimination on the basis of religion in health and education sectors; and to accelerate entry into force of a new programme for the protection of refugees.

E. The impact of the international human rights review processes on child-related law and policy in Ireland

What are the main conclusions to be drawn from this dense summary of the engagement of domestic child advocacy groups in Ireland with international human rights review processes, and in particular, what can be said about the impact that their participation in this array of government review procedures under the CRC and the UPR has had on child policy and law in Ireland?

---

[46] For notification of the closure of the prison institution, see the announcement of the Ministry of Justice in April 2017, which acknowledges the influence of the advocacy of human rights and children's rights actors, available online at http://www.justice.ie/en/JELR/Pages/PR17000117.

According to a number of child rights advocates interviewed, the processes of state review under the human rights treaties are considered by the main civil society groups active in the field to be a crucial lever of domestic change.[47] One leading children's rights scholar and close observer of the field has stated that 'much of the progress made in Ireland's law and policy can be traced to the Committee on the Rights of the Child' and that Ireland 'has taken the recommendations of these bodies very seriously over the years'.[48] The reviews by the CRC Committee over the years have been described by domestic advocates as particularly helpful to gain traction on specific issues related to children's rights, particularly when the issue— such as asylum-seeking children in 'direct provision' accommodation and care, or boys detained in adult jails—lacks domestic salience and political will is consequently lacking.[49] UN-based advocacy has been seen as providing a space and an opportunity for civil society groups to draw attention to important issues which have been domestically neglected, and when domestic politics has failed vulnerable groups of children.[50]

The example of child rights in Ireland is not the classic case of a repressive authoritarian government ignoring or suppressing the claims of human rights groups, but rather the ordinary difficulties faced by domestic actors in attracting attention and resources to issues which have been neglected for more mundane or quotidian reasons, including the lack of leverage of traditionally disempowered groups (whether Travellers, certain groups of children, refugees, etc.), or the lack of media attention and popular salience. The opportunity provided by the review process has not only brought international attention to such issues, but also enabled civil society groups to meet with government actors at various stages including prior to and during the drafting of the state report, as well as during the review process itself when the state came to defend its record before the treaty body.[51] Civil society advocates have also indicated that the use of the treaty body's concluding observations in their follow-up domestic advocacy and campaign work has been very effective.[52]

These observations of domestic child rights advocates are borne out by the record of Ireland's responses to the various human rights monitoring processes in which the government engaged over the past two decades. While academic research conducted in 2002 suggested that the state was initially slow to respond to

[47] Interview with Jillian Van Turnhout, child rights advocate and former Senator.
[48] U. Kilkelly, *Ireland's Law and Policy: Moving towards a Children's Rights Based Approach*, 25 April 2014, available online at https://www.oco.ie/app/uploads/2017/09/KilkellyOCO10thAnniversaryLecture.pdf at 4.
[49] Interview with Tanya Ward, Chief Executive of the Children's Rights Alliance.
[50] Ibid.
[51] According to the Chief Executive of the Children's Rights Alliance, concessions from the state on important issues such as an increase in social welfare payments for child refugee seekers have been made shortly before the treaty body review under the Convention on the Rights of the Child.
[52] Ward (n. 49).

the commitments it had made under the Convention on the Rights of the Child particularly as far as structural changes were concerned,[53] significant changes to child policy in Ireland have been made since that time, and the treaty-reporting and UPR processes appear to have played a distinctive role. Since the time of its first review in 1998, the government has taken action to respond to a substantial number of the recommendations made in the context of the CRC human rights monitoring process. Many of these recommendations originated in NGO shadow reports, which were then picked up on during the review process, and eventually reinforced by the recommendations contained in the concluding observations of the Committee on the Rights of the Child, and at times also in the Universal Periodic Review process.

Three broad categories of reforms can be observed to have taken place in Ireland, including institutional and structural reforms; the adoption of new laws and legislation; and changes to policy and practice. In addition to these various specific legal and policy impacts, the international human rights monitoring system has also been used by domestic actors in the field as a continuous mechanism for national and local accountability, and as an informational and advocacy tool, not only at the time of Ireland's international reviews but on an ongoing basis.

In terms of institutional and structural changes, one of the most important was the creation of the Ombudsman for Children's Office. This had been a declared priority of the Children's Rights Alliance from the time of the first state review before the CRC. As noted above, the idea of an Ombudsman specifically for children is one that originated in Norway but subsequently spread to other jurisdictions, partly under the influence of a recommendation of the Committee on the Rights of the Child.[54] Following years of domestic advocacy and lobbying, the Irish government eventually established the Ombudsman for Children's Office in 2004 after the Committee on the Rights of the Child had recommended the creation of such an institution.[55] The Ombudsman for Children's Office has seen a continued rise each year in the number of complaints made to it since its creation and has proven to be a fairly robust accountability mechanism for children's affairs. It has reported on a range of issues including homelessness and domestic abuse, mental health services, legislation on education, and adoption, as well as making submissions to the international human rights monitoring mechanism and dealing with a vast number of individual complaints.

A further significant institutional change was the creation of a Department of Children and Youth Affairs, including a ministry with full cabinet status. This development has been described as 'rais(ing) the profile of children's issues at a

---

[53] N. Hayes, *Children's Rights, Whose Rights? A Review of Child Policy Development* (2002).

[54] See n. 25 above.

[55] Civil society groups had been campaigning for the creation of the Office since 1995 and advocacy efforts included commissioning a report to investigate the potential models for Ombudsman for Children in Ireland: see Barnardos, *Children's Rights Information Pack* (2008), at 9.

political level' and the minister's presence at the cabinet table has been said to ensure specific budget provision for children's services.[56] A third major institutional change was the creation of a new Child and Family Agency (Tulsa), whose establishment has substantially changed and integrated many aspects of the way in which vulnerable children are protected by the state.[57] And although the CRC Committee did not make any specific recommendation calling for the creation of this agency, domestic advocates used the Committee's recommendations and general jurisprudence to influence the shape of the new agency, by advocating for it to be built around a child-rights approach.[58] By making submissions to the Department of Children and Youth Affairs on the proposed legislation and holding advocacy meetings, civil society groups succeeded in having key provisions of the CRC—including reference to the best interests of the child, stronger family supports and the need to consult with children—reflected in the legislation and in the creation of the Agency. A further specific but important institutional change brought about by advocacy and pressure from the Commission on the Rights of the Child was the closure of a harsh and inappropriate penal institution in which boys—often young Traveller boys—had been incarcerated.[59]

The second group of changes influenced by the engagement of domestic civil society groups and governmental actors in the context of the international human rights monitoring mechanisms was a series of key constitutional and legislative measures in the field of child policy. The first major overarching change was the amendment of the Constitution to include references to children's rights and to the best interests of the child. This change was the outcome of a lengthy campaign on the part of a range of child rights advocates—a campaign which was actively challenged by religious and other groups.[60] The holding of a constitutional referendum on the issue followed a recommendation to include express protection for children's rights by the Constitution Review Group which had been set up to undertake a comprehensive review of the Irish Constitution.[61] The proposal to include explicit recognition of children's rights in the Constitution was later made by the Children's Rights Alliance to the Committee on the Rights of

---

[56]   L. Lundy et al., *The UN Convention on the Rights of the Child: a study of legal implementation in 12 countries* (2010) 55.

[57]   When created, the Tulsa Child and Family Agency brought together a range of hitherto separate services, the Health Service Executive (a government agency) Children and Family Services, the Family Support Agency, and the National Educational Welfare Board. Tulsa also incorporated some psychological services and services for children who have been victims of violence.

[58]   Children's Rights Alliance, *The Child and Family Agency*, available online at www.childrensrights. ie/content/child-and-family-agency.

[59]   See n. 46 above.

[60]   See O'Mahony, 'The UNCRC and the Politics of Children's Rights Reform in Ireland', ccjhr blog, 20 November 2009, available online at https://www.ucc.ie/academic/law/blogs/ccjhr/2009/11/uncrc-and-politics-of-childrens-rights.html

[61]   The Constitution Review Group Report (1996), available online at https://web.archive.org/web/20110721123125/http://www.constitution.ie/reports/crg.pdf . There is an extensive section of the report dealing with provisions of the Constitution governing the family and children.

the Child, and in 2006 they were joined by the Ombudsman for Children and the Irish Human Rights and Equality Commission in making this recommendation. Action was eventually taken by the government following the second review by the Committee on the Rights of the Child in 2006 when an announcement was made by the Taoiseach (Prime Minister) Bertie Ahern that a referendum would be held. This promise to hold a referendum had apparently been agreed between civil society and the government delegation during the state review in Geneva,[62] and it led to widespread mobilization within the sector, including the launch of a campaign to support the proposed amendment by several major child rights and child welfare organizations.[63] The Children's Rights Alliance also engaged in extensive campaigning for a positive vote on the referendum and, as indicated above, the ultimate result was a vote in favour of the inclusion of the provisions on children's rights in the Constitution. The language of the amendment makes clear that children are themselves rights-holders and that the state has a duty to vindicate and protect those rights.[64]

While both the referendum campaign and the constitutional change itself have attracted criticism from various commentators, who argued for example that the wording was weak and that the likely benefits in practice of the change were not obvious, it has broadly been welcomed by child rights advocates as at least a step in the right direction.[65] They have argued that the Constitution did not sufficiently protect children rights, and particularly did not include various principles of the CRC including the need to take account of children's voices and to enable them to participate in decision-making affecting them. They were concerned that previous case law had taken the view that the 'best interests' of the child lay with the married family, and had interpreted the concept paternalistically, and that a constitutional amendment would make a real difference to the way courts and other relevant authorities approached the rights and interests of children.[66] Despite the shortcomings of the referendum process, including inadequate time to campaign or to influence the wording of the proposed amendment, they saw the referendum and the eventual constitutional change as important steps. Recent case law of the Irish higher courts has borne out this expectation, as the Supreme Court and the High Court have delivered important judgments invoking the new constitutional provision on the rights of the child.[67]

---

[62] Interview with Jillian Van Turnhout.

[63] ISPCC, 'Children's Organisations Launch Yes for Children', Press Release, 24 September 2012, https://www.childrensrights.ie/resources/children%E2%80%99s-organisations-launch-yes.

[64] For an analysis of the debate which preceded the constitutional change, see Nolan, 'The Battles over Children's Rights in the Irish Constitutions', 22 *Irish Political Studies* (2007) 459.

[65] See n. 36 above for some of the critical reactions both to the amendment campaign and to the wording and purpose of the amendment itself.

[66] Correspondence with Tanya Ward, Chief Executive of the Children's Rights Alliance, May 2018.

[67] See e.g. *IRM, SJR and SOM v. Minister for Justice and Equality*, judgment of the Irish Supreme Court of 7 March 2018, *IRM v. Minister for Justice and Equality* [2016] IEHC 478, judgment of the Irish

Legal actors also argued that the inclusion in the Constitution in 2015 of language reflecting the key principles of the CRC, in combination with advocacy on the part of NGOs, has had a positive impact on subsequent legislation.[68] Child welfare activists have argued that to have a constitutional basis for the general principles of the Convention makes it easier to advocate for and to secure their inclusion in domestic legislation and, indeed, several pieces of legislation adopted after the referendum reveal this influence.[69] One example is the omnibus Child and Family Relationships Act 2015 which significantly revised Irish family law.[70] A working group headed by the Children's Rights Alliance engaged in extensive advocacy throughout the drafting process of the legislation, making presentations to legislative committees on drafts of the law, mobilizing the children's sector by holding information seminars on the draft, and hosting a meeting including the Minister for Children and featuring presentations on the draft from the Special Rapporteur on Child Protection and various civil society organizations.[71] Ultimately, following a period of sustained advocacy throughout its drafting and adoption, the terms of the draft legislation changed from reflecting what has been described as an 'outdated and arguably paternalistic concept of welfare'[72] and adopted instead a children's rights-based approach. Part V, section 31 of the Act introduced for the first time a lengthy list of factors that must be considered in determining the best interests of the child.[73] The Act also stipulates that children have the right to be heard in both private and public law proceedings in all matters affecting them.[74] Somewhat similar provisions on the best interests of the child and the need to ascertain the views of the child have also since been included in the Child and Family Agency

High Court of 29 July 2016, and, albeit in order to confirm a statutory interpretation on housing rights, *Fagan v. Dublin City Council*, judgment of the Irish Supreme Court of 19 December 2019.

[68] Kilkelly (n. 48) 10.

[69] While the referendum was held in November 2012, the amendment did not enter into law until 24 April 2015, due to the challenge brought before the Irish courts. But although the amendment's entry into force was considerably delayed, nevertheless its wording and the provision of the Convention on the Rights of the Child were very influential during the drafting of the Child and Family Agency Act 2013 and the Child and Family Relationships Act 2015, which were drafted after the referendum but before the amendment formally entered into force.

[70] Amongst other things, s. 63 of the Child and Family Relationships Act 2015 amends the Guardianship of Infants Act by including Part V, s. 31 which lays out the most comprehensive definition of the best interests of the child in Irish law. The right of the child to be heard is also enshrined in a number of different sections of the 2015 Act, including s. 21(8), Part IV, s. 6C(8)(a), and Part IV, s. 6(e) (13). Section 63 of the 2015 Act which introduced Part V, s. 32(1)(b) into the Guardianship of Infants Act 1964 enables the court to appoint a child view's expert in order to determine and convey the child's views in both public and private law matters.

[71] Children's Rights Alliance, 'Putting Children at the Heart of Family Law Reform', Press Release, 30 January 2014, available online at http://www.childrensrights.ie/resources/putting-children-centre-family-law.

[72] Kilkelly (n. 48) 10.

[73] Child and Family Relationships Act 2015, Part V, s. 31.

[74] See n. 70.

Act 2013,[75] the Child Care (Amendment) Act 2015,[76] and the Gender Recognition Act 2015.[77]

In addition to these institutional and legislative changes, advocacy around the Convention on the Rights of the Child has also led to a third group of changes in terms of its impact on policy and practice. In 2010, a UNICEF report noted that most of Ireland's progress in implementing the Convention by that stage had been made in terms of policy rather than legislation.[78] And while important legislative reforms have been introduced since that time, there have been significant changes to policy and practice too. One example of a change in practice which came about following sustained civil society advocacy on behalf of the Ombudsman for Children's Office was the extension of the mandate of this Ombudsman to conduct investigations into complaints received from asylum-seeking children in 'direct provision', something which was previously prohibited by the terms of the legislation creating the Ombudsman for Children's Office.[79] A second example is the way in which sustained campaigning on the basis of the concluding observations of the Committee on the Rights of the Child on corporal punishment gradually led to the complete prohibition on corporal punishment in all settings in Ireland by means of a ministerial order in December 2015.

Another notable change in practice brought about under the influence of a 1998 recommendation made by the Committee on the Rights of the Child in its concluding observations on Ireland concerned the need for better coordination of delivery of services for children in Ireland.[80] In response to the Committee's recommendation, the government drafted the National Children's Strategy 2000–2010, which it described as being 'rooted in the positive vision of the UN Convention on the Rights of the Child'.[81] The Strategy was criticized by some children's rights advocates as being insufficient in its implementation of the Convention, given the paucity of timescales, plans, and resources.[82] However,

---

[75] Section 9 of the Child and Family Agency Act 2013, which is entitled the 'best interests and views of the child', requires the Agency to have regard to the best interest of the child when making decisions in relation to the performance of its functions. When dealing with individual cases, it requires the best interest of the child to be the paramount consideration and further requires the views of the child be ascertained and due weight given to their views.

[76] See ss. 7(8) and 7(9) of the Child Care (Amendment) Act 2015.

[77] See s. 12(6) of the Gender Recognition Act 2015 which provides that the court shall not grant a child aged 16 and above an exemption to the minimum age requirement for gender recognition unless the court is satisfied that such an order is in the best interest of the child.

[78] Lundy et al. (n. 56) 56.

[79] See Ombudsman for Children, 'Ombudsman for Children can now Investigate Complaints from those in Direct Provision', Press Release, 3 April 2017, available online at https://www.oco.ie/ga/news/ombudsman-children-can-now-investigate-complaints-direct-provision/.

[80] UN Committee on the Rights of the Child, *Concluding Observations* (1998) UN Doc. CRC/C/15/Add.85, para. 28: 'The Committee suggests that the State party adopt a comprehensive National Strategy for Children, incorporating the principles and provisions of the Convention in a systematic manner in the designing of all its policies and programmes.'

[81] Department of Health and Children, *National Children's Strategy 2000-2010* (November 2000) Taoiseach's Forward.

[82] See Lundy et al. (n. 56) 54.

following a further recommendation from the CRC Committee in 2006 to adopt a rights-based approach in its strategies,[83] the government expressly included recognition of children's rights as one of five key principles on which its second strategy, the National Policy Framework for Children and Young People 2014–2020 was based.[84] While critics have suggested that this remains more of a statement of intent than an integration of a child rights approach into the strategy itself,[85] the Advisory Council set up under the Framework nonetheless provides further opportunity for influencing policy by bringing together a number of stakeholders in the field and providing a platform for civil society to engage with the relevant government department to help shape the implementation of the Framework.[86]

A final way in which the Convention on the Rights of the Child and the treaty-body process surrounding it, as well as the Universal Periodic Review system, have influenced practice in relation to children's rights in Ireland is in its impact on the activities of civil society groups in the field. As has been seen in the developments described above, the concluding observations of the Committee on the Rights of the Child have been used as an ongoing instrument and measure of accountability for governmental action, and as an advocacy tool for civil society. Since the time of the enactment of the CRC and its ratification by Ireland, there has been a high degree of coordination and cohesion amongst domestic groups focused on the welfare of children and young people, making it relatively easy for them to coordinate advocacy strategies based on the Committee's recommendations. Leading NGOs and civil society groups have provided training sessions to others on how to use the human rights treaty review processes to promote policies advancing children's welfare and rights.[87] In recent years various children's organizations have begun to use a rights-based approach in their advocacy and to press for governmental accountability for the provision of particular services, for example by using a scoring system to grade the government's performance on mental health services,[88] education, and a range of other issues.[89] The child services organization, Barnardos produces an annual 'back to school' costs survey, which in recent years has led with the right to education under the CRC and the Irish Constitution, and which

---

[83] UN Committee on the Rights of the Child, *Concluding Observations: Ireland* (2006) UN Doc. CRC/C/IRL/CO/2 paras. 6–11.

[84] See *Better Outcomes, Brighter Futures: The National Policy Framework for Children and Young People* (2014–2020) 20.

[85] Kilkelly (n. 48) 5–6.

[86] https://www.gov.ie/en/publication/63a1ff-report-of-the-national-policy-framework-for-children-young-people-20/.

[87] See e.g. Children's Rights Alliance, 'Children's Rights Training: A Training Programme on Children's Rights and Effective International Advocacy', available online at https://www.childrensrights.ie/content/children%E2%80%99s-rights-training.

[88] St. Patrick's Mental Health Services, *Submission to Seanad Public Consultation Committee on Children's Mental Health in Ireland* (May 2017).

[89] See e.g. the report card system used by the Children's Rights Alliance, available online at http://www.childrensrights.ie/content/report-card-2018 at 9.

influences the pre-budget submission made by both Barnardos and the Children's Rights Alliance to the government treasury department (department of finance) each year.[90] The Children's Rights Alliance, notably, uses its annual Report Card to integrate recommendations from the Committee on the Rights of the Child, and to highlight where further action on the part of the government is required.[91] The Report Card assigns the government a grade under each section and then provides an overall grade, which in 2018 was a C-.[92] The grading is carried out by an independent panel composed of experts in child law and human rights, and representatives from the business sector, trade unions, and the media, as well as representatives from Ireland's tripartite 'social partnership' of employers, employees representatives, together with government.[93]

One last example of the use of the treaty-body system in between the periods of review to hold the government to account for its commitments under the Convention can be seen in the organization of a 'child summit' by the Children's Rights Alliance, together with the government department of children and youth affairs, some months after the state examination under the CRC in 2016.[94] This summit brought together policy makers and decision makers, government officials, civil society, and young people, as well as two members of the Committee on the Rights of the Child. The aim of the summit was to discuss and debate action that needed to be taken in order to comply with provisions of the Convention concerning children's rights in Ireland.[95] The event assembled a range of stakeholders for the purposes of dialogue, although the presence of the UN Committee members arguably also ensured an additional element of external scrutiny following the CRC review in 2016.

4. Case Study 2: reproductive rights reform in Ireland

The movement for reproductive rights reform in Ireland has been quite different from the movement for children's rights. Even if the latter saw some sharp divisions of opinion as between secular and religious groups, the degree of divisiveness and social contestation surrounding reproductive rights in Ireland has been considerably higher than in the field of child rights. Abortion remained a subject that was almost entirely taboo in the country until the end of the twentieth century, and the

---

[90] See e.g. for the 2020 analysis https://www.barnardos.ie/policy/the-issues/education/the-real-cost-of-school-2020.

[91] See n. 90.

[92] Ibid.

[93] Ibid.

[94] Children's Rights Alliance, 'First Child Summit Brings International Children's Rights Home to Irish Soil', Press Release, 7 September 2016, available online at http://childrensrights.ie/resources/first-child-summit-brings-international.

[95] Ibid.

very small number of women's groups which spoke out or sought to mobilize on the issue were marginalized and often vilified. Catherine McGuinness, who was a Senator in the 1980s when she opposed a constitutional amendment to enshrine the 'right to life of the unborn', recalled how 'organised groups … came along then to shout down anyone who dared speak aloud, or worse still in public, against the proposed amendment … I remember the anonymous letters we received. I remember the phone calls to my home'.[96]

The movement for reproductive rights had begun in the late 1960s and early 1970s, at a time when the influence of the Catholic church on social issues remained strong. Contraception was illegal, divorce was prohibited under the Constitution, and abortion at any stage of pregnancy was punishable as a crime under the 1861 Offences against the Person Act.[97] Indeed, not only did the criminal law prohibit both abortion and contraception, but considerable efforts were made to insulate Irish society from knowledge of or external access to these. The Censorship of Publications Act 1929 banned any publication which made reference to abortion or contraception,[98] and in addition to prohibiting the importation, distribution, and sale of contraceptives, the 1935 Criminal Law (Amendment) Act made their advertisement a criminal offence.[99]

The first stages of liberalization of the law relating to contraception began in the 1970s with a ruling of the Irish Supreme Court in the case of *McGee v. Attorney General* (in which several judges drew on the US Supreme Court case of *Griswold v. Connecticut*) that married couples had a constitutional right to use contraception,[100] although even this very limited exception encountered strong political opposition and the *McGee* judgment was not implemented for years.[101] The judgment followed a long period of sustained work by a small number of organizations such as the Irish Family Planning Association, which had defied the restrictive laws and sought to provide access to contraception to people in Ireland for some time before the *McGee* litigation.[102] Following continued campaigning and activism in the following years, legislation was adopted by a narrow majority in 1985, permitting contraception to be sold to individuals over 18 in limited venues.[103] Further

---

[96] McGuinness, 'I could not resist a moment of triumph after 35 years', *The Irish Times*, 29 May 2019.

[97] This statute, adopted at a time when Ireland was under British rule, remained in force after Irish independence.

[98] Censorship of Publications Act 1929, s. 17. This was strengthened by s. 9 of the Censorship of Publications Act 1946.

[99] Criminal Law (Amendment) Act 1935, s. 17.

[100] *McGee v. Attorney General* [1973] IR 284; *Griswold v. Connecticut* 381 US 479 (1965).

[101] The political resistance to change was demonstrated in the seven-year delay in the adoption of legislation to implement the *McGee* ruling on marital access to contraception, i.e. the 1979 Family Planning Act. Notably the Taoiseach, the Prime Minister whose government introduced the legislation, crossed the floor to vote against it and in accordance with his belief that Irish people were opposed to the creation of a 'permissive society'.

[102] For an account see Cloatre and Enright, 'On the Perimeter of the Lawful': Enduring Illegality in the Irish Family Planning Movement, 1972–1985', 44 *Journal of Law and Society* (2017) 471.

[103] Health (Family Planning) (Amendment) Act 1985.

legislation in 1992 lowered the age at which condoms could be bought to 17, and expanded somewhat the venues in which they could be bought. Eventually the Health (Family Planning) (Amendment) Act in 1993 legalized the sale of condoms and removed the age and venue restrictions on their sale.

If the movement for reproductive rights in relation to contraception represented a struggle, however, the battle over abortion was an even more intense and painful one marked by extensive social and political contestation and divisiveness over more than three decades. The slow and gradual process of change was punctuated by three interrelated sets of developments which together proved central to the movement for reform. The first was a series of individual incidents that came to public attention involving the prohibition of or severe restriction on access to abortion—including access to travel for an abortion overseas—for a number of women and girls in particularly cruel circumstances, including children and women refugees who had been raped, as well as women with pregnancies involving fatal foetal abnormalities and women who were miscarrying. These incidents and the public attention and outrage they generated served as catalysts of different kinds for the growing social movement in favour of reproductive rights in Ireland over the decades, and in several instances also led to important domestic and international litigation which played a role in the process of reform. The second set of developments was a series of four constitutional referenda on a variety of issues related to abortion, beginning with the insertion of express protection for the life of the unborn into the Irish Constitution in 1983, and ending with a referendum in 2018 which repealed that provision and paved the way for the introduction of legislation providing for a relatively liberalized system of access to abortion in Ireland. The third set of developments was an ongoing series of critical interventions by international human rights institutions and actors on aspects of Irish law concerning access to abortion, including the treaty bodies of the ICESR, CEDAW, the ICCPR, and CAT, in addition to the European Court of Human Rights, the Committee of Ministers, and the Human Rights Commissioner of the Council of Europe, as well as a range of UN Special Rapporteurs and the UN Human Rights Council.

The campaign for reproductive rights was different in various ways from the children's rights movement, and not only in its more contested and divisive nature. One difference lies in the fact that the publicity generated by the cases of individual women were more prominent in the movement for abortion law reform, while the child rights movement—although galvanized at times by particularly shocking incidents such as the Kilkenny incest case or the discovery of unidentified children's bodies buried in the grounds of a former 'mother and baby' home—was characterized more often by collective advocacy on broad sets of policies. One feature that the two sets of campaigns did share in common, however, was that the continuous back-and-forth between three sets of actors—activists within the domestic movements, international human rights bodies and processes, and state actors of different kinds—was important in gradually building public support for reform and eventually changing policies.

The gradual mobilization of public support for reproductive rights reform led ultimately to the momentum behind the final transformative constitutional referendum in 2018 which brought about the first substantial reform of Irish law since the criminalization of abortion in 1861. The story of reproductive rights reform is not however a neatly linear one, and the critical catalysing events and interventions were often followed by periods of political resistance or stalemate. Nevertheless, the underlying movement for reform, however repressed and marginalized it was at times, never entirely abated or dissolved, but continued to act and respond to both internal and external events. Ultimately, the eventual set of crucial legislative and policy reforms were brought about by a combination of factors: the ongoing social activism over decades on the part of women and others concerned with reproductive rights; the wider public reaction to a series of particularly painful and shocking cases; pressure and leverage generated by the critical statements and interventions by a range of international human rights bodies as well as domestic bodies including courts, human rights commissions and a specially-convened Citizens Assembly; and finally the eventual public and governmental response to that set of actions and reactions.

A. International human rights law on reproductive rights

Unlike the field of children's rights, which covers a broad range of issues to which the UN Convention on the Rights of the Child is dedicated, the issue of reproductive rights is both more specific and subject to greater social contestation internationally as well as domestically, mainly due to religious convictions about the sanctity of foetal life and the relative weight given to these convictions as opposed to the personal autonomy and reproductive health of women. Further, there is no clear statement of the right of access to abortion in any one human rights treaty, but rather a range of guarantees under a series of different international and regional human rights treaties which protect different aspects of a woman's right to terminate a pregnancy, as well as a growing jurisprudence on the right to reproductive health.

These include, at the international level, provisions of the Convention on the Elimination of All Forms of Discrimination against Women (CEDAW), the International Covenant on Economic, Social and Cultural Rights (ICESCR), the International Covenant on Civil and Political Rights (ICCPR), and the Convention against Torture (CAT), and at the regional level the European Convention on Human Rights (ECHR).

Articles 10, 12, and 16 of CEDAW proclaim the right to education, information, and advice on family planning, the right of equal access to health services related to family planning, and the right of women to decide freely and responsibly on the number and spacing of their children, and the right to information and education to enable them to exercise these rights.[104] Article 12 of the ICESCR protects the right to health, which has been interpreted by the Committee on ESCR to mean that the provision of maternal and reproductive health services is a core obligation,[105] and that there is a right to sexual and reproductive health.[106] Articles 6, 7, 17, and 26 of the ICCPR express protection for the right to life and the right to privacy, as well as protection against cruel, inhuman and degrading treatment and against discrimination on the basis of sex, which have been treated by the Human Rights Committee in different circumstances as protecting women and girls from being prevented from accessing abortion services.[107] The CAT and the ECHR similarly provide legal protection against torture and cruel, inhuman, or degrading treatment,[108] and the ECHR guarantees protection for the right to private and family life, all of which have been interpreted at different times to prevent states from depriving women of access to abortion in a range of particular circumstances. Similarly, freedom of expression and information as protected under the ICCPR[109] and the ECHR[110] have been held to protect women's right of access to information on abortion. Ireland is a party to all of these international instruments, including the various optional protocols which establish individual complaints or communications procedures, other than the optional protocol to the ICESR.

In addition to the specific rights set out in these binding treaties, and the ways in which they have been interpreted by the various treaty bodies in relation to abortion over time, a range of other international norms and guidance have been articulated by broad-based and influential bodies over time, contributing to the growing jurisprudence on reproductive rights. At the United Nations International Conference on Human Rights in 1968, the Proclamation of Teheran was the first

---

[104] See also the decision of the CEDAW committee on individual communication *LC v. Peru*, UN Doc. CEDAW/C/50/D/22/2009, of 17 October 2011, finding violations of Articles 2, 3, 5, and 12 in the state's refusal to provide access to therapeutic abortion and surgery to a raped child who had attempted suicide.

[105] UN CESCR General Comment No. 14: *The right to the highest attainable standard of health* (Article 12) (2000), Adopted by the Committee on Economic, Social and Cultural Rights at the Twenty-second Session, E/C.12/2005/4, 11 August 2000, paras. 14 and 44(a).

[106] UN CESCR General comment No. 22: *The right to sexual and reproductive health* (Article 12) (2016) adopted by the Committee on Economic, Social and Cultural Rights E/C.12/GC/22, 2016.

[107] See e.g. *KL v. Peru*, UN Doc. CCPR/C/85/D/1153/2003 (24 October 2005); *LMR v. Argentina*, UN Doc. CCPR/C/101/D/1608/2007 (28 April 2011); and *AM v. Ireland*, UN Doc. CCPR/C/116/D/2324/2013 (31 March 2016).

[108] For a summary of some of the international jurisprudence, including of the CAT and the ECHR, on denial of access to abortion as cruel, inhuman and degrading treatment, see Zureick, '(En)gendering Suffering: Denial of Abortion as a Form of Cruel, Inhuman, or Degrading Treatment', 38 *Fordham International Law Journal* (2015) 99.

[109] See the comments of the UN Human Rights Committee on the report of Ireland on its obligations under the ICCPR, *Comments of the Human Rights Committee*, UN Doc. CCPR/C/79/Add. 21 (3 August 1993) at para. 15.

[110] Application No. 14234/88 and 14235/88, *Open Door Counselling and Dublin Well Woman v. Ireland* (1993) 15 EHRR 244, (1992) 246 Eur. Ct. H.R. (series A).

international policy document to recognize the importance of family planning, stating that: 'Parents have a basic human right to determine freely and responsibly the number and the spacing of their children.'[111] In 1994, a major UN-coordinated International Conference on Population and Development published the Cairo Programme of Action, which identified unsafe abortion as a public health concern and provided for the first time a definition of reproductive health in an international policy document.[112] Shortly afterwards, the fourth in a series of major UN-coordinated World Conferences on Women, the Beijing Conference, published the Beijing Platform of Action which affirmed the Cairo definition and declared the right to control sexuality and reproduction to be a human right.[113] Most recently, in 2003, the Maputo Protocol to the African Charter on Human and Peoples' Rights became the first international treaty to explicitly grant a right to abortion in specific circumstances.[114]

In terms of national political changes reflecting or paralleling these changing international norms, 42 jurisdictions broadened legal access to abortion between 1967 and 1978.[115] Notably, Ireland's close neighbour, the United Kingdom, enacted the Abortion Act 1967 which allowed women to obtain terminations where their mental or physical health was at risk. This for the first time made it easier for Irish women to obtain abortions, as they could—if they had sufficient resources—travel to the UK where it was lawful and accessible.

B. The emergence of a reproductive rights movement in Ireland and its counter-movement

As indicated above, a social movement in favour of liberalizing Ireland's prohibition on access to contraception had begun in the late 1960s, with the establishment of the Irish Family Planning Association (IFPA, initially called the Fertility Guidance Company) in 1969. The IFPA managed to circumvent the legislative prohibition on the sale of contraception by distributing it freely and encouraging

---

[111] Final Act of the International Conference on Human Rights, Teheran, UN Doc. A/Conf. 32/41 (22 April to 13 May 1968) at para. 16.

[112] Report of the International Conference on Population and Development, Cairo (5–13 September 1994), UN Doc. No. A/Conf 171/13 at 12.

[113] Report of the Fourth World Conference on Women, Beijing (4–15 September 1995), UN Doc. No. A/Conf 117/20 at paras. 17 and 94.

[114] The protocol affirms the right to choose and requires states to authorize abortion 'in cases of sexual assault, rape, incest, and where the continued pregnancy endangers the mental and physical health of the mother or the life of the mother or of the foetus'. For discussion see Ngwena, 'Conscientious Objection to Abortion and Accommodating Women's Reproductive Health Rights: Reflections on a Decision of the Constitutional Court of Colombia from an African Regional Human Rights Perspective', 58(2) Journal of African Law (2014) 183 at 190.

[115] 'Worldwide Laws and Policies on Contraception, Abortion and Sterilisation Affect Service Provision', 6(2) International Family Planning Perspectives (1980) 74 at 75.

'donations'. In 1971 Mary Robinson, a prominent senator who later became president of Ireland and subsequently UN High Commissioner for Human Rights, sought to introduce a bill to legalize contraception in Ireland, but the bill was refused a reading. That same year, a group of women from the Irish Women's Liberation Movement, including prominent feminist activist and journalist Nell McCafferty, travelled to Northern Ireland, within the jurisdiction of the UK, on what became known as the 'Contraceptive Train' and returned with what appeared to be packets of contraceptives which they openly swallowed as an act of defiance in front of customs officials.[116]

These developments were amongst a number of events at the time which had the effect of galvanizing a conservative counter-movement against the emerging Irish reproductive rights movement. One of the founding members of the Pro-Life Amendment Campaign wrote a decade later about the 'seeds of the Irish Abortion movement' which he linked with the establishment of the Contraception Action Programme and several other women's initiatives including the Rape Crisis Centre, the Dublin Well Woman Centre, and the Woman's Right to Choose Group.[117] Meanwhile across the Atlantic, the United States Supreme Court gave its famous judgment in *Roe v. Wade*, in which it ruled that the constitutional right to privacy encompassed the right to have an abortion.[118] The Irish Supreme Court was also by this stage at the peak of its own 'golden age',[119] composed of a new generation of legal scholars who appeared keen to emulate the civil liberties and human rights discourse coming from the United States.[120] Indeed the decision in *McGee v. Attorney General*[121] on marital contraception was handed down only a few months after *Roe v. Wade*.

These indications of a growing move towards social liberalism within Irish society in the 1970s were met with strong resistance from socially conservative and largely Catholic organizations, which mobilized for the adoption of a 'pro-life amendment' to the Irish Constitution, ostensibly to prevent what they feared might be a *Roe*-type decision being handed down by the Irish Supreme Court.[122] The two largest political parties agreed on this move, and the wording proposed for the 8th Amendment to the Constitution was the following:

---

[116] The pills were actually paracetamol rather than contraceptive pills; the group had not realized they required a prescription to purchase contraception in Northern Ireland!

[117] John O'Reilly, as quoted in T. Hesketh, *The Second Partitioning of Ireland: The Abortion Referendum of 1983* (1990), at 5.

[118] 410 US 113 (1973).

[119] Hogan, 'The Supreme Court and the Equality Clause', 4(3) *The Bar Review* (1999) 116.

[120] R Mac Cormaic, *The Supreme Court* (2016) 94–99.

[121] See n. 100 above.

[122] Tom Hesketh (n. 117), at 8, wrote that 'interest in the cause of the unborn flowed naturally from the general unease felt within many traditionalist groups with the way Irish society was perceived to be developing'.

The State acknowledges the right to life of the unborn and, with due regard to the equal right to life of the mother, guarantees in its laws to respect, and, as far as practicable, by its laws to defend and vindicate that right.[123]

The campaign was a bitter and divisive one,[124] but the referendum met with a swell of support from an overwhelmingly Catholic population, despite warnings from the Attorney General and others at the time that the wording was problematic.[125] Indeed, a few months before the vote was held, a young woman named Sheila Hodgers who was suffering from breast cancer had died in great pain in an Irish hospital, when her medical treatment was stopped once it was discovered that she was pregnant. The hospital refused to induce her pregnancy or to perform a caesarean section, and she died in apparent agony after giving birth to a child, who died along with her shortly afterwards.[126] The account of her death was published in a leading Irish newspaper but had no apparent effect on the outcome of the vote. Although the voter turnout was lower than 54 per cent, the Eighth Amendment protecting the right to life of the unborn was passed with 67 per cent of voters in favour of the proposal, and became Article 40.3.3 of the Constitution.

C. From the 1983 referendum to the 2002 referendum via the 'X' case: the issue of information and travel for abortion

Armed with the new constitutional protection for the unborn in Ireland, the antiabortion movement then turned its attention to pregnancy counselling and to the reality that many thousands of Irish women facing unwanted or crisis pregnancies each year travelled to the UK in order to access abortion. In a series of cases, antiabortion groups successfully argued that Article 40.3.3 prohibited the distribution of information on abortion. In *Attorney General (Society for the Protection of the Unborn Child SPUC) v. Open Door Counselling and Dublin Well Woman Centre*, the Supreme Court granted an injunction restraining the defendant women's counselling organizations from providing information on the availability of abortion services in other jurisdictions.[127] The court held that the Society for the Protection of the Unborn Child (SPUC) had standing to argue on behalf of the unborn child, and that there was no constitutional right to information relating to the availability of services abroad.

---

[123] The Pro-Life Amendment Campaign had originally proposed a draft amendment which stated: 'The State recognises the absolute right to life of every unborn child from conception and accordingly guarantees to respect and protect such right by law.' See Hesketh (n. 117) 18.

[124] See the description by historian D. Ferriter, *The Transformation of Ireland 1900-2000* (2005) 716.

[125] Mac Cormaic (n. 120) 283.

[126] 'Sheila Hodgers—a case in question', *The Irish Times*, 2 September 1983.

[127] *Attorney General (Society for the Protection of the Unborn Child SPUC) v. Open Door Counselling and Dublin Well Woman Centre* [1988] IR 593.

In response, Open Door Counselling initiated a case before the European Court of Human Rights. In 1991, the then European Commission on Human Rights took the view that the injunction granted by the Supreme Court in *Open Door* violated the right to freedom of expression, protected by Article 10 of the ECHR.[128] In the parallel case of *SPUC (Ireland) Ltd v. Coogan*, the Irish Supreme Court ruled that SPUC had standing to seek an injunction against University College Dublin's Students' Union, which had provided information on abortion services to its students.[129] SPUC then initiated proceedings against three student unions to stop them publishing the contact details of abortion providers in the United Kingdom in their student handbooks, and the High Court judge (a woman) referred the case to the European Court of Justice as the issue could have implications for European Union law rights.[130] On appeal the Supreme Court awarded the injunction on the basis that the unborn's right to life was an established constitutional right and that there was no competing constitutional right.[131] Meanwhile, the European Court of Justice in Luxembourg ruled that the termination of pregnancy could constitute a 'service' for the purposes of EU law, and that member states could not prohibit the distribution of information about that service.[132] But as there was no commercial link between the student unions and the abortion clinics in the present case, the facts did not come within the scope of European Community law. The case was returned to the Irish High Court, and the injunction was finally lifted by the Supreme Court several years later.[133] In the meantime, the Irish government, fearing further legal challenges, negotiated a protocol to the Maastricht Treaty establishing the European Union, to the effect that nothing under EU law would affect Article 40.3.3 of the Constitution containing the guarantee of the right to life of the unborn.

Hence the counter-movement had successfully not only secured the enactment of the 8th amendment, but had got the Irish courts to rule that this new amendment prohibited the provision of information or counselling on the availability of abortion outside the state. Only the prodding of the European Commission on Human Rights on the violation of freedom of information and expression that this entailed, and perhaps also the fear of a further reference to the European Court of Justice led to the eventual removal of the injunction which SPUC had secured against the students unions and the counselling services.

The more dramatic set of events which precipitated the next bout of activism on both sides, and which led eventually to the second constitutional referendum

---

[128] *Open Door Counselling and Dublin Well Woman v. Ireland* (1993) 15 EHRR 244.
[129] *SPUC v. Coogan* [1989] IR 734.
[130] *SPUC v. Grogan* [1989] IR 753.
[131] Ibid.
[132] Case C-159/90, *The Society for the Protection of Unborn Children Ireland Ltd v. Stephen Grogan* (EU:C:1991:378), [1991] ECR 4685.
[133] *SPUC v. Grogan (No. 5)* [1998] 4 IR 343.

was the X case, the first and most famous in a series of 'alphabet litigation' cases involving restrictions on access to abortion for Irish girls and women. The X case involved a 14-year old girl (known as 'X') who had become pregnant after being raped by a neighbour. Her parents informed the Irish police that they planned to take her abroad for a termination, and queried whether the foetal remains could be used as evidence in a criminal trial. This information was communicated to the Attorney General, who issued proceedings for an injunction in the High Court to prevent the girl from travelling, although she had already left the jurisdiction. When told of these developments, the girl and her parents returned home to Ireland, and she expressed suicidal feelings to her mother.[134] Granting the injunction, the High Court judge weighed the risk that X might take her own life against 'the certainty that the life of the unborn will be terminated if the order is not made'.[135]

The decision was highly controversial and there were protests and counter-protests not just in Ireland and the UK but also in the US.[136] The girl and her family appealed the decision to the Supreme Court, which lifted the injunction after a three-day hearing.[137] The ruling indicated that a majority of the court interpreted Article 40.3.3 to mean that abortion was permissible in Ireland in certain circumstances: if there was a 'real and substantial risk' to the life of the woman, which 'could only be avoided by the termination of pregnancy'.[138] Hence the inclusion of Article 40.3.3 in the Constitution, which had been intended by the anti-abortion activists as a cast-iron protection against the introduction of any abortion in Ireland, had become the vehicle for the introduction of abortion for the first time as a matter of constitutional law, even if in very restrictive circumstances. Other members of the Supreme Court were extremely critical of the government's and legislature's failure to introduce legislation in response to the 8th amendment to clarify the circumstances in which abortion would be legal if there was a tension between the life of the mother and the life of the foetus.

The case also highlighted the fact that the 8th amendment affected not only the rights of women to seek abortion in Ireland but also their ability to travel out of the country for a termination. The realization of this fact in the context of the shocking circumstances of the X case, where a 14-year-old girl was being forced against her wishes and that of her parents to carry a pregnancy to term after rape, led to a shift in public opinion for the first time against aspects of the 8th amendment and the

---

[134] Ibid. 286.

[135] *A.G. v. X* [1992] 1 IR 1 at 12.

[136] Mac Cormaic (n. 120) 288.

[137] Free to travel, Ms X and her family returned to England, but she miscarried before the procedure could be carried out.

[138] *A.G. v. X* [1992] 1 IR 1 at 53–55.

beginnings of support for the availability of abortion in certain circumstances in Ireland.[139]

The legal uncertainty generated by the *SPUC, Open Door,* and *X* cases led to a further referendum to amend Article 40.3.3 of the Constitution in 1995. Three issues arising from those cases were put to the electorate: whether there should be a right to travel for an abortion, whether there should be a right to access information on abortion, and whether the risk of suicide (as had been present in the *X* case) should be explicitly ruled out as grounds for an abortion in Ireland. The first two amendments were overwhelmingly adopted and the third was rejected.[140] Legislation was then adopted in 1995 to give effect to the two amendments, providing that doctors and counsellors could give information on the availability of abortion abroad if women requested it, but that no appointments could be made on their behalf.[141] The restrictive nature of this legislation was later criticized by a UN Special Rapporteur, who emphasized the impact it had on health providers and counsellors in Ireland.[142]

In 1997, it became public knowledge that there was likely to be a 're-run of the "X" case'.[143] A 13-year-old girl had become pregnant after she been raped by a neighbour, and was taken into state care. She became suicidal as a result of her condition, and the Eastern Health Board sought an order to enable her to be brought to England to obtain a termination. The District Court granted that order, which was challenged in the High Court by the girl's parents. The High Court upheld the decision on appeal, noting that C's life was in imminent danger, and that the recent constitutional amendment prevented an injunction being granted against someone who planned to travel for an abortion.[144] A similar case later arose almost 10 years after the *C* case, leading to an eventual recognition by the High Court of the right of a teenage girl who was carrying a foetus with anencephaly to travel for

---

[139] Before the *X* case, a significant percentage of Irish people believed that abortion in all circumstances ought to be illegal. In 1986, a study which was later published by the Crisis Pregnancy Agency found that 38% of the population believed that abortion was not permissible in any circumstances (see *A Survey of the General Population*, Crisis Pregnancy Agency (2004) available online at https://www.esri.ie/system/files/media/file-uploads/2015-07/BKMNEXT066_Summary%20Report_Irish%20Contraception.pdf). By 1997, an opinion poll published in *The Irish Times* newspaper indicated that that figure had shrunk to 18%, and that 77% were in favour of permitting abortion in certain circumstances ('77% say limited abortion right should be provided', *The Irish Times*, 11 December 1997).

[140] For a caustic commentary on what the outcome reflected about the contradictory attitudes of Irish people towards abortion, see Browne, 'Why can't foreigners grasp Irish abortion?', *The Irish Times*, 18 August 1999.

[141] The Regulation of Information (Services outside the State for the Termination of Pregnancies) Act 1995. This legislation was referred to the Supreme Court to test its compatibility with the Constitution in *Re Article 26 and the Regulation of Information (Services outside the State for the Termination of Pregnancies) Bill 1995* [1995] 1 IR 1.

[142] United Nations General Assembly, *Report of the Special Rapporteur on the situation of human rights defenders*, UN Doc. A/HRC/22/47/Add.3 (26 February 2013) at para. 86.

[143] 'A Monster of Legalisms', *The Irish Times*, 19 November 1997.

[144] *A and B v. Eastern Health Board* [1998] 1 IR 464.

an abortion, but only after an attempt was made by the national health service to forcibly prevent her from traveling by contacting the police.[145]

In 1999, the highly restrictive situation governing abortion in Ireland and the fact that women were required to travel abroad came in for criticism from the CEDAW committee, the UN treaty body monitoring Ireland's implementation of CEDAW.[146] The government at the time acknowledged its obligations under international human rights law in a Green Paper on abortion which referred to the state's obligations under CEDAW, the ICCPR, and the CRC, and also acknowledged that an absolute prohibition on abortion would be contrary to the ECHR.[147] International human rights obligations were also regularly cited during the cross-parliamentary committee hearing which followed.[148]

In 2001 a further constitutional amendment was proposed which would have removed suicide as a ground for legal abortion, and introduced legislation to outline when intervention to save the life of a pregnant woman would be appropriate. The ambivalent nature of the proposal however was confusing and did little to clarify the position on abortion or to satisfy many anti-abortion advocates,[149] and it was ultimately defeated in a referendum held in March 2002. Perhaps fatigued by the succession of proposals for reform and referenda, the rejection of this amendment signalled a temporary cessation of political activity on abortion in Ireland. Despite the recommendation of a Constitutional Review Group in 1996 that guidelines should be adopted for appropriate medical intervention in cases where a woman's life was at risk and term limits for lawful abortions,[150] and despite the legality of abortion in such circumstances following the X case, no such guidelines or legislation were adopted and in practice no abortions were carried out in Ireland for another decade and a half.[151] Indeed, under the guidelines of

---

[145] Unreported judgment of McKechnie J of the High Court, 9 May 2007.

[146] United Nations Committee on the Elimination of Discrimination against Women, *Report of the Committee on the Elimination of Discrimination against Women, Twentieth session, 19 January–5 February, Twenty-first session (7-25 June 1999)*, UN Doc. A/54/38/Rev. 1, at paras 185 and 186. The Committee made reference to the particular hardship this created for particular groups of women who could not travel, such as asylum seekers.

[147] *Green Paper on Abortion* (1999) at 24–25 and 34.

[148] *Fifth Progress Report on Abortion* (2000) at 80, A493, A 494, and A509.

[149] 'Abortion referendum as proposed is invalid', *The Irish Times*, 25 February 2002. Groups such as the Pro-Life Campaign and SPUC supported the referendum, whilst groups such as Ireland for Life and the Mother and Child Campaign opposed it for being insufficiently restrictive.

[150] *Report of the Constitution Review Group* (1996).

[151] Annual statistics have been provided by the Department of Health since the 2013 Protection of Life During Pregnancy Act. See https://health.gov.ie/blog/publications/notifications-in-accordance-with-section-20-of-the-protection-of-life-during-pregnancy-act-2013-annual-report-2016/.   An informal report on Irish abortion statistics prior to that time have been put together, which suggest that abortions were first performed in Ireland in 2014, though ectopic pregnancies were no doubt terminated before that. See W. R. Thompson and J. Davidson, *The Past, Present and Potential Futures of Abortion in Ireland*, available online at http://www.johnstonsarchive.net/policy/abortion/ireland_abortion_2018.html. And a 2010 report by Human Rights Watch announced that the NGO had not been able to find a single case of an abortion lawfully carried out in Ireland: *State of Isolation: Access to Abortion for Women in Ireland* (2010).

the Irish Medicines Board of 2001, an Irish doctor could not perform a legal abortion without being disbarred from the medical profession. By 2003, 20 years after the Eighth Amendment was adopted, over 94,000 Irish women had travelled to England for a termination.[152]

D. From the 2002 referendum to the Protection of Life During Pregnancy 2013 Law: the beginnings of real reform

While the period between the failed 2002 referendum and the eventual adoption of legislation in 2013 to give effect to the limited 'X case exception' (risk to life of mother/suicide) saw a temporary decrease or cessation of formal political activity on abortion, the same period saw a significant rise in the engagement by activists with international human rights law and institutions on the issue of abortion. Domestic advocates submitted shadow reports and complaints to an array of treaty bodies, and cases brought by individual Irish women before the European Court of Human Rights brought external visibility to the highly restrictive nature of Irish abortion law and kept a degree of international and domestic pressure on the government.

In 2005 the CEDAW Committee expressed continuing concern about these restrictive laws and urged the government 'to facilitate a national dialogue on women's right to reproductive health'.[153] Ireland was criticized by the Committee on the Rights of the Child for the lack of adequate access for adolescents to necessary information on reproductive health,[154] and by the UN Human Rights Committee on account of the 'highly restrictive circumstances under which women can lawfully have an abortion in the state' during Ireland's third report under the ICCPR in 2008.[155]

A number of cases brought by individual women under the ECHR, which had previously indicated that states had a wide degree of discretion in deciding the point

---

[152] The statistics have been collected from the UK Department of Health by the Irish Family Planning Association, https://www.ifpa.ie/abortion-statistics-show-3265-women-abandoned-by-the-irish-state/.

[153] *United Nations Committee on the Elimination of Discrimination against Women* (22 July 2005), UN Doc. CEDAW/C/IRL/CO/4-5 at para. 39. Meanwhile the CEDAW Committee developed its jurisprudence on abortion in other cases similar to Ireland's *X* case In 2011 in *LC v. Peru* (4 November 2011), UN Doc. CEDAW/C/50/D/22/2009, a 13-year-old child who had become pregnant following rape suffered severe spinal injuries when she attempted suicide, but was refused a spinal alignment treatment because she was pregnant, and became permanently paralysed. The CEDAW Committee declared that Peru was obliged to alter its law to allow women to obtain an abortion in cases of rape and sexual assault.

[154] United Nations Committee on the Rights of the Child, *Concluding observations, Consideration of reports submitted by state parties under Article 44 of the Convention on the Rights of the Child*, UN Doc. CRC/C/IRL/CO/2, at para. 52.

[155] United Nations Human Rights Committee, *Concluding Observations of the Human Rights Committee*, UN Doc CCPR/C/IRL/CO/3 (30 July 2008) at para. 13.

at which a right to life should begin,[156] generated even greater visibility and public attention for the issue of abortion in Ireland. A woman known as 'D' brought her case before the European Court of Human Rights (ECtHR) when she had become pregnant, only to discover at 14 weeks that her foetus suffered from a very serious and often fatal genetic disorder, Trisomy 18.[157] She was unable to receive medical treatment in Ireland, and had to travel to Belfast to have the pregnancy terminated.[158] She argued to the ECtHR, supported by the Irish Family Planning Association, that the need to travel abroad for a termination in these circumstances and the lack of information on abortion services had violated her Convention rights. While her application was dismissed on procedural grounds for alleged failure to exhaust domestic remedies, a notable feature of the case was that the Irish government lawyer argued that cases of fatal foetal abnormalities might not be covered by the 8th amendment to the Constitution, meaning that the 'right to life of the unborn' would not apply, even though the state had never (before or afterwards) accepted this argument or adopted this position.[159] In 2007, the ECtHR ruled in favour of a woman who had been prevented from obtaining an abortion in Poland even though domestic law provided for abortion in cases of a severe risk to health.[160] While the ECtHR did not declare a substantive right to abortion under the ECHR, it ruled that where a state does permit abortion on a specific ground, there must be an effective procedure to assess whether that ground has been met.[161] The ruling was highly relevant for Ireland, given the lack of such procedural rights for women in the absence of any legislation or guidance as to when abortion would be permissible following the *X* case. Indeed this absence was publicly criticized the following year by the Council of Europe Commissioner for Human Rights.[162]

---

[156] *Vo v. France* [2004] ECHR 326. Earlier cases had related to the restriction on abortion in certain circumstances (see *Brüggemann and Scheuten v. Federal Republic of Germany* (1977) 3 EHRR 244) and whether a woman's partner could prevent her from seeking a termination (see e.g. *Paton v. UK* (1981) 3 EHRR 408; *H v. Norway* 73 DR 155 (1992); *Boso v. Italy* App. No. 50490/99, Eur. Ct. H.R. 846 (2002)).

[157] *D v. Ireland* (Admissibility) (2006) 43 EHRR SE 16.

[158] The woman in question had written anonymously to a leading national newspaper on the eve of the 2002 referendum, and her intervention was credited with swaying public opinion in the vote. See ' "Reasonable compromise" beset by a tide of controversy', *The Irish Times*, 8 March 2002.

[159] See for discussion, J. Schweppe and E. Spain, *Legislating for Article 40.3.3: Schweppe and Spain on Art.40.3.3. and the capacity to survive outside the womb* (2013), available online at http://rightsni.org/2013/01/legislating-for-article-40-3-3-schweppe-and-spain-on-article-40-3-3-and-the-capacity-to-survive-outside-the-womb/.

[160] Case 5410/03, *Tysiac v. Poland* [2007] 1 FCR 666 (ECHR). Despite the severe health risk which she faced, the applicant was unable to find a medical professional who would agree to perform an abortion, and had to carry her third pregnancy to term. She was left with such damaged eyesight that Polish social services issued a certificate stating that she was medically unable to care for her children. See para. 31 of the judgment. See also *RR v. Poland* (2011) EHRR 31.

[161] Poland was condemned again some years later for breach of the procedural rights of a 14-year-old child who had been initially denied an abortion despite having been raped, and who was indeed herself subjected to a criminal investigation for alleged 'unlawful sexual intercourse': see *P & S v. Poland* [2013] I FCR 476, App. No. 57375/08, at para. 98.

[162] Council of Europe, Commissioner for Human Rights, *Report by the Commissioner for Human Rights, Mr Thomas Hammarberg on his visit to Ireland, (26-30 November 2007)* (30 April 2008), at 23–24.

In the years afterwards, two further key rulings concerning abortion in Ireland were handed down by the ECtHR and the UN Human Rights Committee respectively, and these were followed by a tragic event which drew enormous public attention to the highly restrictive situation. The rulings were the *ABC* judgment of the ECtHR,[163] and the *Mellet* opinion of the Human Rights Committee,[164] while the tragic event was the death of a pregnant woman named Savita Halappanavar who had been denied a termination following a septic miscarriage. The response to these three events triggered a further series of domestic events and catalysed a fresh wave of social mobilization that led ultimately to the constitutional referendum in 2018 which finally reformed abortion law in Ireland.

In the case of *A, B & C v. Ireland*, three women together brought a case against the state after each of them had to travel to the UK to obtain an abortion, in circumstances in which there were risks to the health of the first two and to the life of the third if they had continued their pregnancies.[165] The Court, to which multiple amicus interventions were made on both sides, found that Ireland had acted within the permissible limits of the Convention (the 'margin of appreciation') in the case of the first two applicants, in part because they had the option of travelling to another jurisdiction for an abortion, but ruled that the third applicant's procedural rights had been violated. Given that Irish law since the *X* case apparently permitted abortion in cases where a mother's life would be at risk if the pregnancy continued, the Court ruled that C had a right to a process to establish whether she met the requirements for a legal abortion in Ireland, and that the state was obliged to enact legislation to clarify how the balance between the rights of the pregnant woman and the rights of the foetus should be resolved. Hence, although the *ABC* ruling was actually a very cautious one, it drew international and public attention once again to the frozen state of the legislature in Ireland on the issue of abortion, and specifically to the fact that the government had not—despite the passage of nearly 20 years—introduced legislation to implement the *X* case and to outline the circumstances in which abortion was permitted.

The European ruling proved very important in sparking a domestic discussion on reform, with its illustration of the unworkability of the status quo, and it had the effect of encouraging other women to come forward and publicize their own tragic stories.[166] One such woman who was encouraged by the ECtHR judgment to come forward was Michelle Harte.[167] She had been diagnosed with an aggressive form of melanoma and had been advised by doctors, as she was in the early stages of

---

[163] *A, B and C v. Ireland*, App. No. 25579/05 (ECHR, 16 December 2010).

[164] Views adopted by the UN Human Rights Committee under article 5(4) of the Optional Protocol, concerning communication No. 2324/2013, Amanda Mellet v Ireland, 31 March 2016.

[165] See n. 163.

[166] 'Why is simple treatment not available even when a mother's life is at risk?', *The Irish Times*, 21 December 2010.

[167] 'Abortion nightmare for cancer sufferer', *The Irish Independent*, 29 December 2010.

pregnancy, to terminate her pregnancy lest it interfere with life-saving treatment. The hospital's ethics forum, however, decided against allowing the abortion, saying her life was not under 'immediate threat' and she was forced to travel to England, which led to a five-week delay in her treatment. The state settled her claim, and she died shortly afterwards.[168] Her story was covered extensively in the media.

In 2010 the international NGO Human Rights Watch published a highly critical report on Irish abortion laws, arguing that the state was violating many of its international human rights obligations by restricting access to abortion services and information both within Ireland and for Irish women seeking services abroad.[169] Other international bodies continued to press the state, including the UN Committee against Torture which urged the Irish government, in its first periodic review of Ireland, to 'clarify the scope of legal abortion through statutory law',[170] and the Commissioner for Human Rights of the Council of Europe who released a critical report on the lack of legislation clarifying the circumstances in which abortion would be available.[171]

The government responded to the combination of international and domestic pressure with small steps, agreeing to form an expert group to address the ruling in *ABC*,[172] and submitting an Action Plan to the Committee of Ministers of the Council of Europe in relation to the implementation of the ruling.[173] The international pressure continued, however, with a highly critical report by the Special Rapporteur on the Right to Health to the UN General Assembly,[174] and recommendations from six other states to Ireland on the reform of its abortion law (including the implementation of the *ABC* ruling) during Ireland's first Universal Periodic Review in October 2011.[175] The Committee of Ministers of the Council of Europe (the enforcement arm of the ECHR system) expressed continued concern at the length of the delay of the government's response.[176] The publicity around

---

[168] 'State settled with cancer patient', *The Irish Times*, 22 November 2012.

[169] *State of Isolation: Access to Abortion for Women in Ireland* (2010).

[170] United Nations Committee Against Torture, *Concluding observations of the Committee against Torture, Consideration of reports submitted by State parties under article 19 of the Convention (9 May–3 June 2011)* UN Doc. CAT/C/IRL/CO/1 (17 June 2011) at para. 26.

[171] Council of Europe, Commissioner for Human Rights, *Report by the Commissioner for Human Rights, Mr Thomas Hammarberg on his visit to Ireland (1-2 June 2011)*, 15 September 2011, at 7.

[172] *Programme for Government* (2011).

[173] *A, B and C v. Ireland, Action Plan, Information submitted by the Government of Ireland* (16 June 2011). Available online at https://health.gov.ie/blog/press-release/action-plan-a-b-and-c-v-ireland-application-no-255792005-grand-chamber-judgment-16th-december-2010-information-submitted-by-the-government-of-ireland-on-16th-june-2011/.

[174] United Nations General Assembly, *Note by the Secretary General, Right of everyone to enjoyment of the highest* attainable standard of physical and mental health, UN Doc. A/66/254 (3 August 2011) para. 11-14.

[175] Report of the Working Group on the Universal Periodic Review, UN Doc. A/HRC/19/9 (21 December 2011).

[176] Council of Europe, Committee of Ministers, 1136th meeting on 8 March 2012, Case against Ireland, Case No. 12, available online at https://search.coe.int/cm/pages/result_details.aspx?objectid=0 9000016805cb729.

the case and the international condemnation it generated led to the establishment of several grassroots advocacy and support groups, including Terminations for Medical Reasons, led by Irish women who had pregnancies involving fatal foetal abnormalities, and the Abortion Rights Campaign in 2012, both of which became important and influential parts of the domestic campaign for abortion reform.[177]

Attempts by a small number of lawmakers, including long-time activist and parliamentarian Claire Daly, to introduce legislation early in 2012 to implement the X case failed.[178] And just a few hours after the 'expert group' which had been tasked by the government with implementing the ABC case issued its report containing various options in November that same year,[179] news of the death of a woman named Savita Halappanavar began to spread. The circumstances surrounding her death became a further crucial catalyst for changes in public opinion on the availability of abortion in Ireland. She was admitted to hospital at 17 weeks of pregnancy and was found to be miscarrying, but despite her repeated requests for a termination, the hospital staff refused, citing amongst other reasons the fact that Ireland was a Catholic country.[180] Even though she was found to have contracted a serious bacterial infection, doctors did not intervene due to the presence of a foetal heartbeat and because they did not believe her life to be in danger. She later received treatment but died from septicaemia a week after arriving at the hospital. An inquiry subsequently found that 'concerns about the law ... impacted on the exercise of clinical professional judgment'.[181]

Shortly after Savita Halappanavar's death, the Council of Europe's Committee of Ministers issued a further sharp rebuke of the government's delay in implementing the ABC judgment of the ECtHR,[182] and this time the government acted by introducing the Protection of Life During Pregnancy Bill. The proposed legislation allowed for abortion in circumstances where a woman's life was at risk from physical illness or suicide, and elicited great controversy amongst members of the legislature despite the fact that it sought only to codify the existing law resulting from the X case.[183] NGOs including Amnesty International and the Irish Council for Civil Liberties made submissions to the relevant legislative committee, citing

---

[177] Minister for Health, Simon Harris, later credited the organization Terminations for Medical Reasons with changing his mind on the need for reform of Irish abortion law. 'Simon Harris: I felt ashamed at abortion treatment and changed my view', *Irish Independent*, 29 December 2017.

[178] 'TDs reject abortion Bill in vote', *The Irish Times*, 19 April 2012.

[179] *Report of the Expert Group on the judgment in A, B and C v Ireland* (November 2012), available online at https://health.gov.ie/wp-content/uploads/2014/03/Judgment_ABC.pdf.

[180] 'Midwife manager "regrets" using "Catholic country" remark to Savita Halappanavar', *The Irish Times*, 10 April 2013.

[181] *Investigation of Incident 50278 from time of patient's self-referral to hospital on the 21st of October 2012 to the patient's death on the 28th of October, 2012*, Health Service Executive, June 2013, at 69.

[182] 'Ireland told to expedite abortion legislation or regulation' *thejournal.ie*, 10 December 2012, available online at http://jrnl.ie/710582.

[183] See e.g. Deputy Eamon Ó'Cúiv, *Protection of Life During Pregnancy Bill 2013: Second Stage (Resumed) (Continued)* 1 July 2013, at 21, available online at https://data.oireachtas.ie/ie/oireachtas/debateRecord/dail/2013-07-01/debate/mul@/main.pdf.

Ireland's international and European human rights obligations,[184] and the legislation was eventually adopted in July 2013.

E. From 2013 until the 2018 referendum: the reform of Irish abortion law

The interaction between domestic advocacy and international human rights bodies in pressurizing state actors continued with increasing intensity in the years that followed these events. The death of Savita Halappanavar prompted extensive public protests and vigils across the country, and injected energy and urgency into the slow and fitful debate which had been taking place in Ireland over the previous decade. Several months after her death saw the establishment of the Coalition to Repeal the Eighth Amendment, an umbrella organization which united a number of existing pro-choice groups with others including doctors, midwives, students' unions, artists, and local and regional community groups. At the same time, a range of international institutions continued both to mirror and to supplement the domestic campaigns, maintaining high-profile public pressure by criticizing the state's restrictive abortion regime, including the Human Rights Committee during Ireland's periodic review in 2014[185] and the UN Special Rapporteur on Torture.[186]

Two further domestic cases captured the headlines once more: the case of a young asylum seeker known as 'Y' who discovered on arrival in Ireland that she was pregnant, apparently as a result of rape in her country of origin. She said she would rather die than have the baby, but due to extensive delays in providing her with travel documents on account of her asylum-seeker status, she was eventually told at 22 weeks that it was too late for an abortion. She was admitted to a maternity hospital where she refused food and drink, and a decision was made to deliver the baby prematurely by caesarian at 24 weeks.[187] Her later claim for battery against the state was settled. In a second case around the same time, a young woman was declared to be brain dead after a fall, and her family wanted to remove her from life support and bury her. However, as she was found to be 12–14 weeks pregnant, medical staff felt themselves obliged by law to consider the right to life of the foetus. For a few weeks after her death, her body was kept on mechanical ventilation and fed and medicated through a tube. This treatment was intended to postpone the deterioration of her body and the collapse of her internal organs up to a point where

---

[184] Joint Committee on Health and Children, *Report on Protection of Life during Pregnancy Bill 2013 (Heads of) Volume 2* (May 2013) at 93, 341, and 363.

[185] United Nations Human Rights Committee, *Concluding observations on the fourth periodic report of Ireland (19 August 2014)* UN Doc. CCPR/C/IRL/CO/4 at para. 9.

[186] 'UN Human Rights Committee Chairman says Irish law treats raped women as a "vessel"', *RTÉ News*, 15 July 2014, available online at https://www.rte.ie/news/2014/0715/630888-un-human-rights/.

[187] 'Timeline of Ms Y case', *The Irish Times*, 14 October 2014, available online at https://www.irishtimes.com/news/social-affairs/timeline-of-ms-y-case-1.1951699.

the foetus would be viable, but her family was strongly opposed to this and wanted her to die with dignity. Her father brought legal proceedings and the court ruled that since the prospects for delivery of a live baby were virtually non-existent, it was in the 'best interests of the unborn' that the treatment be discontinued.[188]

Meanwhile advocates continued to press for change through domestic political as well as legal channels, and through the use of international human rights mechanisms. Ongoing attempts by Clare Daly, Mick Wallace, and other members of the legislature to introduce a bill to allow for abortion in cases of fatal foetal abnormalities in 2015 and again in 2016 were defeated, with the attorney general providing advice that the proposed law was unconstitutional.[189] In its report on Ireland's third periodic review under the ICESR, the UN Committee on Economic, Social and Cultural Rights again criticized Ireland's 'highly restrictive legislation on abortion' and the lack of procedural clarity for women, and recommended a further constitutional referendum to bring the law into line with international human rights standards.[190] Similarly, the Committee on the Rights of the Child, in its report during the third and fourth periodic review of Ireland's compliance with the CRC expressed ongoing concern about the impact of Ireland's restrictive abortion regime on the human rights of girls.[191] Domestic as well as international NGOs such as Amnesty International added their voices to the debate by emphasizing both the hardship and stress for Irish women, as well as the violation of multiple international human rights standards and norms.[192]

A major constitutional initiative was taken the following year to establish a 'Citizens Assembly' which was tasked amongst other things with making recommendations on Ireland's abortion laws.[193] Domestic political activism which had been focused the previous year on a referendum on same-sex marriage was shifted now with greater energy onto reproductive rights. Fresh cases involving Irish

---

[188] *PP v. HSE* [2014] IEHC 622 at para. 40. See Murray, '*PP v Health Service Executive: A Reanalysis—Part 1*', 33(12) *Irish Law Times* (2015) 174 at 177. Little consideration was given to the rights of the woman: see M. Enright, *PP v HSE: Practicability, Dignity and the Best Interests of the Unborn Child*, 28 December 2014, HumanRights.ie, available online at https://inherentlyhuman.wordpress.com/2014/12/28/pp-v-hse-practicability-dignity-and-the-best-interests-of-the-unborn-child/.

[189] 'Dáil defeats Clare Daly's abortion Bill 104 to 20', *The Irish Times*, 10 February 2015, available online at: https://www.irishtimes.com/news/politics/dáil-defeats-clare-daly-s-abortion-bill-104-to-20-1.2098098. See also *Protection of Life in Pregnancy (Amendment) (Fatal Foetal Abnormalities) (No. 2) Bill 2013: Second Stage [Private Members]* Dáil Debate, 30 June 2016, available online at https://www.oireachtas.ie/en/debates/debate/dail/2016-06-30/51/?highlight%5B0%5D=abortion&highlight%5B1%5D=abortion&highlight%5B2%5D=abortion&highlight%5B3%5D=abortion&highlight%5B4%5D=abortion.

[190] United Nations Committee on Economic, Social and Cultural Rights, *Concluding observations on the third periodic report of Ireland (8 July 2015)* UN Doc. E/C.12/IRL/CO/3, at para. 30.

[191] United Nations Convention on the Rights of the Child, *Concluding observations on the combined third and fourth periodic reports of Ireland, (1 March 2016)* UN Doc. CRC/C/IRL/CO/3-4, at paras 57–58.

[192] *She Is Not A Criminal: The Impact of Ireland's Abortion Laws* (2015) 19, available online at https://www.amnestyusa.org/pdfs/Ireland_She_Is_Not_A_Criminal.pdf, see 98.

[193] 'Taoiseach pledges citizens' assembly on abortion issue', *The Irish Times*, 17 December 2015; *Programme for Partnership Government* (2016) 84.

women came to public attention, including one in which a suicidal girl was detained in a mental health unit after requesting an abortion,[194] as well as the case of Amanda Mellet, which she brought as an individual complainant to the UN Human Rights Committee under the ICCPR.[195] Mellet had been 21 weeks pregnant when she discovered that her foetus had fatal congenital defects. Unable to receive medical treatment at home, she was forced to travel to the UK for a termination, from which she had to return immediately as she could not afford to stay overnight. The Human Rights Committee criticized the criminalization of abortion in these circumstances, finding that she had been subjected by the state to 'discrimination and cruel, inhuman or degrading treatment' and urged Ireland to reform its laws.[196] Ireland's abortion laws were also strongly criticized by at least 15 states during the Universal Periodic Review conducted by the Human Rights Council in 2016,[197] although the government refused to accept any recommendations other than to consult with all stakeholders on the possibility of a further constitutional referendum to reform the legal framework.[198] Clare Daly drew attention in parliament to the violation of international human rights law which had been highlighted in the *Mellet* case, and pointed out that it was not just a domestic constitutional issue.[199]

The Citizens Assembly—an initiative that in the years since its establishment has gained considerable attention worldwide as an apparently successful 'mini-public' experiment in deliberative democracy—took place over a period of 10 weekends, beginning in late 2016.[200] The Assembly received over 13,000 submissions from the public, including from NGOs, interest groups, and individual citizens, on the issue of abortion as well as a number of other constitutional topics with which the body had been tasked. Attention was drawn to the incompatibility of the constitutional ban on abortion with numerous human rights provisions, and to the findings of the many international human rights bodies which had expressed their views on the issue.[201] The *Mellet* case, and the fact that the government had accepted the

---

[194] *Child Care Law Report Project* (2017) Vol. 1, available online at https://www.childlawproject.ie/publications/order-detaining-pregnant-girl-seeking-abortion-discharged/.

[195] Human Rights Committee, Communication no. 2324/2103 (2016).

[196] Ibid. para. 99.

[197] United Nations Human Rights Council, *Report of the Working Group on the Universal Periodic Review*, UN Doc. A/HRC/33/17 (18 July 2016). The Committee did, however, note the government's plans to establish a citizens' assembly: see para. 121.

[198] Ibid. paras. 135 and 136.

[199] *Protection of Life in Pregnancy (Amendment) (Fatal Foetal Abnormalities) (No. 2) Bill 2013: Second Stage [Private Members]* Dáil Debate (30 June 2016), available online at https://www.oireachtas.ie/en/debates/debate/dail/2016-06-30/51/?highlight%5B0%5D=abortion&highlight%5B1%5D=abortion&highlight%5B2%5D=abortion&highlight%5B3%5D=abortion&highlight%5B4%5D=abortion.

[200] https://www.citizensassembly.ie/en/previous-assemblies/citizens-assembly-2016-2018-/.

[201] See submission of the Irish Family Planning Association, 'A health and rights approach to abortion in Ireland', *Submission to the Citizens' Assembly* (16 December 2016) at 13; and of the Irish Human Rights and Equality Commission, *Submission to the Citizen's Assembly in its consideration of Art 40.3.3 of the Irish Constitution* (16 December 2016), at 27–29.

findings of the Human Rights Committee, was invoked by several submissions.[202] The impact of abortion law on the human rights of minorities such as the Travelling community[203] and on women with disabilities was also emphasized by others.[204] Several of those who made written submissions were later invited to speak to the Assembly,[205] and the importance of international human rights standards was mentioned alongside domestic law and policy concerns.[206]

While the Assembly was taking place, the UN Human Rights Committee made public its decision in another case brought by an Irish woman, Siobhán Whelan, who had been forced to travel to the UK to terminate her pregnancy on discovering that the baby had a congenital brain defect.[207] In each of these and other striking cases—A, B & C, Ms D, Amanda Mellet, and Siobhán Whelan—it was the publication of the international committee report or judgment and the media interest attracted by these that helped to bring the women's experiences to wider public attention and to catalyse the kind of anger and empathy that further fuelled the domestic movement. Several further sources of external pressure on Ireland to reform its abortion law during the same period, again complementing and interacting with the domestic pressure, included the critical report of the CEDAW committee in its periodic review,[208] the report of the Council of Europe's Commissioner for Human Rights following a visit to Ireland,[209] and the very critical periodic report of the UN Committee against Torture (which acknowledged and encouraged the work of the Citizens' Assembly).[210] When the time came for the Citizens' Assembly to vote on its final recommendations, while views certainly differed as to what kind of reform should be introduced, there was an overwhelming majority in favour of

---

[202] See the Irish Human Rights and Equality Commission, ibid. at 17; Amnesty International Ireland, 'Human Rights Compliant Framework for Abortion in Ireland', *Submission to the Citizens' Assembly* (16 December 2016), at 7, 8, and the National Women's Council, *Submission to the Citizens' Assembly on its Consideration of the Eighth Amendment to the Constitution* (December 2016), at 11.

[203] National Traveller Women's Forum, *Submission to the Citizens' Assembly on the Eighth Amendment to the Constitution*, at 1.

[204] Centre for Disability Law and Policy, *Submission to the Citizens' Assembly on Repeal of the Eighth Amendment to the Constitution* (15 December 2016).

[205] The groups were Amnesty International Ireland, Atheist Ireland, Coalition to Repeal the Eighth Amendment, Doctors for Choice, Doctors for Life Ireland, Every Life Counts, Family & Life, Irish Catholic Bishops' Conference, Irish Family Planning Association, Parents for Choice, Pro Life Campaign, General Synod of the Church of Ireland, Iona Institute, National Women's Council of Ireland, Union of Students in Ireland, Women Hurt, Youth Defence.

[206] See e.g. the presentation by Coalition to Repeal the Eighth Amendment, *Paper of Coalition to Repeal the Eighth Amendment delivered to the Citizens' Assembly on 5 March 2017*, at 3, and the presentation by the Union of Students in Ireland, *Paper of the Union of Students in Ireland (USI) delivered to the Citizens' Assembly on 5 March 2017*, at 2.

[207] *Whelan v. Ireland*, Human Rights Committee, Communication no. 2425/2014 (2017).

[208] United Nations Committee on the Elimination of Discrimination against Women, *Concluding observations on the combined sixth and seventh periodic reports of Ireland*, 9 March 2017, UN Doc. CEDAW/C/IRL/CO/6-7, at para. 42.

[209] Council of Europe, Commissioner for Human Rights, *Report by the Commissioner for Human Rights, Nils Muižniek on his visit to Ireland (22-25 November 2016)* (29 March 2017), at 19.

[210] United Nations Committee Against Torture, *Concluding Observations on the second periodic report of Ireland*, para. 31.

amending Article 40.3.3 of the Constitution. The government established a parliamentary committee to examine the Assembly's findings and to recommend reform, and over the months which followed the committee heard evidence and recommendations from many sources and held many question and answer sessions, including on the issue of Ireland's international human rights obligations.[211]

The parliamentary committee published its recommendations at the end of the year, advising that Article 40.3.3 of the Constitution should be replaced with a provision enabling the parliament to adopt legislation to regulate abortion, and recommending that a referendum be held to that end. Amongst the reasons given by the Committee was the ongoing breach of Ireland's international human rights obligations, as indicated in the *Mellet, Whelan, ABC*, and other cases.[212] Reference was also made to these decisions in the parliamentary debates which followed,[213] and ultimately the opposition leader of the socially conservative party, Micheál Martin of Fianna Fáil, announced his intention to support repeal of the restrictive constitutional provision. This was followed by the decision of the prime minister (Taoiseach) at the time, Leo Varadkhar, and the entire cabinet to support its repeal, despite deep schisms within the various political parties on what had long been an emotive and bitterly divisive issue in Ireland. Despite litigation which threatened to complicate the constitutional position in relation to the rights of the unborn,[214] a referendum bill was published proposing to repeal Article 40.3.3, and to replace it with a clause stipulating that 'provision may be made by law for the regulation of termination of pregnancies'. In addition to repealing Article 40.3.3, the referendum bill outlined the main elements of the legislation which the government planned to introduce, which included the legalization of abortion up to 12 weeks without specific grounds and afterwards on grounds of risk to health or life (both physical and mental), the decriminalization of any woman's request for abortion, and the provision of abortion in case of fatal foetal abnormalities.[215]

---

[211] See e.g. the evidence of Peter Boylan, former head of the national maternity hospital, *Business of Joint Committee on the Eighth Amendment of the Constitution* (18 October 2017), and of Christina Zampas, Joint Committee (4 October 2017), at 22-26.

[212] *Report of the Joint Committee on the Eighth Amendment of the Constitution* (December 2017), at 5. Three dissenting members of the Committee published their own report, arguing amongst other things that 'consistent pressure to expand abortion in Ireland lacks a basis in international law': *Minority Report/Joint Assessment of Peter Fitzpatrick TD, Mattie McGrath TD and Senator Ronan Mullen on the work of the committee on the Eighth Amendment and its conclusions* (20 December 2017), at 7.

[213] See Deputies Bríd Smith and Catherine Connolly in Dáil Debates, 17 January 2018, available online at https://www.oireachtas.ie/en/debates/debate/dail/2018-01-17/25/, and Alan Kelly in Dáil Debates, 25 January 2018, available online at https://www.oireachtas.ie/en/debates/debate/dail/2018-01-25/26/.

[214] See the case of *IRM v. Minister for Justice* [2016] IEHC 478, in which a High Court judge ruled that an unborn child had constitutional rights beyond the right to life in Article 40.3.3; but this holding was overturned on appeal to the Supreme Court: *IRM v. Minister for Justice* (2018) paras. 11.21–11.25, which ruled that the unborn did not constitute 'children' for the purposes of other constitutional rights, but that the state was nonetheless entitled under statute to act to protect the interests of the unborn (para. 10.63).

[215] For details, see the government's *Policy Paper: Regulation of Termination of Pregnancy*, Department of Health, 8 March 2018.

An intense and passionately argued two-month referendum campaign involving extensive public participation and media coverage followed the publication of the referendum wording and the proposed legislation. The campaign to repeal Article 40.3.3 was composed of a range of civil society groups including the National Women's Council, the Abortion Rights Campaign and the Coalition to Repeal the 8th Amendment. Campaigning against the repeal and in favour of the retention of a strict anti-abortion regime were a collection of other civil society groups including 'Save the Eighth' (comprising the Life Institute and Youth Defence) and 'Love Both' (run by the Pro Life Campaign). In the course of the campaign, a variety of arguments and issues were raised, but a particularly prominent part in the public debate was played by women who came forth for the first time to speak about the fact that they had sought abortions, travelled for abortion, or been refused abortion in a range of difficult circumstances. Whereas abortion had previously been a matter of shame and secrecy for many Irish women, and had remained an unspoken subject for so long, the gradual emergence into the public gaze of women such as Amanda Mellet and Siobhan Whelan, and the widespread shock and sympathy generated for the women and girls affected in the *X*, *Y*, and *ABC* cases, and by the death of Savita Halappanavar, meant that unlike in earlier debates on the subject, the suffering of particular women and the presence of vulnerable human faces and voices were connected to the issue of abortion. Bolstering and supporting these individual human stories was the articulation of legal and policy arguments based partly on international human rights law, such as the campaign launched by the Irish Council for Civil Liberties highlighting the impact on the rights of women of Article 40.3.3 of the Constitution.[216]

On 25 May 2018, the referendum to repeal the 8th amendment to the Constitution took place. The voter turnout was 64 per cent, and the referendum was passed by a majority of 66 per cent of the population. Thirty-five years after its adoption in the 1983 referendum, Article 40.3.3 of the Constitution was finally repealed, and a much less restrictive legislative scheme on abortion was approved.

5. Conclusions

The two examples provided in this chapter illustrate in different ways the slow but ultimately very significant changes brought about in Ireland in the fields of children's rights and welfare on the one hand, and reproductive rights on the other, through social advocacy campaigns which included the ongoing engagement by domestic activists with international human rights law and institutions over several decades. Although the way in which the campaigns were conducted and

---

[216] Irish Council for Civil Liberties, *Her Rights*, available online at https://www.iccl.ie/her-rights/.

evolved, and the nature and number of the groups spearheading them and the degree of underlying social support they enjoyed varied, both sets of campaigns drew extensively and continuously on international human rights law and institutions and worked through a dynamic of ongoing engagement through mobilization and pressure 'from below' as well as the activation of external accountability and pressure on the state 'from above' to press for legal and political change.

The social, political, and constitutional influence of Catholicism in Ireland presented a significant challenge for groups which sought to bring about reform in these areas. The greater emphasis in the Constitution on the authority of the family than on the rights of the child and the underlying set of social priorities which this reflected presented an obstacle for advocates seeking to promote child welfare policies that took account of the autonomous interests, needs, and rights of children. In the field of reproductive autonomy, on the other hand, social and religious beliefs about the sanctity of unborn life had made the issue of abortion virtually taboo in Ireland, and the enactment of the Article 40.3.3 of the Constitution in 1983 at the behest of conservative groups fearing the growth of a liberal social movement had seemed to lock-in the most restrictive position possible. Yet in the case of each of these issue areas, change was brought about through a long-term process which included the persistent invocation and use by domestic advocates and activists of international human rights law and institutions, and the publicity, accountability, and pressure brought to bear from both above and below on a range of governmental and other actors, while building social support for the causes. None of this is to suggest that law in general or international human rights law in particular was the driving force behind child rights and reproductive rights reform in Ireland. As noted in Chapter 2, it would be difficult if not impossible to sustain a clear and simple argument about the unambiguously causal effect of international human rights law in bringing about change. Throughout these decades in Ireland, changes were taking place in attitudes towards the Catholic church and its authority as a result of numerous intersecting social forces and events, including the coming to light of specific horrors such as widespread child sexual abuse by clergy and the effective imprisonment of unmarried mothers and their children in brutal 'mother and baby' homes run by religious institutions. Nevertheless, the way in which grassroots and domestic advocacy on children's rights engaged with international human rights law and activism as part of their campaigns for reform formed an important part of the wider set of national and transnational social and political processes within which child rights reform and abortion law reform were brought about in Ireland.

The example of child welfare reform in particular demonstrates how a coalition of hitherto separate child-focused organizations and groups came together following Ireland's ratification of the Convention on the Rights of the Child, and re-oriented their work and their advocacy around the idea of children's rights. By bringing issues before the Committee on the Rights of the Child, and requiring the government to engage repeatedly with the Committee and with the meaning and consequences in practice of the obligations taken on under the Convention, they injected fresh impetus into existing domestically focused campaigns, opened a public conversation about children's rights, and placed Ireland's practices and attitudes towards children and the family in the context of international and transnational standards. They developed and pursued new initiatives and ultimately succeeded in pressing for the adoption of a range of important legislative and policy reforms.

The study of the process of abortion law reform—and reproductive rights more generally—which is a more specific issue area than the broader field of child rights but also historically an even more divisive and difficult one in Ireland, points to the ways in which domestic activists as part of their strategies drew upon and engaged a variety of international human rights institutions and laws (including courts, treaty bodies, and other international actors) over a number of decades both to keep pressure on the government and the state to introduce change, as well as to create public awareness of the suffering of specific women and to highlight existing and emerging international norms on reproductive rights. While domestic advocacy and the effort to change social attitudes to abortion in Ireland was at the heart of the campaign, at the same time the output of international human rights institutions and the amplification of their interventions in the Irish media played an important part in that effort to change the way abortion was viewed and understood in the country.

The cases brought by or on behalf of particular Irish women and girls to the ECtHR and the Human Rights Committee of the ICCPR were not only intended to draw attention to the situation in Ireland and to generate external accountability and additional pressure on the state, but they were also part of the iterative process of articulating, contextualizing, and developing the existing international human rights norms governing reproductive rights. Thus the procedural rights of women to access services which are lawful in the state, which had initially been enunciated in the *Tysiac* case against Poland,[217] were further articulated and clarified in the Irish *ABC* case of the ECHR, in which they were applied to the situation of a woman whose life would be threatened by the continuation of her pregnancy. And the decision of the Human Rights Committee to condemn the domestic criminalization of abortion in the circumstances of Amanda Mellet, whose foetus had a fatal abnormality and who had to travel to the UK for an abortion, strengthened and reinforced the development which had begun in international human rights law towards recognizing the denial of abortion in various circumstances as cruel, inhuman, and degrading treatment.[218] At the same time the painful stories of many other women, which for decades had remained secret and concealed, were

---

[217] See n. 161.
[218] See Zureick (n. 108).

encouraged to be shared by the example of these few women whose cases were brought to international attention by being litigated or considered by regional and international tribunals and treaty bodies. The bringing of those cases to international institutions gave support to the women and legitimacy to their complaints by highlighting and confirming that the treatment they had endured violated very basic and widely shared international standards. At the same time, the publicity given to their stories was amplified by the international context, and by the sense that Ireland was an outlier in the harshness and restrictiveness of its treatment of women, and that this treatment constituted a violation of basic human rights.[219]

The story of children's rights reform was a less turbulent one—though it certainly encountered opposition and resistance—than the campaign for reproductive rights reform. It was driven mostly by a sector of professional civil society which organized and coalesced to engage with government and other domestic institutions to promote change, as compared with the more powerfully contested and wider grassroots campaign of social mobilization for abortion law reform. Yet international human rights law played a significant part in each of the two different campaigns for change, by helping to highlight and publicize specific injustices, channelling external attention, providing a focal point for domestic advocacy, articulating and developing standards and rights to be asserted, strengthening arguments for legislative and policy reform, increasing pressure on the state to act, and providing support and legitimacy for the domestic campaigns. Even while the reforms in question took place in the context of a much broader and complex set of cultural, socio-political, as well as economic transformations unfolding in Ireland over those decades, it is clear that the targeted advocacy campaigns for children's rights and reproductive rights drove those reforms, and that the continuous interaction between domestic advocates and international human rights institutions and bodies played an important part in the ultimate success of those campaigns.

[219] To understand better the role that key actors within the abortion law reform campaigns saw international human rights law playing in those campaigns and in the wider movement for law reform, a number of interviews were carried out with some of these actors in the preparation of this chapter. Those interviewed include Senator Ivana Bacik; Clare Daly TD; Mairead Enright, Reader at Birmingham University and founding member of Lawyers for Choice; Gráinne Gilmore, spokesperson for Together for Yes and Lawyers for Yes, Liam Herrick and Meabh O'Rourke, Irish Council for Civil Liberties, Colm O'Gorman of Amnesty International, and Denise Roche of the National Women's Council of Ireland.

6

The past and future of human rights

The lessons derived from the advocacy campaigns discussed in earlier chapters can help to test the experimentalist account of human rights but also to evaluate the potential for the human rights movement to confront the major challenges of the current era. On the one hand, those campaigns suggest that the experimentalist practice of human rights advocacy is reasonably resilient and adaptive. On the other hand, internal contestation from within the movement as well as external critiques in recent years have helped to galvanize reform and to push activists and advocates to think more innovatively about the changes needed to strengthen their ability to engage with problems as diverse and fundamental as illiberalism, climate change, digitalization, pandemics, and economic and other forms of inequality.

1. Reflections on past human rights advocacy

A. Lessons from the case studies

I argued in earlier chapters that some of the prominent critiques of the failings of the human rights movement have tended to exaggerate its deficiencies, to understate its achievements, and to misunderstand or mischaracterize its many ways of working in practice. They do so while calling on current and future generations to abandon the flawed human rights movement, at a time when illiberal authoritarianism has been taking hold in many parts of the world, facilitated and exacerbated in ways by the COVID-19 pandemic, and when human rights advocates and defenders are facing increasing threats to their safety and their lives.

The studies of particular human rights campaigns in different parts of the world described in the preceding chapters were chosen in part as a response to such critiques. The aim was to illustrate, through detailed examples of a range of campaigns in different countries and different contexts, some of the ways in which international human rights law and advocacy has been effectively used to advance progressive change around the world. The campaigns chosen do not focus on some of the classic civil and political rights—such as torture or freedom of expression—which have been the subject of several previous studies of the impact of human rights law. Instead they focus on rights which do not fall easily on one or other side of the civil-political/socio-economic rights divide, including gender equality, educational access, reproductive freedom, and an array of children's rights. Further,

Reframing Human Rights in a Turbulent Era. Gráinne de Búrca, Oxford University Press (2021). © G de Búrca.
DOI: 10.1093/oso/9780198299578.003.0006

they are campaigns which were pursued not within formally authoritarian regimes but in a variety of democratic systems—settled, hybrid, and unstable—with a view to examining human rights advocacy in contexts where there is acknowledged scope for civil society activism.[1]

These examples were chosen also to exemplify the experimentalist account of international human rights law and advocacy advanced in Chapter 2. I have offered this account as an alternative to theories of human rights effectiveness which assume either a bottom-up or a top-down dynamic, since it emphasizes not only the crucial role of both domestic activism and international accountability, but also the interactive, mutually constitutive as well as iterative dimensions of international human rights in practice. The three sets of campaigns chosen are clearly just only instances, intended to exemplify and illustrate aspects of human rights experimentalism, but many others might have been chosen.

Each of the studies provides some support for the experimentalist account of human rights effectiveness proposed in Chapter 1. Each indicates a range of ways in which human rights, including the treaty bodies that provide ongoing monitoring and interpretation of human rights provisions, were used as part of powerful campaigns for social change driven by civil society advocates. Activists drew on the experience, visibility, and external accountability provided by international human rights bodies and networks of support to bolster their campaigns for domestic reform, and in each case there was an ongoing and eventually productive back-and-forth between domestic advocates, international human rights bodies, and other domestic institutions and actors in pushing for change. Women's groups and organizations established to promote gender justice in Pakistan engaged repeatedly with the Convention on the Elimination of all Forms of Discrimination Against Women (CEDAW) and Universal Periodic Review (UPR) processes over the years, as well as with international and regional networks of support; disability rights activists in Argentina used an array of Convention on the Rights of Persons with Disabilities (CRPD) processes; and children's rights and reproductive rights campaigns in Ireland brought and supported cases before the regional human rights court as well as numerous international treaty bodies to bolster their domestic mobilization for legal and policy reform. The campaigns were lengthy and contested, and international processes such as human rights litigation, treaty body reporting, and UPR were often complex, bureaucratic, and difficult to navigate. As observers have noted, the voices and concerns of activists are almost inevitably

---

[1] See however on the ubiquity of 'societal authoritarianism' within all kinds of regimes, democratic as well as autocratic, see Chua, 'Legal Mobilization and Authoritarianism', 15 *Annual Review of Law and Social Science* (2019) 355. On the difficulty of mobilizing for human rights in highly authoritarian political systems, see 'Struggles from Below: Literature Review on Human Rights Struggles by Domestic Actors', Research and Innovation Grants Working Papers Series' (21 February 2017), available online at https://www.usaid.gov/sites/default/files/documents/2496/Struggles_from_Below_-_Literature_Review_on_Human_Rights_Struggles_by_Domestic_Actors.pdf.

diluted, altered, and diffused when they encounter the international human rights system.[2] Nevertheless, in each of the examples studied, long-term campaigns that brought together domestic activism and international human rights processes resulted eventually in a range of significant social and legal reforms, and in some cases the international norms were also developed and changed in response.

Much of the focus throughout this book has been on the crucial role of domestic mobilization—of activism and advocacy on the part of civil society actors and those affected—in promoting human rights. But the case studies also suggest that domestic mobilization for human rights in many circumstances may not be necessarily be sufficient or most effective if it remains entirely a bottom-up process, despite how important social mobilization is to a successful outcome. In all of the campaigns described in the studies, the strategies used by activists to promote human rights relied at important junctures for impact and leverage on the way they engaged with international norms and ideas, external institutions, or processes of accountability, and with transnational networks of support. Just as much, however, it is equally clear that the process of human rights reform in each of the campaigns was very far from being a top-down process where the pressure on governments to take action to realize rights commitments came mainly from external actors or elites, whether other governments, international committees, courts, rapporteurs, or transnational networks. Instead it was through ongoing interactions between multiple domestic and external sets of actors, processes, and institutions—domestic, regional, and international—over time that progress in the various campaigns for reform and development and implementation of the rights claimed in practice took place.

In that sense the three studies in this book provide some support for the proposition that it is in ongoing mobilization around a set of transnational human rights ideas or norms, and through continued iterative engagement between sets of actors and institutions at the national and international levels, that the levers of human rights reform can be seen to work. The impetus, energy and ideas that drove eventual reform in all three country studies originated with those who experienced the impact of its absence and their advocates, i.e. social movements and civil society actors of various kinds. Women's groups and gender-focused NGOs in Pakistan, disability activists and their supporters in Argentina, and child rights advocates and reproductive rights activists in Ireland mobilized to draw attention to their cause and to demand change. They were bolstered by their networks—transnational and regional networks which provided them at different times with

---

[2] See Billaud, 'Keepers of the Truth: Producing Transparent Documents for the Universal Periodic Review', in H. Charlesworth and E. Larking (eds), *Human Rights and Universal Periodic Review* (2015). Also Cowan and Billaud, 'Between Learning and Schooling: The Politics of Human Rights Monitoring at the Universal Periodic Review', *Third World Quarterly* (2015) 1175. Also MacDowell Santos, 'Mobilizing Women's Human Rights: What/Whose Knowledge Counts for Transnational Legal Mobilization?', 10 *Journal of Human Rights Practice* (2018) 191.

material and ideational support, resources, shared experiences, and strategies International human rights bodies and institutions provided a focal point, an external, information-generating accountability forum, a medium through which their claims and demands at particular moments were channelled and aired, and a mechanism through which the normative standards contained in the various human rights treaties were discussed and interpreted. Independent domestic institutions, including courts, Ombuds offices, media, and parliamentary actors and others, helped to raise the profile of the issue on the domestic public agenda, supplied veto points, and helped to maintain pressure on governmental actors to introduce reform. The picture of international human rights law and advocacy emerging from the studies is not a bottom-up or top-down mechanism, but a dynamic and interactive movement in which multiple actors at multiple sites engage in an (often highly contested and resisted) iterative process which helps to promote legal, policy, and practical change affecting those who assert their rights. The rights-related reforms eventually introduced in each of the three case studies included constitutional, legislative and policy change, as well as a range of changes in practice.

One of the interesting intermediate effects of human rights law seen in each of the studies has been the impact of treaty ratification on domestic civil society. At least three sets of effects of this kind are evident from those campaigns. First, in several of the contexts discussed, a range of service groups or organizations focused on the welfare of particular population groups, whether women, persons with disabilities, children, or others, were already in existence; and one effect of human rights treaty ratification and the introduction of the international review process associated with it was to prompt some of those groups over time to shift their focus and approach to a rights-based advocacy strategy. This was seen in Ireland in relation to children's rights, in Argentina with disability rights, and to a lesser extent in Pakistan with some of the prior women's organizations. A second effect of treaty ratification in particular instances was to bring different kinds of groups together into coalitions that had not previously existed, in other words to catalyse greater cooperation amongst NGOs and other social groups in using the new opportunities created by the treaty ratification to pursue broadly shared goals. This was clear in Ireland with the formation of the Children's Rights Alliance from a multiplicity of existing NGOs after the ratification of the Convention on the Rights of the Child (CRC). A comparable alliance was created among numerous child rights organizations in Argentina after the CRC was ratified there, and similarly the influential REDI civil society alliance was established in the field of disability rights following Argentina's ratification of the CRPD. Even when NGOs did not come together to create formal or permanent alliances, they often collaborated intensively in the context of participating in the treaty body review process and preparing shadow reports. A third such effect of human rights treaty ratification on domestic civil society was to trigger the creation of entirely new organizations which had not previously existed, such as Sisters in Islam, and Musawah, which sought to integrate feminist readings of the Koran with the international human rights framework in countries with a Muslim-majority population. These findings are consistent with those of Kiyoteru Tsutsui in his book on the engagement of domestic minority movements with international human rights in Japan.[3] Tsutsui argues that engagement with international human rights norms and institutions 'transformed movement actorhood' in the country, 'altering actors' subject positions to reshape their goals and approaches.'[4] And while acknowledging that the relative impact of advocacy in different areas requires closer examination, he argues nonetheless that the use of international institutions and rights in all cases in his study made a difference to the domestic campaigns and to policy change.[5]

It is important to emphasize again, however, returning to the argument of Chapter 1, that any strong causal claim as to the role of international human rights in changing substantive law and policy is likely to be impossible to substantiate, and even mistaken in its conception. The processes of reform described in the various examples in this book are embedded in a whole range of social, political, and economic changes and developments. This seems most obvious when the campaigns pursue major and controversial change over decades, such as the Irish abortion law reform, or policies to challenge the subordination of women in Pakistan, but strong causal claims about the role of human rights law seem equally inapt in most cases. Even in the context of quite focused and discrete campaigns such as the provision of certificates of completion of education for persons with disabilities, or the establishment of an Ombuds office for children in which the role of human rights law was very prominent, any attempt to isolate the specific impact of human rights law and advocacy from other social and political processes of change is problematic. This point has been made at times by social scientists to question the impact and significance of human rights law.[6] However, the argument of this book is not that human rights law and advocacy have by themselves brought about the reforms discussed, but that they have played an important and even arguably indispensable part in these processes of reform. The values, discourse, institutions, and tools of human rights have provided a moral, political, and legal frame for activists and social movements in their campaigns for change, and these have altered dynamics at important stages of those campaigns, providing crucial leverage for reform.

At the same time, each of the cases studied has also yielded a range of insights in terms of the limits and failures of particular campaigns, as well as their successes, and in the variations between them. While the general proposition that international human rights law and advocacy has helped human rights campaigns to

---

[3] K. Tsutsui, *Rights Make Might* (2018).

[4] Ibid. 216.

[5] Ibid. 218.

[6] Chilton and Posner, 'The Influence of History on States Compliance with Human Rights Obligations', 56 *Virginia Journal of International Law* (2016) 211.

further progressive change through ongoing iterative interaction between a range of domestic and international actors and institutions finds support in all three sets of country studies, they also differed from one another in a range of relevant respects.

B. Argentina

The Argentina study described a number of campaigns for human rights reform, some quite specific and centred on individual cases concerning disability rights, as well as others which were broader and more diffuse such as those relating to pension reform or child rights. The processes of activism and the outcomes produced by the various campaigns invoking human rights differed in a number of respects. The two main instances of advocacy for inclusive education involved a clear and specific objective on an issue which was not especially divisive (even though it was not uncontested)—the right to reasonable accommodation within an educational course, and the recognition of education through adequate certification of completion. In these two instances, the bringing of legal and administrative proceedings by two individuals, drawing on the CRPD and its application to that context, and with the support of domestic disability rights organizations, led to broadly satisfactory outcomes for both, and to legal and policy changes—at least initial changes, even if further reform is still sought—on the issues in question. The two cases concerned discrete policy changes which were not particularly costly for the state to implement and were not particularly socially controversial. The issue complained of in each situation had been mainly the consequence of failure to recognize the distinctive position and needs of persons with disabilities, including what would be required to include them fully in the existing educational context. No major campaign to generate and mobilize popular support proved necessary to reach a fairly successful outcome for each: their advocacy with the backing of disability rights groups and the CRPD committee and its jurisprudence, and with the involvement of courts and the support of the media, was enough to yield a positive outcome and at least the first steps towards reform of the practices challenged.

By comparison, the issue of pensions for persons with disabilities was one which was costly to the government and affected significant numbers of people across the country. In this case, although litigation invoking the CRPD was brought to challenge the measure, it was the social pressure created by angry public protests, critical media coverage and popular outrage, rather than litigation, that led the government to reverse its decision to cut these pensions, although the CRPD was also frequently invoked as part of the media coverage and in the protests. The ongoing campaign on the part of reproductive rights activists to reform Argentina's abortion law, on the other hand, while it has generated a significant social movement (*ni una menos*, building on existing 'national women's encounters' in Argentina) including large-scale protests and engagement with international human rights law and institutions took several years to provoke legislative reform to overturn the existing ban on abortion other than in cases of rape or risk to life.

The Argentine examples suggest that in the case of wider and costlier policies such as pension reform and child poverty which implicate socio-economic inequalities, as well as for more socially divisive issues such as abortion, the building of a strong social movement, and the mobilization of significant and demonstrable public support is likely to be very important to supplement legal and other tools of human rights campaigning and litigation, and particularly when the distributive implications of reform are significant.

C. Pakistan

The study of Pakistan examined the use of CEDAW by domestic activists to promote the rights of women through an array of campaigns on different issues ranging from family law to gender-based violence, harassment, political participation, institutional reforms, and others. Perhaps unlike the example of disability rights and inclusive education in Argentina, most if not all of the injustices on which women's groups have been campaigning in Pakistan are less a consequence of neglect or oversight than a consequence of deliberate and entrenched patriarchal social and political structures, and of the centrality of religion to political and social life. None of the changes sought was uncontroversial, and most of the reforms came about only after decades of struggle and advocacy. While there has been a women's movement for quite some time in Pakistan, it has not always been strong and prominent, and the movement for women's human rights remains divided along urban and rural lines, with women from the professional and elite classes being those most prominently involved in activism. Organized civil society groups and NGOs dedicated to gender equality have regularly used international human rights institutions and drawn on transnational networks of support, as well as leveraging support from domestic institutions. Their advocacy has yielded results in the shape of numerous hard-won legislative reforms both at federal and provincial level, many of which refer explicitly to international human rights law. But at the same time, and despite the lengthy struggle to get these laws enacted, the implementation in practice of the legal reforms has lagged significantly behind. This is evidently a consequence of the ongoing lack of political will and inadequacy of resources dedicated to implementation. Hence the example of women's rights in Pakistan suggests that human rights advocacy aimed at reforming a system which reflects deeply socially entrenched practices will require more than legally targeted reform, even with the backing and support of international as well as domestic law and institutions. It requires the building of a wider and stronger social movement against misogynistic and patriarchal practices—something which recent women's marches in Pakistan have begun to reflect and to generate—to underpin legal and other advocacy strategies, to mobilize around particular outrages against women and girls, and to press more powerfully for implementation.

D. Ireland

While both the child rights and reproductive rights campaigns in Ireland included the kind of iterative engagement with domestic and international human rights institutions and networks by domestic activists that the experimentalist account describes, there were also key differences between the two campaigns and in the factors that were important to their relative success. The subject of child welfare, although not without controversy in Ireland, was significantly less socially divisive than abortion. In the case of reproductive rights, while domestic advocacy around international institutions proved important in the process of mobilizing for change, ultimately it was the building of a strong social movement including protests and demonstrations but also the sharing and highlighting of individual stories of suffering that proved decisive in shifting public opinion to support reform. The language of human rights was also less prominent in the abortion campaign than in the children's rights campaigns, although international human rights institutions played an important if underappreciated role in highlighting and giving prominent voice to the hardships of particular (formerly silenced) women and emphasizing Ireland's outlier status on abortion. By comparison, in the context of child rights reform, a strong coalition of children's advocacy groups came together around the Convention on the Rights of the Child and managed to press successfully for an array of important human-rights inspired institutional and policy reforms over two decades, without any significant social movement or broader social mobilization emerging to support the introduction of these changes. Nevertheless, despite the successes of child rights advocacy in bringing significant changes to Irish law and policy in this regard, two caveats should be entered. In the first place, some of the changes, such as the insertion of a provision in the Constitution to enshrine the best interests of the child, were criticized (e.g. for being poorly worded or not adding sufficiently to the status quo) and the relevant referendum turnout was low. This would suggest that even when an issue is relatively uncontroversial or of low salience, the pursuit of particular human rights reforms likely to result in significant change—such as a constitutional amendment—would be better done after first building wider public awareness of and support for the reform. In the second place, as has also been the case in Argentina, one of the major and persistent challenges for child rights advocates in Ireland is the high rate of child poverty. Reforms entailing significant and visible distributive consequences generally require the mobilization of extensive social support both for generating broader legitimacy as well as for supplying sufficient political pressure, and it is less likely that low-profile human rights advocacy on the part of specialized NGOs who are mainly in dialogue with the government will succeed, even with the backing of international norms and institutions, in the absence of that wider underlying social support.

One significant qualification to or refinement of the experimentalist hypothesis that international human rights law helps to promote progressive social change through the iterative interaction of domestic civil society, international institutions, and independent domestic institutions, which emerges from the case studies is therefore the following: human rights advocacy campaigns that have not built a broad base of social support are less likely to succeed in bringing about change, particularly when the change sought is controversial or costly, even where there is sustained interaction with and support from international human rights institutions and actors, and from independent domestic institutions. The importance of social movements and of building wider support for particular causes is clear in different ways in all three studies. This also raises a question which is the reverse of the argument in this book (that social mobilization helps to promote human rights), namely whether human rights can bolster social movements. Human rights might, for example, strengthen social movements by anchoring some of their legitimacy in universalist values, providing a basis for generating wider social support, or helping to provide traction in their campaigns. Certainly, it is noteworthy that participants in many of the social protests which took place around the world in 2019 invoked the language of human rights, including both socio-economic and political rights, suggesting that they saw it as important to their claims. Similarly, the co-founder of the Black Lives Matter movement which erupted so powerfully again in the United States in 2020 has described it as in essence a human rights movement, combining both civil-political and socio-economic rights in its demands.[7]

2. Contemporary challenges for human rights

The various examples outlined in the book describe human rights campaigns for reform that took place over lengthy periods of time, in some cases over decades. The reasons for looking more closely at campaigns in different parts of the world include responding to scepticism about the influence of human rights law and advocacy, and presenting an alternative account of the functioning of international human rights law to that of some prevailing accounts. Yet even if the examples used are sufficiently convincing in their account of the role played by human rights law

---

[7] Tometi and Lenoir, 'Black Lives Matter Is Not a Civil Rights Movement', *Time Magazine*, 10 December 2015: 'Black Lives Matter is often called a "civil rights" movement. But to think that our fight is solely about civil rights is to misunderstand the fundamental aspirations of this movement ... It is about the full recognition of our rights as citizens; and it is a battle for full civil, social, political, legal, economic and cultural rights as enshrined in the UDHR'.

and advocacy in advancing rights-based reform in these instances, and in suggesting a plausible account of the effectiveness of human rights in those cases, a more urgent question is whether any lessons to be drawn from those examples and from the experimentalist account remain relevant for the future.

Many of the events examined in the various examples from Pakistan, Argentina, and Ireland took place during a period in which the international human rights system and its array of laws and institutions had become solidly established, when the language of human rights had become broadly accepted in many parts of the world, and before the powerful contemporary backlash had begun to spread in earnest. The period from the 1950s until the early years of the twenty-first century was, broadly speaking, one of establishment, expansion, and consolidation of the legal and institutional framework of international human rights. It was during the decades described in the Argentina, Ireland, and Pakistan case studies that a substantial number of UN and regional human rights treaties were adopted, widely signed, and ratified (even if with numerous reservations and opt-outs) and that the Universal Periodic Review was created. The various institutional mechanisms for monitoring and enforcing those human rights treaties gained a degree of legitimacy and acceptance amongst states and civil society during these years, and many if not most of the governments which had signed on to the treaties accepted at least in principle their obligation to comply with the commitments undertaken. None of this is to suggest that it was an uncontentious period, that there were not major challenges to the doctrines and practice of human rights as well as ongoing and widespread human rights violations, or that all states were comfortably on board with a strong system. Nevertheless there was a clear sense that the human rights regime was increasingly a matter of fairly broad international consensus and that a wide array of states supported the ratification and implementation of multiple human rights treaties and the establishment of human rights institutions.

The current era, on the other hand, is a very challenging one for human rights. It is a turbulent and rapidly changing time in terms of the shifting geopolitical order, widening inequality, the outbreak of a major pandemic, the spread of digitalization, and fundamental doubts about the sustainability of the planet. There are of course numerous other pressing issues confronting human rights advocates, and a multiplicity of serious injustices and challenges that could be added to those addressed here. For present purposes, however, several developments which are of particular contemporary salience have been chosen for the specific challenges they pose to the human rights movement, including in the ways in which they intersect with one another. Below, some of the implications for human rights advocacy of the rise of political illiberalism, the digital revolution, the onset of climate change, rising inequalities and the pandemic outbreak will be discussed, with a view to considering whether a model of human rights law and advocacy which may have had success in previous decades is really fit for the current time.

A. The rise of political illiberalism

The past decade has seen significant changes taking place in the global political landscape, which have brought with them a set of increasingly insistent challenges to human rights laws and institutions. Prominent amongst them is the rise of nationalist political illiberalism with its concomitant backlash against international institutions and against human rights.[8] While it was certainly not uncommon in previous decades for governments at times to reject particular rulings of human rights courts, to ignore recommendations of human rights treaty bodies or special rapporteurs, and even to reject or withdraw from a treaty or a regional system,[9] the more sustained pushback against human rights in recent years is arguably different in scale and degree.[10] Fuelled by a notable rise in political movements on the extreme right, illiberal nationalist parties and leaders entered government in many parts of the world including the Philippines, Turkey, India, Brazil, Hungary, and Poland, some of which were formerly liberal democratic states. Many governments and leaders have become overtly hostile to human rights laws and institutions, including treaties and systems to which their states had been party for many years. The United Kingdom and the United States under conservative governments joined numerous other states in expressing increasing scepticism towards human rights laws and institutions. In addition to challenging the role and legitimacy of human rights courts and bodies, some states have cut their funding and have withdrawn or threatened to withdraw from them, as in the case of the United States from the Human Rights Council or Russia's long-running threat to withdraw from the European Convention on Human Rights.[11] Observers and human rights advocates fear that international institutions in response to these moves have begun to self-censor and to weaken their monitoring.[12] Many states have also taken steps to limit the freedom of action as well as the funding of civil society organizations

---

[8] Helfer, 'Populism and International Human Rights Law Institutions: A Survival Guide', in G. L. Neuman (ed.), *Human Rights in a Time of Populism: Challenges and Responses* (2020) 218.

[9] See e.g. Helfer 'Overlegalizing Human Rights: International Relations Theory and the Commonwealth Caribbean Backlash against Human Rights Regimes', 102 *Columbia Law Review* (2002) 1832. On Venezuela's withdrawal from the American Convention on Human Rights in 2012, see Mejía-Lemos 'Venezuela's denunciation of the American Convention on Human Rights', 17 *AJIL Insights* (2013). And more generally for the somewhat fractious relationship of the UK and the European Convention on Human Rights system over time, see K. S. Ziegler, E. Wicks, and L. Hodson (eds), *The UK and European Human Rights: a Strained Relationship* (2015).

[10] For a useful summary see Vinjamuri, 'Human Rights Backlash', in S. Hopgood, J. Snyder and L. Vinjamuri (eds), *Human Rights Futures* (2017). See also Helfer, 'Pushback Against Supervisory Systems: Lessons for the ILO from International Human Rights Institutions', Duke Law School Public Law & Legal Theory Series No. 2019-55.

[11] See for the US reduction in support to UN and regional human rights bodies over reproductive rights, https://ijrcenter.org/2019/04/08/u-s-resists-international-oversight-reduces-iachr-funding-over-reproductive-rights/.

[12] See e.g. Stiansen and Voeten, 'Backlash and Judicial Restraint: Evidence From the European Court of Human Rights', 17 August 2018, available online at SSRN https://ssrn.com/abstract=3166110; also Helfer (n. 10) 273.

and NGOs involved in the promotion of human rights, and there has been a per-ceptible increase in repression and violence against human rights defenders, often with tacit support from the state in question.[13] In short, in many different parts of the world, human rights laws are being dismissed or ignored, the institutions and courts charged with interpreting them are being criticized and efforts made to weaken and de-fang them, and the activists and advocates who mobilize to im-plement these rights are being constrained and targeted. More generally, the rise of political illiberalism is challenging and undermining democracy in many places, even when autocratic governments assert, as in Hungary, that in reality they rep-resent a new form of 'illiberal democracy'.[14] Instead, illiberal governments have moved to weaken or undo any constraints or checks on their authority, to capture institutions so as to entrench their power, and to silence critics and opponents as well as to limit rights and freedoms which might be used to challenge them.[15]

B. The era of digitalization

A second major recent transformation which presents significant challenges to the human rights project as it has developed to date is digitalization. Digitalization—the process of integrating digital technology into many if not all aspects of life—has been profoundly transforming social and economic life, as well as practices of government worldwide. Technology is no longer primarily a tool to be used for specific and defined purposes. It is an immensely powerful force which not only shapes most of modern communication but also increasingly and fundamentally organizes the way we live, work, and are governed. While many of the positive changes and innovations brought by technology have the potential to enhance and strengthen human rights advocacy and activism and even to transform some of its modalities and practices, the dark side of digitalization is also profoundly challen-ging to human rights.

The loss of privacy resulting from the constant and ubiquitous gathering and use of data on individuals and groups by private companies and—lagging somewhat behind them but no less eagerly—by governments is perhaps only the most ob-vious of these risks. The centrality of surveillance has long been associated with the authoritarian state, but the nature and rapidity of technological change is such that

---

[13] See Buyse, 'Squeezing Civic Space: Restrictions on Civil Society Organizations and the Linkages with Human Rights', 22 *International Journal of Human Rights* (2018) 966 and Amnesty International, *Laws Designed to Silence: The Global Crackdown on Civil Society* (2019).

[14] For a challenge to the argument that 'illiberal' democracy can constitute a form of democracy, as opposed to a new form of majoritarian authoritarianism, see Chopin, 'Démocratie Illibérale ou Autoritarisme Majoritaire', Notre Europe, Policy Paper No. 235 (19 February 2019), and W. Sadurski, *Poland's Constitutional Breakdown* (2019), Ch. 9.

[15] See e.g. A. Polyakova *et al.*, *The Anatomy of Illiberal States: Assessing and Responding to Democratic Decline in Turkey and Central Europe*, Brookings Institute, February 2019.

centralized surveillance of this kind is now becoming common in all kinds of democracies, with many organizations warning of the rise and spread of digital authoritarianism.[16] While China's high-tech repression of the Uighur population and the country's social credit system may have initially garnered the most headlines, the emergence and creation of somewhat similar systems of social credit are not confined to authoritarian states.[17] Governmental as well as private digital ID systems gather and rely on multiple forms of biometric information—fingerprints, facial recognition, iris scans, palm veins, DNA, and more—and an increasing number of states condition access to various public goods on participation in and compliance with such systems.[18] And the enthusiasm during the COVID-19 pandemic for the development of contact-tracing smartphone apps, which have been presented as an effective way of helping to control the resurgence and spread of the virus, have raised related concerns about privacy, equity, and freedom, as well as doubts about the effectiveness of such digital tracing mechanisms.[19]

Today, decision-making by algorithm abounds. Algorithmic decision-making gives rise to numerous human rights-related risks, including its disproportionate impact on those living in poverty.[20] Indeed many of the possible risks have not been considered in advance, yet the technology continues to advance rapidly and to be put into practice.[21] Artificial intelligence and automation are fundamentally changing the workplace, while digital exclusion and data inequality can significantly affect life chances in an era in which access to public services including education, health, and welfare are increasingly conditioned on internet access

---

[16] See e.g. https://freedomhouse.org/report/freedom-net/2018/rise-digital-authoritarianism A. Polyakova and C. Meserole, *Exporting Digital Authoritarianism: The Russian and Chinese Models*, Brookings, August 2019, available online at https://www.brookings.edu/research/exporting-digital-authoritarianism/, J. Sherman, *The Long View of Digital Authoritarianism*, New America Weekly, 20 June 2019, available online at https://www.newamerica.org/weekly/edition-254/long-view-digital-authoritarianism/. Shoshana Zuboff has written powerfully about surveillance capitalism and the implications for democracy and human freedom of a ubiquitous global digital architecture: The Age of Surveillance Capitalism (2019).

[17] See e.g. M. Elgan, *Uh-oh: Silicon Valley is Building a Chinese-style Social Credit System*, 26 August 2019, available online at https://www.fastcompany.com/90394048/uh-oh-silicon-valley-is-building-a-chinese-style-social-credit-system; Greenfield, 'China's Dystopian Tech Could be Contagious', *The Atlantic*, 14 February 2018; and M. Variyar and J. Vignesh, *The New Lending Game Post-Demonetization*, 6 January 2017, available online at https://tech.economictimes.indiatimes.com/news/technology/the-new-lending-game-post-demonetisation/56367457.

[18] The number of countries adopting digital ID systems on every continent is growing too rapidly to count—one private sector company mentions over 70 but the number is constantly rising: https://www.gemalto.com/govt/identity/2016-national-id-card-trends. Some of those whose systems have given rise to human rights challenges include India, Kenya, Ireland, the UK, and Tunisia.

[19] See A. Soltani, R. Calo, and C. Bergstrom, *Contact-Tracing Apps Are Not A Solution to the COVID-19 Crisis*, Tech Stream, Brookings, 27 April 2020.

[20] On the problems of the emerging digital welfare state, see the Report of the Special rapporteur on extreme poverty and human rights to the UN General Assembly of 11 October 2019, A/74/48037.

[21] For an analysis of some of the ways in which artificial intelligence may impact human rights, see the report prepared by the Council of Europe's Committee of Experts on Internet Intermediaries, *Study on the Human Rights Dimensions of Automated Data Processing Techniques (In Particular Algorithms) and Possible Regulatory Implications* (2017).

and other forms of digital connection and fluency. In short, the multiple ways in which technology has been transforming social, political, and economic life are all-encompassing and profound, and thought has only recently begun to be given to the ways in which it may undermine rather than advance human welfare, freedom, dignity, and justice.

C. Climate change

A third fundamental challenge confronting the international human rights system is climate change. In addition to the basic existential threat it poses to the future of the planet, the rapid progress of global warming presents particular challenges to many existing social and political practices, including those of the human rights movement. Reports from the UN Office of the High Commissioner for human rights and from other international environmental and human rights actors have noted the impact of extreme weather events on rights throughout the world, including the right to life, health, housing, water, and sanitation, food, self-determination, culture, and development.[22] Less developed countries in the global south and states that are particularly geographically situated—as well as those living in poverty everywhere—suffer disproportionately from the negative impacts of climate change.[23] The scale, speed, and force of the impacts of global warming mean that the challenges they pose for political, economic, and social life and practice are widespread and profound.

D. Increasing inequality

Fourth, the widening of existing socio-economic inequality, while by no means a new or recent challenge in the way that the digital revolution and the pandemic are, has nonetheless accelerated and become more prominent in recent decades. In particular, the set of neoliberal economic policies which prevailed in the United States and Europe from the 1980s Reagan-Thatcher era onwards, together with the 'Washington consensus' policies pursued globally by international financial institutions, unapologetically promoted the interests of capital and the enrichment of the wealthy, while undermining the provision of public goods and services through unchecked privatization and presiding over increasing income inequality. Thomas Piketty's powerful study in 2014 presented twentieth century capitalism as

---

[22] See https://www.ohchr.org/EN/Issues/HRAndClimateChange/Pages/AboutClimateChangeHR. aspx.
[23] See the report of the UN Special Rapporteur on Extreme Poverty and Human Rights on 'Climate change and Poverty' of 25 June 2019, A/HRC/41/39. See also the climate vulnerability index developed by the Intergovernmental Panel on Climate Change.

a facilitator of plutocracy and brought the issue of economic inequality to the fore-front of current political debate.[24] And the growth of both left-wing and right-wing populist parties over the past decade as well as the vote of the British people in favour of leaving the European Union in 2016 have been widely seen as a response—at least in part—to rising socio-economic inequality.

The pervasiveness of such inequality challenges human rights in multiple ways, violating a range of economic and social rights,[25] as well as civil and political rights.[26] And while extreme inequality is by no means a new challenge, its expansion over recent decades including in wealthier countries has been magnified and exacerbated by the other challenges mentioned here. At the same time, as noted in Chapter 1, critics have argued with increasing force that the human rights movement is implicated in this problem; that it has been weak and inadequate when confronted with socio-economic inequality; that it has accompanied and facilitated structural injustice and inequality; and that it is not up to the task of change going forward. The inadequacy of the human rights framework in tackling the deep economic and political structures which maintain a grossly unequal world has been a refrain of many critical scholars including David Kennedy, Martti Koskenniemi, Naomi Klein, Susan Marks, and Wendy Brown for several decades, joined more recently by historically-oriented scholars such as Jessica Whyte, Samuel Moyn, and others.

E. COVID-19

A fifth major challenge, already noted above in its intersection with the spread of digitalization and surveillance, is the COVID-19 pandemic which originated in late 2019 and spread worldwide. The pandemic has had rapid and pervasive effects on almost every aspect of social, economic, and political life. Amongst these effects are many which have serious implications for an array of human rights as well as for the human rights movement. In the first place, the pandemic has provided opportunities for existing authoritarian governments to introduce additional repressive measures that further limit an array of freedoms, as well as for democratic-backsliding governments to do the same, and even for fairly stable and robust democratic regimes to introduce emergency measures and to derogate from existing human rights commitments. Further, and apart from the introduction of emergency measures and human rights suspensions and derogations, including

---

[24] T. Piketty, *Capital in the 21st Century* (2014).

[25] See e.g. Young, 'Inequality and Human Rights', 5 *Inference* (2019) 1 and Dehm, 'Righting Inequality: Human Rights Responses to Economic Inequality in the United Nations', 10 *Humanity* (2019).

[26] See the Report of the Special Rapporteur on extreme poverty and human rights, Philip Alston, Human Rights Council, Twenty-ninth session, Agenda item 3, A/HRC/29/31 (27 May 2015).

increased policing and repression to enforce pandemic measures, the fact that some of the tools proposed in many jurisdictions for responding to COVID-19 have involved increased digital surveillance has raised concerns on the part of human rights organizations.

In addition, and even without the fresh interventions of governments to repress civil liberties and suspend formal human rights guarantees, the immediate impact of the pandemic has been to exacerbate all of the existing socio-economic inequalities and to hit poorer and marginalized communities much harder than middle class or wealthy parts of the population within states, as well as to mirror and worsen existing global inequalities among states. The racial disparities in the harmful effects of COVID-19 have been very evident in many countries. The effects of the pandemic on those living in crowded or inadequate accommodation in which social distancing is not possible, on those with precarious jobs and few or no savings, and on those living in countries with weak, inegalitarian, or non-existent healthcare systems have been particularly devastating.

F. Implications for human rights law and advocacy

While several of the contemporary challenges described here—particularly the onset of climate change—have been looming for quite some time, few of them were prominent during the period when the various human rights campaigns discussed in this book took place. The increasing salience of rising inequality and the rapid spread of political illiberalism—including within formerly liberal democratic states—and the pushback against human rights law and institutions have gathered pace mainly since the global economic crisis of 2008, and the digital revolution has similarly gained rapid momentum over the last decade. The profound effects of global warming have also significantly accelerated in recent years, and the epoch-making COVID-19 outbreak began only in 2019. Each of these challenges alone and certainly all of them together present human rights advocates and activists with a different and more turbulent global political, social, and economic landscape compared to that which pertained during the various campaigns described in earlier chapters.

What are the implications of these challenges for the account of human rights law and advocacy presented in the book so far? The rise of illiberalism and the backlash against human rights law and institutions is perhaps at first the most obvious threat, in the sense that the account of human rights law and advocacy I have advanced is premised on the interaction between domestic social movements and civil society activists, international human rights institutions and actors, and independent domestic institutions, putting pressure on states to introduce change. If illiberal and populist governments are increasingly challenging the authority and legitimacy of international human rights norms and institutions, limiting the freedom and resources of civil society to mobilize and advocate, and undermining independent domestic institutions which might check their power, the potential for human rights law and advocacy to advance social change is likely to be significantly affected. And even if it remains, for now, a specific group of states that is most openly challenging and undermining international human rights law and institutions, the wider legitimacy and status of institutions can gradually and even rapidly be eroded if other states begin to follow suit. Ryan Goodman and Derek Jinks have written persuasively about the ways in which states are socialized or acculturated into joining human rights treaties and processes by virtue of their proximity to and relations with other states which are members of these, and there is little reason to think that the isomorphic behaviour is not equally likely to manifest in the other direction.[27] In other words, if powerful and influential states within global governance groupings are reneging on, challenging, and withdrawing from human rights treaties and systems, it seems likely that other states will take the opportunity follow suit, thereby also weakening and diluting the regime for those that remain.

The digital revolution also presents new and difficult questions for those seeking to advance social justice through human rights advocacy. While, unlike the growth of illiberalism, technological change can also greatly benefit and enhance human rights advocacy even as it poses risks, nevertheless the experimentalist account of human rights law and advocacy may not seem well-equipped to address certain aspects of the digital revolution. One example concerns the factor of time.[28] The case studies of particular human rights struggles examined in previous chapters each involved persistent and long-term campaigns which in some cases continued for several decades before change was eventually brought about. This gradual and long-term approach does not seem well suited to the rapid pace of technological change. Another factor is the target of human rights advocacy. The conventional target of much if not most human rights advocacy to date has been the state, since even when the private sector is the dominant source of human rights abuse, advocates have tended to seek durable and broadly applicable solutions in public regulation rather than through aiming activity at particular corporations or private actors.[29] Yet in the digital era, it is the private sector that is driving technological change and any meaningful effort to shape a human rights-respecting

---

[27] R. Goodman and D. Jinks, *Socializing States: Promoting Human Rights Through International Law* (2013). See also B. Greenhill, *Transmitting Rights: International Organizations and the Diffusion of Human Rights Practices* (2016).

[28] See e.g. C. Rodríguez-Garavito, 'For Human Rights to Have a Future, We Must Consider Time', Open Global Rights, 10 June 2019, available online at https://www.openglobalrights.org/for-human-rights-to-have-a-future-we-must-consider-time/.

[29] For an argument that civil society actors are beginning to mobilize more effectively to target corporate accountability for human rights, see Birchall, 'The Role of Civil Society and Human Rights Defenders in Corporate Accountability' (forthcoming 2020) in S. Deva and D. Birchall (eds), *The Edward Elgar Research Handbook on Human Rights and Business*, available online at SSRN https://ssrn.com/abstract=3566318.

digital environment will need to engage more frontally with the role of the private sector. A third factor is the highly specialized nature and opacity of much advanced technology, which renders it difficult for advocates and those affected to challenge, even where adverse effects are evident or likely.

Climate change also starkly presents the experimentalist account of human rights law and advocacy with its limitations. As in the case of challenges of digitalization, the ongoing and long-term character of the account of human rights advocacy outlined in this book seems ill-suited to the urgency of many of the threats posed by climate change.[30] The collective rather than individual character of climate harms also suggests that some of the traditional tools of human rights law will be less helpful in addressing the widely felt impacts of global warming. Further, the combination of the climate challenge, which has given rise to increasing grassroots advocacy, with that of growing illiberalism, has resulted in environmental activists and advocates being made a particular target of repressive governmental measures as well as harassment and violence. As the stakes have grown higher, the crackdown on climate activists has become ever more aggressive.[31] Finally, the anthropocentrism of the human rights project may seem ill-suited to the realities of climate change in which the planet and the biosphere are in need of protection just as much as the human inhabitants of the planet, and in many cases in need of protection from human use and exploitation.[32]

Similarly, the COVID-19 outbreak confronts the model of human rights advocacy described in this book with major challenges. Quite apart from the immensity of the impact on the pandemic on social and economic life and the widespread hardship it has caused with particular impact on already disadvantaged communities, the extensive social restrictions and other repressive measures which have been put in place to contain the spread of the virus have drastically limited rights such as freedom of assembly, association, and protest. And since the experimentalist approach to human rights law and advocacy derives much of its energy and effectiveness from social mobilization and activism, these restrictions present real difficulties for the work of human rights advocates. At the same time, the derogations and states of emergency introduced by many states complicate the monitoring functions of the array of international human rights bodies which also play an important role.[33]

---

[30] Rodríguez-Garavito (n. 28).

[31] See the report by Global Witness, 'Enemies of the State? How the Government and Businesses Silence Land and Environmental Defenders', 30 July 2019, available online at https://www.globalwitness. org/sv/campaigns/environmental-activists/enemies-state/. See also Matejova, Parker, and Dauvergne, 'The Politics of Repressing Environmentalists as Agents of Foreign Influence', 72 *Australian Journal of International Affairs* (2018).

[32] Humphreys, 'Climate Change and Human Rights: Anthropocentric Rights', *Global Policy Journal*, November 2015. See also S. Humphreys (ed.), *Human Rights and Climate Change* (2010).

[33] For a compilation of Venice Commission reports on states of emergency published by the Venice Commission in response to the rash of COVID-19 related states of emergency, see CDL-PI(2020)003, Strasbourg, 16 April 2020, available online at https://rm.coe.int/16809e38a6. The UN Office of the

3. Can human rights rise to the challenge?

The scale and complexity of the various challenges are immense, and the question is what role the international human rights movement can play in shaping and promoting meaningful responses. While that might seem to beg the question of whether humanity as a whole is able or prepared to respond, there is ultimately no alternative. Various critics have pointed to undoubted shortcomings, hypocrisies, and failures of the human rights movement to argue that it is not fit for purpose in the years ahead, and all the more so when it comes to tackling the really major issues that are rooted in inequalities of various types. But like most such movements, the balance sheet is neither all good nor all bad. There is a great deal in the history of the human rights movement to underscore its immense mobilizing potential and to show that the ideals, energy, and institutional support that have made it an often powerful, dynamic, and resilient movement in recent decades, will be much needed in the struggle for justice in the current turbulent era. To abandon rather than reform and renew human rights mobilization, as many contemporary critics have advised those seeking progressive change to do, would leave that struggle significantly poorer and less well-equipped to meet those challenges.

A. Illiberalism

It is clear that human rights advocates and activists seeking to work in a current and future political environment, in which international human rights institutions and networks are challenged and defunded, civil society actors are targeted and their freedoms curbed, and governments are systematically removing domestic institutional checks and balances on their power, will face significantly greater obstacles than before. Nevertheless, even under such conditions of spreading illiberalism, leverage can still be generated by engagement between domestic activists, external forums for accountability, and independent domestic institutions, even if the actors and institutions may not always be the same as those which were central during the consensus era of international human rights. Human rights movements often grow and strengthen during periods of political repression, as it is generally when rights and freedoms are under threat that resistance movements develop, as seen across Latin America during the dictatorships and more recently in Hong Kong and other parts of the world. Even if they are at greater risk due to rising political illiberalism, social movements and civil society activism tend not to give up or disappear.

High Commissioner for Human Rights also offered guidance in April 2020: https://www.ohchr.org/Documents/Events/EmergencyMeasures_COVID19.pdf.

Further, even as international human rights institutions are being challenged and undermined by illiberal governments, one of the strengths of the international human rights system is its plural, dispersed and even fragmented nature. The international order more generally is a pluralistic and fragmented one, with few pretensions—despite the improbable warnings made by some against the risks of a world government—towards any kind of centralized structure or ordering.[34] And the human rights regime as a sub-system of that international order is itself highly decentralized, with regional human rights courts and commissions on several continents, as well as a multiplicity of human rights treaty bodies, special procedures, rapporteurs, and commissions of inquiry, as well as the global political monitoring of the Universal Periodic Review. There is also a proliferation of domestic human rights institutions, including national human rights institutions and commissions, Ombuds offices, as well as domestic court systems to hear human rights claims and complaints. And while some scholars have recently called for a move towards greater centralization and advanced proposals for a world court for human rights, others have strongly challenged the wisdom and desirability of such a move.[35]

Similarly, while the decline of a unipolar or hegemonic global order has meant the loss of a powerful potential ally that could at times be called in to backstop a particular human rights campaign, the rise of a multipolar world requires more strategic thinking but also broadens the options for drawing in a different range of actors, or combination of actors, in support of human rights campaigns. If one institution or court has become captured, if a particular state has withdrawn from the Human Rights Council, if support is not forthcoming from certain formerly influential human-rights-friendly governments, then other sources of external accountability and leverage can be sought, including coalitions of smaller or medium-sized states willing to take a stand.[36] Human rights advocates need to be nimble in finding the most promising sites of external accountability and normative reinforcement to bolster domestic advocacy and mobilization. To use the example of Poland, in which civil society advocates have been mobilizing to protect human rights in the face of an increasingly illiberal government which has captured many formerly

---

[34] Nonetheless it remains a concern for some commentators. See e.g. I. Somin, *A Cosmopolitan Case against World Government*, 16 August 2017, available online at https://2bf6d7da-e054-43b3-a9a8-7b2fd4133c39.filesusr.com/ugd/bdf8dc_038b5c5ba11a49ef8f04cb80c0653fe1.pdf.

[35] M. Scheinin, *Towards a World Court for Human Rights*, 30 April 2009, available online at http://www.eui.eu/Documents/DepartmentsCentres/Law/Professors/Scheinin/WorldCourtReport30April2009.pdf and Nowak, 'A World Court for Human Rights', in G. Oberleitner (ed.), *International Human Rights Institutions, Tribunals, and Courts. International Human Rights* (2018). For criticisms of the idea, see Alston 'Against a World Court for Human Rights', 28 *Ethics and International Affairs* (2014) 197 and Tigroudja, 'La création d'une Cour mondiale des droits de l'homme est-elle contra victima? Libres propos introductifs', in O. de Frouville (ed.), *Le système de protection des droits de l'homme des Nations Unies: présent et avenir* (2017) 163. For a historically informed overview, see de la Rasilla, 'The World Court of Human Rights: Rise, Fall and Revival', 19 *Human Rights Law Review* (2019).

[36] See K. Roth, *The Pushback Against the Populist Challenge*, Human Rights Watch World Report (2018), available online at https://www.hrw.org/world-report/2018/pushback-against-the-populist-challenge.

independent domestic institutions: if, as some observers fear, the European Court of Human Rights over time becomes a weaker venue for human rights claims due to the pressure imposed on the institution by backlash from various governments,[37] domestic advocates might—depending on the issue—choose the European Court of Justice, the Venice Commission on Democracy Through Law, the Council of Europe's Commissioner on Human Rights, the UN Human Rights Committee, or some combination of these and other venues or institutions appropriate to the subject and jurisdiction. This, in fact, is what civil society groups in Poland have been doing in recent years as the government has grown increasingly authoritarian. And as others have noted, international human rights institutions have long operated in unfavourable political settings and have survived by playing a long game, as well as working proactively to shape the external environment in which their decisions are received and supporting the work of civil society in counter-mobilizing.[38]

Equally, if some of the independent domestic institutions such as higher courts become politically captured or weakened within particular states, there are likely to be others which remain sufficiently independent—such as an Ombuds office, a Human Rights Commission, or even certain media actors—to provide support and leverage for human rights activists and advocates. Regional networks can also often become a source of support when the domestic environment grows particularly repressive.[39] Another development which has gathered pace in recent years is the integration of human rights into domestic parliamentary processes, with a view to 'democratizing' human rights and spreading the enforcement and promotion of human rights beyond the usual realm of litigation and judicial action.[40] While not all parliaments or parliamentary committees may be sufficiently independent of government at particular times to provide an autonomous counterpoint, nonetheless the greater the number of domestic institutions engaged with human rights issues, the better the chance of having one or more avoid control or capture and to be available to reinforce and support domestic activism.

Further, while repressive measures to restrict and control domestic civil society are continuing to spread and abound, including restrictions on 'foreign' funding,

---

[37] See e.g. Madsen, 'The Challenging Authority of the European Court of Human Rights', 79 *Law and Contemporary Problems* (2016) 141; Petrov, 'The Populist Challenge to the European Court of Human Rights' NYU Jean Monnet Center Working Paper 3/18.

[38] Helfer (n. 8).

[39] Civicus, a leading global alliance of civil society organizations 'dedicating to strengthening civil society and citizen action throughout the world', maintains a directory of regional and international organizations and networks available to support civil society: http://www.civicus.org/images/Civil_Society_Support_Directory_March2017.pdf.

[40] See for discussion M. Hunt, H. Hooper, and P. Yowell, *Parliaments and Human Rights: Redressing the Democratic Deficit* (2015), and M. Saul, A. Follesdal, and G. Ulfstein, *The International Human Rights Judiciary and National Parliaments* (2017). See also the Annual Report of the UN Office of the High Commissioner for Human Rights on 'The Contribution of Parliaments to the Work of the Human Rights Council and its Universal Periodic Review', 17 May 2018, A/HRC/38/25. See also the work of the Inter-parliamentary Union, available online at https://www.ipu.org/our-impact/human-rights/parliaments-and-human-rights.

philanthropic and other groups have been working to find ways to support civic activists without falling foul of these.[41] For example, innovative proposals have been made to establish a fully global rather than national or philanthropic fund to promote capacity-building and to support civil society in the implementation of the UN Sustainable Development Goals in a way that would avoid the growing set of restrictions on foreign funding.[42] Others have begun to point to the importance of adopting a time-sensitive and longer term perspective than civil society funders have traditionally done, and to recognize the long-term nature of the project of strengthening and supporting civil society, particularly in view of the resurgence of illiberalism and democratic backsliding.[43]

Indeed, at a time when illiberal forms of nationalism are rising and there is pushback against many international institutions, one of the few global agendas to have gained the support of all UN member states is that of the Sustainable Development Goals (SDGs), also known as Agenda 2030. Launched in 2015 as a successor to the Millennium Development Goals, the SDGs set out 17 broad goals aimed at poverty reduction which states have agreed they will strive to reach by 2030. While these goals—ranging from zero hunger, to health, to clean water, gender equality, climate action, access to justice, sustainable cities, and more—have gained universal agreement from UN member states in part precisely by avoiding the language of human rights, nonetheless the content of many of the SDGs is closely related to those of many human rights. On one analysis, over 90% of the goals and targets of the SDGs correspond to human rights obligations.[44] Organizations including the Office of the High Commissioner of Human Rights and the Danish Institute for Human Rights have created resources to highlight the close relationship between the SDGs and international human rights.[45] The Danish Institute in particular

---

[41] See e.g. the work of the organization Funders Initiative for Civil Society, founded in 2016: http://global-dialogue.eu/funders-initiative-for-civil-society/. See also the collective brainstorming in the essays contained in S. Brechenmacher and T. Carothers (eds), Examining Civil Society Legitimacy (2018), and the advice provided by the Global Greengrants Fund in their report Closing Civil Society Space: What Environmental Funders Need to Know (February 2019).

[42] See e.g. the proposal by Forus, which describes itself as a global network of national NGO platforms and coalitions from five continents, working to 'strengthen the capacities of civil society' and to advocate for 'better resourcing of civil society and the defense of an enabling environment for civil society organizations to influence public policy at the national, regional and international level', available online at http://forus-international.org/en/influence/resourcing-of-civil-society.

[43] M. Sovner, B. Gaberman, and W. Moody, Sustaining Civil Society: Lessons from Five Pooled Funds in Eastern Europe, CUNY, Center on Philanthropy and Civil Society (October 2019). Also T. Carothers, The Closing Space Challenge: How are Funders Responding?, 2 November 2015, available online at https://carnegieendowment.org/2015/11/02/closing-space-challenge-how-are-funders-responding-pub-61808.

[44] S. Rattray, Human rights and the SDGs—Two Sides of the Same Coin, UNDP, 5 July 2019, available online at https://www.undp.org/content/undp/en/home/blog/2019/human-rights-and-the-sdgs---two-sides-of-the-same-coin.html.

[45] See G. Curry, Human Rights, the SDGs and the 2030 Agenda for Sustainable Development, January 2019, available online at https://www.ohchr.org/Documents/HRBodies/UPR/SDGs_2030_Agenda.pdf and The SDG-Human Rights Data Explorer, The Danish Institute for Human Rights, available online at https://www.humanrights.dk/sdg-human-rights-data-explorer.

created a database linking monitoring information from the international human rights system to the goals and targets of the SDGs, with a view to developing a human rights-based approach to the SDGs.[46] And while some observers have been sharply critical of the SDGs precisely because of their failure to mention human rights, let alone to articulate an explicit rights-based agenda,[47] others have joined the United Nations Development Programme (UNDP) and the Danish Institute in seeing potential for this new global framework to advance the social justice causes espoused by the human rights movement at a time when it is difficult to find common ground or to build international agreement.[48] Indeed the SDGs are not only supported by a fairly dynamic network of civil society activists but a framework consisting of international, regional and national actors and institutions is already in place that could facilitate an experimentalist monitoring and implementation of these goals and the rights to which they correspond.[49] In a cautiously optimistic assessment of the potential of the SDGs to advance an ambitious social and environmental agenda, one human rights scholar has suggested that a reason for optimism is that the agenda's 'broader normative consensus on development is backed by an array of civil society actors that possess a particular interest in the norms for which they have fought', such that uptake by a mobilized civil society could make all the difference.[50]

A final reflection on the prospects for human rights law and advocacy to thrive in the face of growing illiberalism concerns the interaction between the different dimensions of that practice. The experimentalist account of human rights depends on the interaction of domestic activists with international institutions, transnational networks and domestic independent actors and institutions. And while one of these dimensions—international human rights institutions in particular—has been weakened in recent years with the rise of authoritarian nationalist governments, another dimension—that of social movements and domestic civic activism—may be strengthening with the recent spread of civic protests all around the world. Many of these, such as the Algerian Hirak movement,[51] the Lebanese protest movement,[52] the Iraq

---

[46] See https://sdgdata.humanrights.dk/.

[47] See e.g. Jeffrey Smith and Alex Gladstein, who criticize the attractiveness of the SDG Agenda to authoritarian regimes which do not support democracy or human rights, 'How the Sustainable Development Goals Undermine Democracy', Quartz Africa, 7 June, 2018.

[48] T. Piccione, *Breaking the Human Rights Gridlock by Embracing the Sustainable Development Goals*, Open Global Rights, 17 April 2018.

[49] J. Monkelbaan, *Governance for the Sustainable Development Goals* (2019), in particular Ch. 2.

[50] Langford, 'Lost in Transformation? The Politics of the Sustainable Development Goals', 30 *Ethics and International Affairs* (2016) 167.

[51] D. Nouri, 'The Future of the Algerian Hirak Following the COVID-19 Pandemic', Arab Reform Initiative, 7 April 2020, available online at https://www.arab-reform.net/publication/the-future-of-the-algerian-hirak-following-the-covid-19-pandemic/.

[52] 'Lebanon: 'Anti-government movement continues despite coronavirus "social distancing" orders with car protests', *The New Arab*, 21 April 2020, available online at https://english.alaraby.co.uk/english/news/2020/4/21/anti-government-movement-continues-in-lebanon-with-social-distancing-protests.

protests,[53] the Hong Kong demonstrations,[54] and Black Lives Matter in the United States, amongst others, have adapted to the restrictions of the COVID-19 pandemic by using face masks during physical demonstrations, as well as organizing virtual and other forms of protest. There is evidence of ongoing determination and renewed commitment to these movements despite the pandemic and other setbacks.[55]

It is not easy to predict what the longer-term effects of the protest movements which have erupted in many countries in recent years are likely to be, but their emergence suggests a re-energization of one of the crucial components of human rights advocacy described in this book, namely an active and mobilized citizenry asserting rights and demanding change. The relationship between organic social mobilization and protest movements on the one hand and organized civil society engaged in human rights advocacy on the other, will be discussed further below.

B. Digitalization

The rapid development of technology and its impact on social and political life is, as discussed above, a challenge with which human rights actors have recently begun to grapple.[56] Unlike the rise of illiberalism, however, the development of technology ('the fourth industrial revolution') should not in itself be a threat to human rights. Technology is a force which could ideally be used to enhance and promote human rights as much as to impede or undermine them.[57] The concern about the impact of rapid digitalization on human rights, however, has not been the idea that technology is necessarily harmful in itself, but rather that a range of both public and private uses of technology to date are having negative impacts as well as unpredictable and transformative effects on human freedom and welfare. The constant surveillance and tracking of human beings via their ever more frequent use of technology creates risks not just to privacy but to many other aspects of personal freedom, even when the surveillance and data-gathering is not carried out by authoritarian governments.[58] And despite the promise of digital inclusion and digital development for addressing poverty, discrimination and exclusion are

---

[53] Jaafari, 'Young Iraqis Regroup after the Pandemic Paused their Mass Protests', *Public Radio International News*, 5 May 2020.

[54] Hui, 'Post-Pandemic, Hong Kong Protests Will Likely Return', *Princeton Alumni Weekly*, 8 May 2020.

[55] T. Carothers and D. Wong, *The Coronavirus Pandemic is Reshaping Global Protests*, Carnegie Endowment, 4 May 2020, available online at https://carnegieendowment.org/2020/05/04/coronavirus-pandemic-is-reshaping-global-protests-pub-81629.

[56] See M. Land and J. Aronson (eds), *New Technologies for Human Rights Law and Practice* (2018).

[57] For an earlier recognition of the potential of technology to enhance the work of civil society internationally, see the essays in D. Schuler and P. Day (eds), *Shaping the Network Society: The New Role of Civil Society in Cyberspace* (2004).

[58] See e.g. S. Zuboff, The Age of Surveillance Capitalism (2019).

only some of the more obvious risks that digitalization and algorithmic decision-making pose to human rights.[59]

The pace of technological change raises questions whether the often drawn-out and long-term approaches of human rights advocacy are up to the challenge or will inevitably be left behind by rapid digital developments.[60] There is on the other hand the converse risk that rapid technologically-focused responses and strategies, while important, are not a replacement for longer-term, robust, and durable solutions building on human relationships, even if these are slower to grow and develop. As one commentator recently suggested, 'new eras of protest will have to learn how to combine the ease and speed of online connectivity with the long-term face-to-face organizing that gives physical protest its strength and staying power'.[61]

Can an experimentalist approach to human rights advocacy respond to the transformative effects of the technological revolution? Or given that it was fundamentally shaped by the needs and circumstances of an earlier era, is the human rights movement simply not capable of meeting the profound changes brought by the digital era? On the one hand, the digital revolution presents major new challenges for human rights, but it is also true that the power of many existing forms of domestic and transnational human rights mobilization and activism have been enhanced by digital technology. There is ample evidence of actors and institutions at all levels of the human rights system beginning to adapt, both using and confronting technology and its transformative effects in a range of ways. The added difficulties created for human rights advocacy organizations by the COVID-19 pandemic-related restrictions on in-person gathering and mobilizing also further increased their engagement with digital tools and strategies.

The challenge for human rights activists, just as for the broader community of policymakers, scholars, and activists focusing on the social, economic, and political effects of digitalization, is to learn the ways in which the power of technology can be used to strengthen and reinforce human rights, as well as the ways in which the repressive, dystopian, and inegalitarian dimensions of technology can be predicted and resisted. The positive dimension is inevitably the easier and more exciting aspect of the challenge, and human rights activists and advocates have for years already been benefiting from the ways in which technology enhances communication and facilitates novel forms of advocacy and networking.[62] Persons

[59] See Livingston and M. Risse, 'The Future Impact of Artificial Intelligence on Humans and Human Rights', 33 *Ethics and International Affairs* (2019) 141.

[60] See S. Elsayed-Ali, *Our Human Rights Need to Adapt, and Fast, if They Are to Keep Up with Technology'*, World Economic Forum, 9 December 2016, available online at https://www.weforum.org/agenda/2016/12/five-ways-technology-is-shaping-the-future-of-human-rights. See also the cautionary note by Rodríguez-Garavito (n. 28), about the need for timefulness on the part of human rights actors, referring to the book by Marcia Bjornerud, *Timefulness* (2018).

[61] Antonia Malchik in 'The Problem with Social Media Protests', *Atlantic magazine*, 6 May 2019.

[62] See e.g. *Civil Society Innovation and Populism in a Digital Era*, International Civil Society Center and Just Labs Innovation Report (2019). Also Hall, Schmitz, and Dedmon, 'Transnational Advocacy and NGOs in the Digital Era: New Forms of Networked Power', 64 *International Studies Quarterly*

with disabilities and their advocates, for example, have generally welcomed the potential of technology to transform previous barriers to their access to justice and to other public goods.[63] Human rights defenders organizations have worked with tech companies to develop new tools and strategies for gathering, recording and sharing information on human rights breaches, to fight misinformation, and to provide digital security.[64] New organizations like Grassroots Unwired and The Engine Room have been created to advise social activists and human rights advocates on how to make the most of data and technology to increase their impact,[65] and an annual global gathering on human rights in the digital age brings numerous groups and actors from different disciplines and fields of practice to 'build a global agenda for human rights in the digital age'.[66]

Social movements and grassroots actors have been agile and innovative too. In Hong Kong, to give one example, democracy activists in 2019 followed the practices of earlier social movements in countering the use of surveillance technology such as smart lampposts, using apps and phones not just to decide on immediate tactics such as where to march, where to retreat in the face of teargas and conveying information large numbers of people in real time, but also voting on 'homegrown apps' on next steps.[67] In Russia, as the government sharply increased its repression of civil society in general and human rights organizations in particular, civil society groups have used technology to circumvent some of those restrictions and to continue their work.[68] One Russian NGO working in the field of freedom of information which was forced by the government to close down, describes how it re-formed as an informal association of lawyers and journalists (Team 29), which began to use new media technologies in the nonprofit sector.[69] They used 'online handouts' to advise people of their rights, and have created popular 'text quest' interactive games to advise users on how to communicate with the police and security services, as well as how to protect themselves and their families, and

(2019) 159; and Schmitz *et al.*, 'Democratizing Advocacy? How Digital Tools Shape International Non-Governmental Activism', 17 *Journal of Information Technology & Politics* (2020) 174–191.

[63]   See The Global Initiative for Inclusive ICTs and International Disability Alliance, *Technology and Effective Access to Justice* (2018). More generally, see J. Lazar and M. A. Stein, *Disability, Human Rights and Information Technology* (2017).

[64]   https://www.witness.org/our-work/tech-advocacy/.

[65]   https://www.theengineroom.org/.

[66]   https://www.rightscon.org/.

[67]   See Z. Tufekci, *In Hong Kong, Which Side Is Technology On? Both*, WIRED, 22 October 2019, available online at https://www.wired.com/story/hong-kong-protests-digital-technology/. For the author's earlier work on social protest in the age of technology, see *Twitter and Tear Gas: The Power and Fragility of Networked Protest* (2017).

[68]   See e.g. Deutsche Welle, *Russia Orders Closure of Prominent Human Rights Group*, 1 November 2019 and Freedom House, *Russia: Parliament Approves Repressive Legislation Package Targeting Independent Voices*, 22 November 2019.

[69]   https://team29.org/en/.

their information.[70] The games are popular and sell well, and the revenue thereby generated by the organization has been a welcome source in the face of increasing government restrictions on foreign funding, leading them to help other NGOs in developing and using similar pro-social apps and games for similar purposes.[71] Similar experimental and innovative uses of technology by local activists and movements are to be found in many parts of the world.

More generally, the digital era has seen the emergence of dozens of digital rights NGOs at the national, regional, and international level—many from the global north but increasing numbers also from the global south—which are focused on the risks and challenges to human rights of the uses of technology.[72] At the same time, an array of international institutions and actors have begun to engage with the human rights dimensions of digitalization, including the Office of the High Commissioner for Human Rights, the UN Human Rights Council, UN General Assembly, the Committee on the Rights on the Child UN, as well as a range of special rapporteurs including those on privacy, freedom of expression, and extreme poverty. Regional actors—in particular the European Union and its institutions—have made rights protection in the digital era a key part of their policy. In other words, in addition to the array of new and emerging organizations and actors focused specifically on the impact of technology for social justice advocates, existing human rights institutions as well as multiple actors at grassroots, national, regional, and transnational level are adapting their practices and focus to encompass the specific challenges of digitalization and technological change.

And while the rapid progress, production, and exploitation of technology initially outpaced political, democratic, and regulatory awareness and response, significantly more attention has more recently been paid to the risks as well as the benefits of the digital revolution, and to the kinds of responses which may be needed. Scholars as well as policymakers and lawmakers are actively debating the ways of harnessing the promise of technology while guarding against the risks and dangers.[73] It is not only the human rights community and system that finds itself confronted with new challenges by the technological revolution: the same is true

[70] See T. Tolsteneva, *Technology and Gaming Innovations Bring New Life to Russian NGOs*, Open Global Rights, 12 September 2019.

[71] Ibid.

[72] A selection of leading Global South organizations include Derechos Digitales (Chile and across Latin America), Colnodo (Colombia), CIPESA (Southern Africa), Afroleadership (Cameroon), ASUTIC (Senegal), Unwanted Witness (Uganda) IPANDETEC (Panama and across Central America), Software Freedom Law Centre (India), Digital Empowerment Foundation (India) amongst many others, while some of the prominent global north organizations to date include AccessNow.org, Alt Advisory, Digital Freedom Foundation, Digital Rights Foundation, European Digital Rights, Digital Rights Watch, Electronic Privacy Information Center, The Global Initiative for Inclusive ICTs, Open Rights Group, along with many more. Others like the Association for Progressive Communication are global networks that include organizations from all continents.

[73] See e.g. McGregor, Murray, and Ng, 'International Human Rights Law as a Framework for Algorithmic Accountability', 68 *International and Comparative Law Quarterly* (2019) 309–343.

for virtually all existing systems, including political, economic, and social systems and practices. Frank Pasquale recently described a 'second wave of algorithmic accountability' research and activism in which more structural concerns have begun to be addressed, following the first wave which focused mostly on existing algorithmic systems with a view to making them fairer.[74] In his terms, the second wave of accountability goes beyond improving existing systems and asks 'whether they should be used at all—and, if so, who gets to govern them'. Social movements, human rights advocates, and activists have also begun to ask these questions, and while they may lag behind technological expertise and corporate interest in their engagement, it would at best be premature to conclude that the human rights movement is not capable of rising to those challenges, and there is already some evidence to the contrary. Nevertheless, given the specialized, complex, and fast-moving nature of the tech sector, the advice of those involved in rethinking human rights strategies to develop new forms of coalition and collaboration and to work with non-traditional allies going forward seems critical.[75]

C. Climate change

Unlike digital expansion, climate change does not bring with it potential advantages and benefits for human rights. It is a very fundamental and overwhelming challenge to the future of the planet and the welfare of its population, albeit one whose risks are unevenly distributed and which in the shorter term affects certain geographic areas and poorer populations much more severely than others.[76] Some of the effects of global warming pose immediate and urgent threats to the rights and welfare of specific groups and populations, while others are more relevant to future generations.

Although it is only relatively recently that the overwhelming risk posed by climate change has been widely acknowledged and become highly salient in social and political terms, there are by now few groups concerned with social justice or human rights whose work does not focus to some extent on its impact.[77] This has

---

[74] F. Pasquale, 'The Second Wave of Algorithmic Accountability', Law and Political Economy, 25 November 2019, available online at https://lpeblog.org/2019/11/25/the-second-wave-of-algorithmic-accountability/.

[75] See Rodríguez-Garavito, 'Disrupting Human Rights: Existential Challenges and a New Paradigm for the Field', in N. Bhuta et al. (eds) (forthcoming 2021).

[76] See e.g. S. N. Islam and J. Winkel, 'Climate Change and Social Inequality', UN DESA Working Paper no. 152 (2017). Also the Report to the UN Human Rights Council of the Special Rapporteur on extreme poverty and human rights on Climate Change and Poverty, 25 June 2019, A/HRC/41/39.

[77] For some aspects of the gradual turn by human rights organizations and NGOs towards the issue of climate change, and of environmental organizations towards human rights, see Rodríguez-Garavito, 'International Human Rights and Climate Governance: The "Rights Turn" in Climate Litigation' (forthcoming 2021), and Setzer and Vanhala, 'Climate Change Litigation: A Review of Research on Courts and Litigants in Climate Governance', Wiley Interdisciplinary Reviews: Climate Change (2019).

meant that human rights advocates and activists, NGOs and their networks, international organizations, and institutions, as well as domestic political actors and institutions in many parts of the world are by this stage squarely focused on the ways in which climate change risks undermining human and social welfare and survival.

But to what extent is the experimentalist model of human rights law and advocacy a useful or effective vehicle for addressing the overwhelming impacts of global warming? It is clear that an adequate response to the profound challenges of climate change will require enormous political and social commitment and coordinated global as well as domestic action. To that extent, human rights advocacy is just one of multiple approaches that might play a part in the response. The relevant question, then, is whether human rights advocacy can play a useful part in the set of strategies needed to mount a powerful and coordinated response to the risks and effects of climate change. Yet as noted above, the particular relevance of time including the urgency and immediacy of some of the harms and the transgenerational nature of others, the collective rather than individual nature of the kinds of damage caused or threatened, and the anthropocentrism of human rights law would seem to imply that the strategies, tools, and assumptions of human rights are unlikely to be a good match for the challenges of climate change. On the other hand, human rights advocates and institutions have recently begun to grapple with the risks and effects of climate change in ways that suggest the movement's tools and approaches offer promise, and that suggest openness to the kind of innovation and collaboration that those involved in rethinking the human rights movement have been advocating.

Domestic and local as well as international human rights NGOs have begun to work together with environmental activists and funders on ways of integrating climate change into their work, and on making it a more central and urgent priority.[78] One notable development in recent years has been an explosion in climate litigation, with advocates resorting to cases before domestic courts all over the world.[79] A recent report described 1023 climate cases brought in the US, and a further 305 across 27 countries, and noted both human rights and science playing an increasingly important role in the litigation.[80] The cases are being brought against governments for breach of environmental and human rights obligations to pressure them to take more ambitious climate action, as for example in recent high-profile cases against Ireland, Pakistan, and the Netherlands, and against corporate emitters seeking compensation for damage caused, such as those brought against

---

[78] A first Global Climate Summit was held in New York in 2019 to bring together human rights activists with a view to 'scaling up efforts on climate justice', see https://www.amnesty.org/en/latest/news/2019/07/announcing-peoples-summit-on-climate-rights-and-human-survival/.

[79] See *The Status of Climate Change Litigation: A Global Review* (2017).

[80] J. Setzer and R. Byrnes, *Global Trends in Climate Change Litigation: 2019 Snapshot*, LSE Grantham Research Institute (2019). See also the *American Journal of International Law* Unbound Symposium edited by Peel and Lin, 'Transnational Climate Litigation: The Contribution of the Global South', 114 *AJIL Unbound* (2020), and Rodríguez-Garavito (n. 77).

Exxon Mobil and other large 'carbon majors'.[81] Cases have been brought in low and middle-income countries as well as in highly developed economies, and before regional human rights courts such as the Inter American Court on Human Rights and the European Court of Human Rights as well as the European Court of Justice, and before international human rights bodies including the UN Human Rights Committee and the Committee on the Rights of the Child.

In addition, these and numerous other UN human rights treaty bodies have regularly declared in their concluding observations that human rights obligations require states to address their contribution to climate change including through their emissions or export of fossil fuels.[82] In 2019, five human rights treaty bodies issued a joint statement on human rights and climate change, identifying the risks to human rights posed by global warming, the multiple obligations imposed on states under international human rights law to take action to address climate change and the harms caused by it, and underscoring their own ongoing role in monitoring and holding states to account for their obligations to mitigate and adapt to climate change.[83] The Paris Climate agreement signed in 2015 has been described—despite its somewhat weak language in this respect—as a human rights treaty.[84] And while it falls short of being an experimentalist system, the Paris agreement nonetheless introduced elements of a bottom-up approach to the reduction of carbon emissions by permitting countries to make their own pledges as to individual emission reduction targets, with a process of periodic review.[85] Some of the recent climate litigation has involved litigants asking courts to treat the climate goals of the Paris agreement as benchmarks by which to judge government action, while using human rights provisions and enforcement mechanisms to hold those governments to account.[86] Increased civic activism and mobilization to generate greater pressure on states to revise and increase their contributions, including through litigation, could help to strengthen the Paris climate accord and to create a more effective experimentalist system.

Other new and potentially promising initiatives bringing human rights strategies to bear on climate causes include the move to accord rights to nature, such as

---

[81] For an account of the rise of such 'private' climate litigation against corporations, see Ganguly, Setzer, and Heyvaert, 'If at First You Don't Succeed: Suing Corporations for Climate Change', 38 *OJLS* (2018) 841.

[82] See *States Human Rights Obligations in the Context of Climate Change: Note on the Concluding Observations and Recommendations on Climate Change adopted by UN Human Rights Treaty Bodies*, Center for International Environmental Law (2018).

[83] Joint Statement on Human Rights and Climate Change by CEDAW, CESR, CPRMW, CRC, CRPD, 16 September 2019.

[84] Knox, 'The Paris Agreement as a Human Rights Treaty', in D. Akande *et al.* (eds), *Human Rights and 21st Century Challenges* (2020) Ch. 15.

[85] See D. Victor and C. Sabel, *An Experimentalist Approach to Governing Global Climate Change* (2017), available online at https://ostromworkshop.indiana.edu/pdf/seriespapers/2017fall-colloq/victor-paper.pdf.

[86] See Rodríguez-Garavito (n. 77).

to rivers (in Bangladesh, Ecuador, New Zealand, Colombia, and northern India),[87] the move to recognize intergenerational rights,[88] and the emerging recognition of a human right to a healthy and sustainable environment.[89] An important innovation in a recent environmental treaty signed between countries of Latin America and the Caribbean states is the inclusion of provisions protecting the human rights of environmental defenders. The Escazu Agreement, which is similar in parts to the Aarhus Convention on access to information, public participation, and justice in environmental affairs, is the first such agreement to recognize and attempt to provide protection against the enormous danger increasingly faced by environmental rights activists. Under Article 9 of the treaty, states guarantee 'a safe and enabling environment for persons, groups and organizations that promote and defend human rights in environmental matters', and to take 'adequate and effective measures' to recognize and promote many of the rights of environmental defenders including their rights to life, personal integrity, freedom of expression, and more, as well as to take action to prevent, investigate, and punish intimidation, threats and attacks against them by others. While the treaty is relatively recent, being adopted only in 2018, and so far (at the time of writing) signed by 24 states, the inclusion of these provisions is an important move in recognizing and taking steps to guarantee protection for human rights and environmental defenders who have been harassed and murdered in ever greater numbers in recent years.[90]

But arguably the greatest cause for optimism as to the potential for human rights-based activism to contribute effectively to combat climate change is the powerful set of domestic and global social movements which have recently arisen to protest against the failure of states and corporations to effectively address it. The climate strike movement led by Greta Thunberg and the grassroots Extinction Rebellion movement have galvanized hundreds of thousands of activists across the world to take to the streets demanding action. To have a strong base of social support and activism underlying a cause is, as argued in this book, often a crucial

[87] See O'Donnell and Talbot-Jones, 'Creating Legal Rights for Rivers: Lessons from Australia, New Zealand and India', 23 *Ecology and Society* (2018) 7. Tanasescu, 'Rivers get Human Rights: They Can Sue to Protect Themselves', *Scientific American*, 19 June 2017. For the international campaign to recognize the rights of rivers, see https://www.internationalrivers.org/campaigns/the-rights-of-rivers.

[88] See e.g. Duwell and Bos, 'Human Rights and Future People—Possibilities of Argumentation', 15 *Journal of Human Rights* (2016) 231, Lewis, 'The Rights of Future Generations within the Post-Paris Climate Regime', 7 *Transnational Environmental Law* (2018) 69. For a discussion of the role played by the rights of future generations in the climate case taken by a group of young people in Colombia against the state, see Rodríguez-Garavito, 'Here is how litigation for the planet won in Colombia', *Dejusticia*, 7 May 2018.

[89] See the Report to the UN General Assembly of the Special Rapporteur on Human Rights and the Environment, David Boyd, on global recognition of the right to a safe, clean, healthy and sustainable environment, 19 July 2018, A/73/188. See also D. Boyd, *Rights as a Response to Ecological Apocalypse*, Open Global Rights, 20 March 2019.

[90] See the report of the NGO Global Witness, 'Enemies of the State: How Government and Business Silence Land and Environmental Defenders' (July 2019) and Butt, Lambrick, Menton, and Renwick, 'The Supply Chain of Violence', *Nature Sustainability* (2019) 742.

component of effective human rights advocacy and reform, particularly when the changes demanded are extensive and have major distributive and other implications and costs.

D. COVID-19

The COVID-19 pandemic has also presented an additional set of challenges, mentioned above, both for the human rights movement and for the protection of human rights more generally. The reaction of many states by introducing states of emergency and derogating from human rights treaties and monitoring mechanisms, expanding policing and surveillance, and intensifying existing moves towards repression have already made this clear.[91] The severe exacerbation of existing inequalities by the impact of the pandemic undermines a great many socio-economic as well as civil and political rights. And the widespread pandemic restrictions have created fresh difficulties for social movements and activists in finding ways of mobilizing at a time when gathering or working in-person is limited or prohibited. Nevertheless, the reaction of multiple human rights groups and social protest movements to the pandemic thus far suggests that they are remaining vigilant and are seeking ways to challenge and resist some of the excessively repressive measures introduced, to find creative ways around COVID-related restrictions on their organizing, and to highlight the inequalities and injustices exacerbated by the pandemic. International human rights institutions have also thus far responded rapidly to the pandemic, and particularly to the derogations on the part of states from human rights treaties and their introduction of states of emergency, monitoring these measures, issuing opinions and recommendations, and publishing guidelines as to their permissibility and limits.[92] Various NGOs have also compiled and provided access to the wide array of measures and statements adopted by the range of international human rights bodies on the human rights obligations of states in relation to the pandemic,[93] and academics and activists have organized virtual workshops and events on how to advance justice during the pandemic.[94] While it is too soon to tell, at the time of writing, how effective human rights advocacy and action will be in relation to the consequences of COVID-19, the initial burst

[91] For a useful compilation and virtual hub of information on how states worldwide reacted to the COVID-19 crisis and the measures they introduced, see https://www.democratic-decay.org/covid-dem.
[92] See e.g. the UN Office of the High Commissioner for Human Rights Guidance on Emergency Measures and COVID-19 of 27 April 2020; the Venice Commission (European Commission on Democracy Through Law) Compilation of Opinions and Reports on States of Emergency, 20 April 2020.
[93] See e.g. the compilation assembled by The International Justice Resource Center: https://ijrcenter.org/covid-19-guidance-from-supranational-human-rights-bodies/.
[94] See e.g. J. Huckerby and S. Knuckey, *Advancing Human Rights During the Pandemic: An Online Event Series,* Just Security, 27 May 2020. See also the course on 'Social Justice lawyering in a Pandemic' offered by the City University of New York, see https://www.law.cuny.edu/blog/courses/social-justice-lawyering-in-a-pandemic/.

of activity suggests at least that many of the relevant actors and institutions—civil society, international human rights bodies, transnational networks and domestic institutions—are intently focused on them.

E. Increasing inequality

Inequality is of course far from being a new challenge for human rights. Inequality of all kinds has been a pervasive feature of human society, and the struggle against discrimination—whether racial or ethnic discrimination, gender inequality, or multiple other kinds—has been an important dimension of the human rights movement. However, the widening of socio-economic equality not only as between different parts of the world but within states and increasingly also within wealthy, developed states has become an issue of particular and increasing political salience in recent decades with the continued strengthening and entrenchment of the neoliberal economic model.

As outlined above, the challenge of inequality for the human rights movement lies not only in the fact that extensive socio-economic inequality undermines a wide range of economic and social rights as well as civil and political rights. It lies also in the fact that the human rights movement has been significantly more successful in promoting and addressing civil and political rights than it has in promoting socio-economic rights and addressing socio-economic inequality. One response of human rights scholars and practitioners to the differential impact of human rights advocacy on economic and social rights as compared with civil and political rights has been to point by way of explanation to the different international legal regimes governing the two sets of rights.[95] Despite the language of indivisibility of all human rights and the declarations of international human rights institutions to that effect, the reality is that the drafting of the two UN Conventions dealing with the two categories of rights reflected a considerably more diluted commitment on the part of signatory states to the guarantee and enforcement of socio-economic rights as compared with civil and political rights. While one of the reasons typically offered for this distinction between the two Covenants is that civil and political rights were assumed to be capable of enforcement mainly through non-interference rather than through expenditure by comparison with socio-economic rights whose enforcement would inevitably be expensive, this distinction has been convincingly challenged by scholars pointing out the cost of

---

[95] For accounts of the drafting and development of the two Covenants, see M. Craven, *The International Covenant on Economic, Social, and Cultural Rights: A Perspective on Its Development* (1998) and B. Saul (ed.), *The International Covenant on Economic, Social, and Cultural Rights: Travaux Préparatoires* (2016). On the ICCPR, see W. Schabas and M. Nowak, *Nowak's Commentary on the UN International Covenant on Civil and Political Rights* (2019).

all kinds of rights and the invariably distributive implications of almost all meaningful human rights enforcement.[96]

Nevertheless, the drafting of the two UN Covenants was premised on a distinction between civil and political rights on the one hand and socio-economic rights on the other. Unlike the International Covenant on Civil and Political Rights (ICCPR), the obligations imposed under the International Covenant on Economic Social and Cultural Rights (ICESCR) are phrased in more gradual and contingent terms, requiring states to 'take steps' towards the 'progressive' realization of rights subject to their 'available resources'. The civil and political rights listed in the ICCPR—which has been ratified by the US but not by China—more closely reflected the liberty-focused agenda of capitalist democratic states while the social and economic rights listed in the ICESCR—which has been ratified by China but not by the United States—more closely reflected the welfare priorities of socialist and communist states. Reflecting these divisions, a number of the major American human rights NGOs, notably Amnesty International and Human Rights Watch, did not consider socioeconomic rights as 'real' human rights and did not include socio-economic justice within their mandates for many decades.[97]

Pointing to the international legal origins of the unequal focus of human rights advocacy on socioeconomic rights does not, of course, provide an answer to the critique that the human rights movement has not been up to the challenge of inequality, and indeed the explanation might seem to confirm the critique. A second and more substantive response to that critique, however, has been to challenge the claim that 'human rights has nothing to say about inequality' and to highlight the work of multiple human rights institutions and organizations over many years in combatting inequality.[98] Economic justice causes, as scholars and activists have pointed out, have been actively promoted by a great many local and grassroots human rights organizations around the world.[99]

---

[96] See e.g. S. Holmes and C. Sunstein, *The Cost of Rights: Why Liberty Depends on Taxes* (2000). Sandra Fredman, in *Human Rights Transformed* (2008), argues convincingly that human rights of all kinds, whether socioeconomic or civil and political, entail positive duties and require active state intervention for their realization.

[97] The founder of Human Rights Watch, Aryeh Neier, was a prominent critic of economic and social rights. In his article 'Social and Economic Rights: a Critique', 13 *Human Rights Brief* (2006) (No. 2) 1–3, he argued that distributive concerns should be pursued through the regular political process and should not be pursued as human rights. For a history of Amnesty International's initial exclusion but gradual incremental acceptance of economic and social rights as part of its mandate, see Goering, 'Amnesty International and Economic, Social, and Cultural Rights', in D. A. Bell and J.-M. Coicaud (eds), *The Ethical Challenges of International Human Rights NGOs* (2006).

[98] For the claim that human rights have nothing to say about inequality, see S. Moyn, *Not Enough* (2018) 216. For a rebuttal, see I. Saiz, *Economic inequality and human rights: towards a more nuanced assessment*, 26 April 2018, available online at http://www.cesr.org/economic-inequality-and-human-rights-towards-more-nuanced-assessment; also Margot Salomon and Martin Scheinin in their review of Moyn's book, 32 *Leiden Journal of International Law* (2019) 609. See also Young (n.25) and Dehm (n.25).

[99] See D. Chong, *Freedom from Poverty: NGOs and Human Rights Praxis* (2010). Also *Twenty Years of Economic and Social Rights Advocacy* (2013). On campaigns around the right to water and right to housing, see O'Connell, 'Contesting the Displacement Thesis', 69 *Northern Ireland Legal Quarterly*

Nonetheless, even if critical arguments about the impotence and silence of human rights in the face of inequality are exaggerated or inaccurate, the fundamental underlying charge that the human rights movement has not adequately addressed structural injustice, and particularly structural economic injustice, is a difficult one to refute. Economic inequality has grown ever more extreme in recent decades, and the intergenerational transmission of entrenched poverty in countries of the global north and south alike has ensured that millions of people and their families have few prospects of enjoying basic human rights to health and healthcare, to housing, water, food, education, and a decent living, amongst many others. It is true that prominent campaigns and developments such as the Occupy movements, the World Social Forum, the Jubilee Debt cancellation campaign, the Seattle protests against the World Trade Organizations, Oxfam's twenty-first-century turn to a rights-based approach, and scholarly interventions such as Thomas Piketty's *Capitalism in the 21st Century* and Branko Milanovic's *Capitalism Alone* have significantly raised the public profile of the issue of economic inequality and its relationship to capitalism. But despite such campaigns, protests, and interventions, no political or social movement, including the human rights movement, has really weakened the class structure of society or displaced the model of neoliberal capitalism which became so dominant in the latter decades of the twentieth century.

Should this be taken to mean that the human rights movement is not up to the task and that those interested in economic justice should abandon it? For prominent scholarly voices of the global north, including Hopgood, Kennedy, and Moyn, the 'complicity' or 'companionship' of human rights with neoliberal capitalism provides ample reason to jettison the human rights movement and to find some other path to a more egalitarian society. Hopgood is perhaps the most damning, arguing that 'inequality ... built the human rights movement', that 'the neoliberal consumerist mentality [is] at the heart of human rights' and that 'human rights evacuate the left's principal weapon in demanding distributive change—mass mobilisation to gain political power'.[100] In his book of the same title, Moyn asserts that human rights are 'not enough', that 'the human rights movement cannot disrupt its companionship with neoliberalism simply by pivoting to equality'. He argues that welfare needs to be championed by a different movement 'that will not look like our human rights movement'.[101] In similar vein, David Kennedy, who has long pointed out the limitations of the human rights movement, argues that 'human rights is

(2018) 19. For a list of multiple organizations and actors working on economic and social rights see Sarah Knuckey in a 7-part Twitter thread beginning at https://twitter.com/SarahKnuckey/status/989199192399761410.

[100] S. Hopgood, *Fellow Travelers: Human Rights and Class Inequality*, The Toqueville Review, 10 July 2018.

[101] Moyn (n. 98) 219.

no longer the way forward' in the face of challenges such as 'pandemics, global warming, financial instability and inequality'.[102] The human rights revolution, he declares, 'was a status quo project of legitimation and an establishment career option for those who might otherwise have contributed to a new global politics'.[103]

These and other critical scholars train their lens on the failures of human rights actors and institutions to challenge entrenched structures of economic and political power. Their accounts share a view of human rights advocacy as an elitist and expert-driven practice that defuses protest, de-fangs politics, sets itself against mass mobilization. and impedes redistributive politics. Yet this view is a particular and partial one which focuses on elite institutional actors and large global north NGOs such as Amnesty and Human Rights Watch, but excludes some of the dimensions that give the human rights movement much of its power and potential. This book has argued that the human rights movement is a much broader, more globally diverse, dynamic, and internally contested one than that presented by such critics. In particular, by reframing to include rather than screen out the social movements and grassroots activism as well as civil society diversity that underpins much human rights advocacy, the dynamism and energy that fuel the human rights movement are brought into view. While the ideals of human dignity, welfare, and freedom that underlie the human rights system and the international norms and institutions that provide a legal framework for them are crucial dimensions, without the mobilizing energy and determination of social movements and activists, the capacity of the human rights movement to pursue transformative change would be minimal.

Further, by advancing an account of human rights which presents it as incompatible with mass mobilization and redistributive goals, and as undermining past distributive projects, the critics choose to ignore the many political and social movements which invoke both economic and social rights as well as civil and political rights as core aspects of their demand for progressive and distributive change. Prominent members of the democratic socialist movement in the United States such as Bernie Sanders and Alexandria Ocasio-Cortez have built their progressive political agenda around human rights to healthcare, education, and housing.[104] The Black Lives Matter movement has been described by its co-founder as a human rights movement rather than a civil rights movement, given its integration of economic, social, and cultural rights.[105] And scholars have begun to point to the kinds of changes in strategy that human rights advocates and institutions need to make

---

[102] Kennedy, 'The International Human Rights Regime: Still Part of the Problem?', in R. Dickinson et al. (eds), *Examining Critical Perspectives on Human Rights* (2012) 19, 33–34.

[103] Ibid.

[104] For the Democratic Socialist social and economic bill of rights, see https://www.dsausa.org/strategy/a_social_and_economic_bill_of_rights/.

[105] See n. 7 above.

in order to tackle questions of political economy, and to become a transformative movement in the face of neoliberalism.[106]

None of this is to deny that the human rights movement has failed to address important dimensions of justice or that it is in need of renewal and 'disruptive reform'.[107] Few if any social movements as yet, the human rights movement included, have made serious progress in tackling structural injustice and socioeconomic inequality. And the scale and nature of contemporary challenges, as well as its own blind spots and failures, unquestionably call for rethinking and change within the human rights movement. But to return to the argument made in Chapter 1, human rights are not an alternative to politics or to social mobilization: they are a set of ideals based on commitments to human dignity, welfare, and freedom to frame and orient political and social action, as well as an array of laws and institutions which provide leverage, amplification, pressure, and support for the claims of social movements and advocates. Rather than heeding the exhortation of critics who call for the human rights movement to be abandoned for some unspecified alternative, the challenge is to learn from both the past successes and failures of the human rights movement and to build on its best elements in finding the most effective ways of challenging and addressing structural injustice going forward.

4. The Future of Human Rights

In a report on civic space in 2020, the authors describe a grim set of developments with the potential to crush the foundations of civic activism, including 'far-right, anti-democratic and fundamentalist civil society actors aligning with authoritarian and illiberal powers and oligarchs to re-shape the political, economic and social landscape in line with their values and visions'.[108] Yet they go on to argue that 'there are huge openings for progressive forces too. The growing recognition that economic liberalism and globalization have pushed the planet to its limits and widened inequality is motivating more and more people to engage in political activism to shape their future'.[109] This book joins the latter perspective in arguing that despite the daunting set of developments and challenges, there are important opportunities in the current turbulent era for real transformation and change.

---

[106] On human rights and health in particular, see Kapczynski, 'The Right to Medicines in an Age of Neoliberalism', 10 *Humanity* (2019) 79 and Yamin, 'Struggles for Human Rights in Health in an Age of Neoliberalism: From Civil Disobedience to Epistemic Disobedience', 11 *Journal of Human Rights Practice* (2019) 357.

[107] C. Rodríguez-Garavito, *Disrupting Human Rights: Existential Challenges and a New Paradigm for the Field* (forthcoming 2021).

[108] B. Hayes and P. Joshi, *Rethinking Civic Space in an Age of Intersectional Crises*, May 2020, available online at https://global-dialogue.org/wp-content/uploads/2020/05/FICS-Rethinking-Civic-Space-Report-FINAL.pdf.

[109] Ibid.

The examination of campaigns such as those for gender justice in Pakistan, inclusive education in Argentina, and reproductive autonomy in Ireland has shown some of the ways in which human rights advocacy has helped to advance rights-based change in earlier contexts. And despite the grim contemporary developments and fundamental challenges, the rise of social activism and of rights-based movements including climate strikes, Black Lives Matter, #Me Too marches, and socio-economic protests across multiple continents, as well as the outpouring of solidarity and community activism during the COVID-19 pandemic, give reason to hope that human rights mobilization will continue to drive progressive change.

Understanding the human rights movement to include social mobilization and protest, rather than only organized civil society and international institutions and networks, however, is not to suggest a picture of harmonious coordination amongst these various elements. On the contrary, there is frequent disagreement and contention within and between different parts of the human rights movement. Sharp contestation between different civil society groups and NGOs advocating for similar causes is a regular feature of human rights advocacy, as was evident in several of the campaigns described in previous chapters. Further, the unequal and problematic relationships between international and local NGOs, between funders and civil society, and between global north and global south organizations working on similar issues has been a subject of considerable debate and challenge for human rights practitioners.[110] Apart from north-south and international-local tension, the relationship between communities and grassroots groups affected by rights violations and injustices on the one hand, and the advocates and NGOs who aim to represent them on the other, is also often fraught.[111]

Finally, the relationship between organized civil society and social movements is complicated and far from symbiotic.[112] Not all social movements which pursue social justice agree with the assumptions and strategies of the human rights movement nor see themselves as part of it. Social movements and civil society are two generally different modes of popular organization and the relationship between

---

[110] Jackson, 'Towards Transformative Solidarity: Reflections from Amnesty International's Global Transition Program', 34 *Emory International Law Review* (2020) 705. See also M. Younis, *The Hazards of International NGOs Going Local*, Open Global Rights, 22 May 2018, available online at https://www.openglobalrights.org/the-hazards-of-international-ngos-going-local/ and Open Democracy', *An Open Letter to International NGOs who are Seeking to Localize their Operation*, 5 March 2020, available online at   https://www.opendemocracy.net/en/transformation/an-open-letter-to-international-ngos-who-are-looking-to-localise-their-operations/.

[111] See e.g. S. Babu Pant, *How a Human Rights Movement Gets Disempowered*, 17 June 2017, available online at https://medium.com/@sunilbabupant/how-a-human-rights-movement-gets-disempowered-1348d5d62b7a.

[112] Mary Kaldor, for example, has argued that NGOs could be seen as 'tamed' social movements: Connectas Human Rights, 'Interview with Mary Kaldor', *Sur: International Journal on Human Rights*, March 2014, available online at https://sur.conectas.org/en/interview-with-mary-kaldor/. And Kate Nash has warned against the assumption that human rights advocacy networks are sustained by social movements and argues for careful sociological analysis of the relationship between them: Nash, 'Human Rights, Movements, and Law: On Not Researching Legitimacy', 46 *Sociology* (2012) 797.

them at any given time—whether as allies, competitors, or otherwise—will depend on the particular political and social context.[113] Civil society organizations often position themselves as intermediaries between government and citizens, they are generally more institutionalized and professionalized, and tend to be significantly more influenced by funding considerations. Social movements on the other hand can be more radical, spontaneous, nimble, and disruptive, more directly engaged with political struggle, and less concerned about or constrained by relationships with policymakers or by dependence on funding. Yet while social movements and organized civil society may be quite distinct and often at odds in their methods and activities, to the extent that they pursue similar goals and outcomes they can, and often do, interact constructively, linking the mobilizing energy, knowledge, legitimacy, and power of the former with the longer-term and policy-focused orientation of the latter.[114]

Contestation, friction, and different modalities notwithstanding, a common commitment to advancing human rights and social justice unites grassroots activists and protest movements as well as domestic and international NGOs as part of a broad and pluralist human rights movement, along with national and international institutions, courts, bureaucracies, and other actors that engage in different ways. Indeed, contestation within the movement as well as external criticism and the array of contemporary challenges are amongst the factors which have prompted reflection and reform in recent times.[115] Human rights activists and organizations have been engaged in exercises of self-examination and critique on issues such as the role of funders, inclusion, the need for coalition-building rather than competition between organizations, new kinds of collaboration, and questions of long-term versus short-term goals and strategies. Critiques of human rights as being an excessively narrow and purist discipline mainly for legally-focused advocates who pay too little attention to cognate social justice fields and strategies have begun to be taken seriously. Amongst the many kinds of reform which have been called for include the need for human rights NGOs to work more actively to support social movements, without trying to dominate or domesticate them, and for human rights funders to be prepared to do similarly.[116]

---

[113] Motta, Esteves, and Cox, ' "Civil Society" vs Social Movements', 1 *Interface: A Journal for and about Social Movements* (2009) 1.

[114] See Lettinga and Kaulingfreks, 'Clashing Activisms: International Human Rights Organizations and Unruly Politics', 7 *Journal of Human Rights Practice* (2015) 343.

[115] See e.g. C. Rodríguez-Garavito and K. Gomez (eds), *Rising to the Populist Challenge: A New Playbook for Human Rights Actors* (2019), C. Rodríguez-Garavito, 'The Future of Human Rights: From Gatekeeping to Symbiosis', 20 *Sur: International Journal on Human Rights* (2014), available online at https://sur.conectas.org/en/the-future-of-human-rights-from-gatekeeping-to-symbiosis/ and 'Towards a Human Rights Ecosystem', in D. Lettinga and L. van Troost, *Debating the Endtimes of Human Rights: Activism and Institutions in a Neo-Westphalian World* (2014); Alston, 'The Populist Challenge to Human Rights', 9 *Journal of Human Rights Practice* (2017) 1, and the responses by Ron Dudai and Vijay Nagaraj, in 9 *Journal of Human Rights Practice* (2017), 16 and 22.

[116] Hayes and Joshi (n. 108).

One prominent scholar-practitioner who has led the call for self-reflection and change in the movement argues for greater collaboration between different human rights organizations, for the human rights movement to learn from other fields and disciplines (e.g. collaborative investigative journalism), to develop new narratives, form new coalitions, adopt 'multiple boomerang' tactics, assert new types of rights, and pay greater attention to questions of time.[117] Others are promoting a paradigm of grassroots legal empowerment, aimed at enabling justice movements to be led by the grassroots with advocates and other professionals in supporting rather than leading roles.[118] Renewed thinking on the ways in which civil society organizations can support, learn from, and facilitate grassroots movements, avoid an NGO 'monoculture', and build synergies between professional advocacy bodies and social movements is taking place.[119] Leading human rights practitioners advise focusing on the relationship between looser, fragmented 'self-activism' and focused organizational action, emphasizing the need for organizations to be 'liquid' enough to adapt to the mobilizational and other advantages presented by an era of protest and activism, in which there is widespread disenchantment with the institutions of representative government and a search for more effective ways of advancing rights-based change.[120] These internal debates on reform of the human rights movement are not of course new, and there has been active discussion for many years within different branches of the human rights movement over particular practices and approaches.[121] But one of the more hopeful and even exciting features of the current period of global turbulence is precisely that so much critical thinking and self-questioning is taking place amongst human rights practitioners on the future of the movement, and on how it needs to adapt in a period of profound destabilization and change.[122] There is an openness to new approaches, to

[117] Rodríguez-Garavito, 'Disrupting Human Rights: Existential Challenges and a New Paradigm for the Field', in N. Bhuta *et al.* (eds) (forthcoming 2021). On the need to consider new types of rights, see W. F. Schulz and S. Raman, *The Coming Good Society: Why New Realities Demand New Rights* (2020).

[118] See e.g. the global network organization Namati, https://namati.org/, and the discussion by Satterthwaite, 'Legal Empowerment for Human Rights', in G. de Búrca (ed.), *Legal Mobilization for Human Rights* (forthcoming 2021). On the campaign to 'shift power' towards local ownership of the agenda in the field of global funding and philanthropy, see the #shiftthepower movement, https://globalfundcommunityfoundations.org/what-we-stand-for/.

[119] B. Halloran and W. Flores, *Mobilizing Accountability: Citizens, Movements and the State* (2017), available online at https://www.transparency-initiative.org/wp-content/uploads/2017/03/movements-and-accountability-final.pdf.

[120] Nader, 'Solid Organizations in a Liquid World', *Sur: International Journal on Human Rights* (2014) 483.

[121] The *Journal of Human Rights Practice*, established in 2009, has provided a forum for such debates. For some examples, see Ergas, 'Human Rights Impact: Developing an Agenda for Interdisciplinary, International Research', 1 *Journal of Human Rights Practice* (2009) 459; Evans, 'Trade Unions As Human Rights Organizations', 7 *Journal of Human Rights Practice* (2015) 466; Gready, 'Reflections on a Human Rights Decade', 11 *Journal of Human Rights Practice* (2019) 442.

[122] Apart from scholarly reflection and thinking, many of the leading funders and international NGOs are also engaged in thinking about how the field and their practice may need to change to meet the challenges of the current time: see e.g. S. Gwynne, *Amnesty International wants to 'make human rights popular'*, 29 July 2019, available online at https://www.campaignlive.com/article/amnesty-international-wants-make-human-rights-popular/1592146; Byrne, 'George Soros Fights Back against

disruptive thinking and reform, and to the pluralistic, heterarchical, interactive, and multi-level forms of engagement envisaged by experimentalism.

The experimentalist account of human rights advanced in this book comprises both a descriptive reframing and a normative reorientation. It aims to provide a descriptive account of many existing human rights practices which emphasizes their pluralistic, participatory, diverse, dynamic, and iterative character. The human rights movement understood in experimentalist terms is comprised not just of international human rights bodies and an array of domestic and international institutional actors and networks, but also of civil society organizations and social movements to advance justice. Human rights are understood not as strictly defined standards detailed in advance but as norms that are invoked and developed in an ongoing process of contestation and engagement between social movements and civil society activists, international networks and institutions, and state and independent domestic institutions and actors. Importantly, the experimentalist account also emphasizes ongoing re-evaluation, renewal, and reform of practices and norms and even of the movement itself, domestically and internationally, in the continuing struggle to advance human rights.

At a time when there is growing disenchantment with traditional political systems and representative government, and when multilateralism and international political cooperation are on the wane, the activism of a mobilized citizenry and civil society engagement with international and national institutions to advance human rights can also help to broaden domestic participation and strengthen transnational governance. A time of turmoil and crisis, despite the suffering it brings, can create openings for creative thinking and progressive action, for renewed mobilization to catalyse transformation and change. Frightening though the threat of climate change may be, disturbing as the rise of illiberal authoritarianism and widening inequality are, disruptive as the digital revolution is and disorienting as the COVID pandemic has been, these developments have unquestionably shaken up the political status quo as well as the human rights movement, and are triggering rethinking and reform. The ideals and language of human rights retain power and significance for those marching for justice; human rights laws, institutions, and networks both internationally and domestically provide forms of leverage for activists and advocates, and widespread social movements legitimate and strengthen their demands for change.

The experimentalist account of human rights described in these chapters, far from being an elitist, ineffectual, or bureaucratic practice is a dynamic, diverse, and evolving one. It comprises a multi-actor, multi-level engagement between an

Populist Foes', *Financial Times*, 15 January 2018; T. Coombes, 'Why the Future of Human Rights Must Be Hopeful', Open Global Rights, 19 February 2019, available online at https://www.openglobalrights. org/why-the-future-of-human-rights-must-be-hopeful.

expanding set of participants to define and redefine human welfare, dignity, and freedom in an ongoing struggle to advance justice. In a turbulent era, rather than abandon human rights, we should redouble our efforts to bolster, renew, and reinvigorate a movement that has mobilized so many constituencies and communities around the globe in pursuit of a better world.

Index

For the benefit of digital users, indexed terms that span two pages (e.g., 52–53) may, on occasion, appear on only one of those pages.